MARKETING *and* SOCIAL ISSUES:
an action reader

The Wiley Marketing Series

WILLIAM LAZER, Advisory Editor *Michigan State University*

Contents

PART TWO

Foundations of Marketing

PART THREE

Some Specific Societal Problems and Response to Those Problems

PART FOUR

Future Directions

MARKETING *and* SOCIAL ISSUES:
an action reader

INTRODUCTION *to the Book*

During the past three decades the technological accomplishments of the United States have been greater than those of any other nation in any other period of history. Our society has achieved a record standard of living. We have put men on the moon in less time than was forecast. We have provided much aid to other nations. Our management methods have been copied throughout the world and our business schools are exporting their expertise to many nations. In fact, the spectacular growth of American industry in other nations has resulted in what J.J. Servan-Schreiber calls the American Challenge. These past successes, however, do not indicate that past methods are sufficient to meet the challenges of the future.

The marketing perspective necessary for the 1970's is different from that of the 1940's to 1960's. The descriptive work and case studies in marketing departments helped to bring about the boom of managerial marketing in the 1950's and 1960's. In addition, the managerial perspective was demonstrated to be useful in dealing with the realities of a depression, a war, and a police action. Given this background, it was only natural that our Schools of Business should concentrate on the micro problems of profit-making business enterprises.

During the period of the 1940's to the early 1960's our national perception was that of the biggest and best in everything. In this attitudinal environment we selectively perceived only the factors that enhanced our self-image. And we maintained beliefs about survival of the fittest and rugged individualism. That view has changed in the last two years. There is a "crisis in our national perception." We realize that our past achievements are not enough and that the life of a society is like that of the individual, an unending hurdle race over ever-evolving and perhaps more difficult challenges. The marketing system in the United States, which has played a crucial role in the past, can play a crucial role in resolving the major issues our nation faces today and in the future. We now realize that we have the technical ability and resources to eliminate socioeconomic injustices within our society. Therefore, it seems that solutions are possible if we investigate, organize, and allocate with a new orientation.

The insurrections in our cities, the draft protestors, and other young critics of the society have focused attention on the forgotten minorities. The problems of the 1970's are societal. We have organizations. We have managerial marketing experts. But we are not organized or trained to resolve the problems that are now most critical. These problems require the integrated efforts of private and public organizational groups if they are to be resolved. These problems require new forms of organizations and new ground rules. For these reasons the managerial perspective is not sufficient to cope with the new range of problems that now offer the most immediate challenge to our society.

The problems that continue to be most formidable are the military-industrial complex, racism, and economic issues such as high prices in rural and inner city stores, difficulties in housing construction, and pollution.

It is only as a result of the prolonged period of economic growth that we can have the privilege of addressing ourselves to the above second-order effects. In essence our society has solved the problems of producing large quantities of goods and services. The major issue that we now face is improvement of the quality of life.

There are a growing number of people in our country who believe:

Meaningful employment should be provided for all.

Everyone should be provided with opportunities to achieve a standard of living considerably above the poverty level.

Everyone has a right to have the goods he sees on television.

Everyone should be free from corrupt and misleading practices in the marketplace and in advertising.

Pollution can and must be controlled.

Businesses and other bureaucracies ought to serve people.

Everyone should be adequately fed and sheltered in a peaceful society.

In order for marketing to contribute to the solution of these problems, marketers must develop a broader perspective than the managerial viewpoint of the past three decades.

We agree with those who suggest that we broaden the concept of marketing. Just as important, we must continue to search for those ways in which marketing can contribute to the continued betterment of mankind. At present, the future of the human race is unclear. If we are to survive, we must as individuals and as members of professions be concerned about the quality of life.

The traditional definition of marketing which has dominated the literature of the 1960's is not sufficient. The definitions committee of the American Marketing Association defined marketing as:

> The performance of business activities which direct the flow of goods and services from producer to consumer in order to make a profit and satisfy customers and accomplish the company's objectives.

However, the societal challenges of the 1970's and the requirements of the marketing system have changed. A broader definition of marketing relevant to the present must deal with:

> The total delivery of a standard of living.
> All functions that take place between producers and consumers.
> Meeting needs and creating demand without the problems of brainwashing.
> Development of higher ethics in marketing.

We offer three definitions that are more consistent with the requirements of the 1970's than the definitions that have dominated the literature of the past two decades.

> HOLLOWAY AND HANCOCK: Marketing is "those activities necessary and incidental to bringing about exchange relationships."
> DRUCKER: Marketing "looks upon the entire buriness from the point of view of its ultimate purpose and justification, that is, from the customer."
> SHAFFER: "The market is an organizing or coordinating institution—a system of relationships involved in a group of transactions. Characteristics of markets include the rules governing the participants, the commodities or services in transactions, the number and size of participants, the location, etc."

The need for a new concentrated action by all persons engaged in exchange is clear when we examine our nation's response to the crises described by the National Advisory Commission on Civil Disorders. Quoting from *One Year Later:*

> The commission's [National Advisory Commission on Civil Disorders] description of the immediate consequences of the present policies sounds strikingly like a description of the year since its report was issued; some change but not enough, more incidents but less full scale disorder, because of improved police and military response; a decline in expectations and therefore in short run frustrations. If the commission is equally correct about the long run, the nation in its neglect may be sowing the seeds of unprecedented future disorder and division. For a year later, we are a year closer to being two societies, black and white, increasingly separate and scarcely less unequal.

That is not the prognosis of a bright, happy future in a land free from want with freedom and justice for all. It is the prognosis of a nation that must develop a new, broader perspective for solving its social problems. It is the prognosis of a socio-economic system that must take advantage of the latent resources of its marketing subsystem. It is the prognosis of a society that must learn to operate as a whole as capably as some of society's smaller parts operate in their microspheres of influence.

Solving our present predicament is, of course, an unending process. However, the first crucial step toward progress is the recognition that we all have a role to play and a contribution to make. C. Wright Mills captured this idea in the following quotation:

> In our time we have come to know that the limits of human nature are frighteningly broad. We have come to know that every individual lives, from one generation to the next, in some society; that he lives out a biography, and that he lives it out within some historical sequence. By the fact of his living he contributes, however minutely to the shaping of this society and to the course of its history. (*The Sociological Imagination,* p. 6.)

PART ONE *A Changing Society and a Marketing Perspective*

INTRODUCTION *to part one*

The times are changing and these times require that we take a new look at the present situation and future trends which are evident today. Part I discusses the present situation and future trends, as well as the role of marketing in these changing times and the organization of marketing knowledge for application to the problems of the 1970's. The two introductory selections present some general concepts for the reader's consideration.

Next, John K. Galbraith, Peter F. Drucker and William D. Patterson discuss *Some Indications of Change* in Section A. The objective of these selections is to provide an overview of what is happening and will be happening to the form and purpose of organizations in our society. Given this background, the question for marketers is, "Where and how does marketing fit into this changing panorama?"

Philip Kotler and Sidney J. Levy's article, "Broadening the Concept of Marketing" (Section 6), under Section B, *The Role of Marketing,* has generated a great deal of discussion among marketers. The article suggests that marketing is a function of all organizations, not just business organization. This recognition of the role of marketing in all organizations (and, for that matter, all persons) is important if marketing knowledge and techniques are to receive the broadest possible application.

Under Section B, Robert J. Lavidge and Wroe Alderson discuss the responsibilities and missions of marketers. For example, Alderson describes three major tasks of marketing today.

1. *Finding better ways to move goods to the market.* Our urban ghettos and rural markets are two major population segments that require improved quality and lower cost of the goods they desire.

2. *Product innovation that meets the needs of our population.* We must place more effort on anticipating the application of new technologies to meet present and future needs.

3. *Bringing new people into the market economy.* Many persons in the United States are not really participating in the "affluence" that some enjoy.

An integration of Wroe Alderson and Philip Kotler and Sidney Levy's work is suggested in the diagram below.

The Role of Marketing

Who participates in and helps direct the marketing process		On what tasks should marketers focus their energies	
	Finding the shortest path to the market	The introduction of new products	Expanding the market economy
All organizations— not just business organizations	All organizations should focus energies to find better means of distributing goods and services to consumers. The shortest path may include a thermal reduction tower on a new nuclear generating plant for a major utility to prevent long-run thermal pollution.	All organizations should focus energies for making new products available to the consumer which better satisfy his needs. This includes pollution control and birth control as well as suds control on new detergents.	All organizations should focus energies on bringing greater numbers of people into the economy in which middle-class Americans are participating and will participate.

1. *The Calf Path in Changing Times*

S. W. MOSS

One day through the primeval wood
a calf walked home as good calves should:

But made a trail all bent askew,
a crooked trail as all calves do.

Since then three hundred years have fled,
and I infer the calf is dead.

But still he left behind his trail
and thereby hangs my moral tale.

The trail was taken up next day
by a lone dog that passed that way!

And then a wise bellwether sheep
pursued the trail o'er vale and steep

And drew the flock behind him, too
as good bellwethers always do.

And from that day o'er hill and glade,
through these old woods a path was made.

And many men wound in and out,
and dodged and turned and bent about,

And uttered words of righteous wrath
because 'twas such a crooked path:

But still they followed . . . do not laugh
the first migrations of that calf.

This forest path became a lane,
that bent and turned and turned again.

This crooked lane became a road,
where many a poor house with his load
toiled on beneath the burning sun
and travelled some three miles in one.

And thus a century and a half
they trod the footsteps of that calf.

The years passed on in swiftness fleet;
the road became a village street;

And this, before men were aware,
a city's crowded throughfare.

And soon the central street was this
of a renowned metropolis.

And men two centuries and a half
trod in the footsteps of that calf.
A hundred thousand men were led
by one calf near three centuries dead.

For men are prone to go it blind
along the calf paths of the mind.

And work away from sun to sun
to do what other men have done

They follow in the beaten track,
and out and in and forth and back,

And still their devious course pursue,
to keep the path that others do

They keep the path a sacred groove
along which all their lives they move.

But how the wise old wood gods laugh
who saw the first primeval calf!

But we can't afford to walk today,
the beaten track of yesterday.

The tempo's changed — the drummer's new;
the day demands a different view.

For us the cue is, "Help and heal
the world which dies beneath our heel,"

For how the wise old wood gods fear
the issues now which face our sphere.

The bomb, pollution and despair,
are signs which say to all "beware"

Should they not hear the warning ring
that the times, they are a changing.

2. *Marketing and Social Change*

S. H. GAMBLE

*It is evident to all alike that a great Democratic Revolution is
going on among us, but all do not look at it in the same light. To
some it appears to be novel but accidental, and, as such, they
hope it will be checked; to others it seems irresistible because it is
the most uniform, the most ancient and the most permanent
tendency that is to be found in History.*

ALEXIS DE TOCQUEVILLE, *Democracy in America*

These words, written almost 150 years ago, are especially appropriate today if
one reviews the crises of recent times. The statement represents a consolidation of
many current American attitudes as they anticipate the challenges and
opportunities that will be important during the 1970's and beyond.

This article covers three topics:

The general role of marketing in the future.

Some major existing social problems.

Evidence that the next decade will be a period of tremendous growth which will
provide opportunities for social change.

The Role of Marketing

Many writers[1] have described the increasing importance of marketing activities to
developing nations. But other than simplified selling, buying, distributing, and

---

[1] John Wish and Kelly Harrison, *Marketing: One Answer to Poverty—Food Marketing and
Economic Development in Puerto Rico, 1950-65,* University of Oregon, College of Business
Administration, in cooperation with the Center for International Business Studies, Eugene
Oregon, 1969.

Norman Collins and Richard Holton, "Programming Change in Marketing in Planned
Economic Development," *Kyklos,* Vol. 16, January 1963, pp. 123-134.

John Galbraith and Richard Holton, *Marketing Efficiency in Puerto Rico,* Cambridge Mass.:
Harvard University Press, 1954.

Reed Moyer, "Marketing and Economic Development," Occasional Report No. 1, East
Lansing: Institute for International Business Studies, Michigan State University, 1965.

Charles Slater et al., *Market Process in the Recife Area of Northeast Brazil,* Research Report
No. 2, Latin American Studies Center, Michigan State University, East Lansing, Michigan.

direct word-of-mouth promotion, the small backward trading center does little marketing. In sharp contrast, the United States offers highly complex and challenging opportunities for applying marketing expertise. The existing opportunities for marketers are both exciting and frightening. They are exciting because the United States, as the most affluent and industrialized nation the world has ever known, has opportunities to apply marketing in ways that have never existed or even been conceived before. But marketing opportunities are frightening because the United States also faces serious social problems—by-products of our economic affluence and industrialization. These problems demand new kinds of marketing efforts.

Given the opportunities and challenges for marketing in the coming years, what are the major areas in which marketing can make a contribution? Included are:

Improving distribution systems for food and other basic goods to permit delivery of quality goods at lower prices.

Communicating fully the actual effects of air, water, and life pollution, broken homes, prison conditions, and all forms of social violence.

Raising greater concern about product quality, sales methods, and services.

Identifying consumer needs and improving customer satisfaction, including better job opportunities, housing, and education.

In other words, marketing must identify consumer needs and participate in the process of ensuring that those needs are met. More specifically, marketers must make greater efforts to identify the needs of our society which are either unmet or poorly met, must communicate the existence of these needs to society, and must direct the resources of society toward satisfying these needs.

Major Issues for the 1970's

Many major issues that face American society today are discussed throughout this book. Not all of them are usually thought of as problems related to marketing. However, using our revised perspective of marketing, each of the issues discussed below can benefit from effective marketing action.

Recently, *discrimination against minorities* has received extensive attention in mass media. Demonstrations, activist meetings on college campuses and in many other locations—farms in California, orange orchards in Florida, and the ghettos of our major cities—all illustrate the continuing seriousness of the minority-group discrimination issue. The descriptions of Claude Brown remain a reality. His people are alive but not well in the United States.

Poverty is closely related to the issue of minorities. The poor still lack economic and legal equality in our society. Moreover, present priorities and the complexity of the problem suggest that the effects of poverty will continue during the 1970's and even into the 1980's.

The President's Commission on the causes and prevention of violence (CCPV) recently predicted a potential disquieting situation for the American city in the 1980's and 1990's. The have-nots of our society provide a tremendous challenge to the United States. They represent the most substantial threat of a violent, disruptive revolution. Only a revolution in priorities and a revolution in the efforts to solve these problems can prevent a destructive change in the coming decades.

Product quality and our environmental pollution have received considerable attention in recent months. Increasingly, business is being challenged to provide quality and reliability in the goods it produces. Virginia Knauer and Ralph Nader have successfully led this crusade. Consumer concern for the environment will be an additional important consideration in the coming decade. Of course, concern is not enough. Large organizations and individuals must recognize the need for providing better product quality and reliability and for improving our polluted environment. The valuable business opportunities that these problems represent must also be seen.

Additionally, the United States must determine the role it will play in directing the *survival and growth* of the human race. Clearly, significant steps must be taken to reduce the tension among superpowers who have such destructive potential. Also the United States and other developed nations must identify new techniques for dealing with the problems of developing nations. These techniques must include more effective means for providing resources for these nations while allowing them to assume responsibility for their development and sovereignty. It is clear that America's survival is closely tied to its ability both to cut military armaments in industrial nations and to find new means of sharing its fortunes with less developed nations. The identification and communication of solutions to these international dilemmas are, perhaps, the major challenge facing our society today.

The problem of dialog without *communication* transcends all of the problems we have discussed thus far because it is part of each one of them. The seriousness of this problem is illustrated by the present situations between Arabs and Israelis, parents and college students, Catholics and Protestants, blacks and whites.

The following story, by Howard Warshaw, professor of art at the University of California, Santa Barbara, which recently appeared in *The Center Magazine,* is a colorful illustration of dialog without communication.

The large room through which I must pass to get to my office-studio is scheduled for drawing. However, due to the popular misconceptions that drawing is unnecessary to painting and that painting is unnecessary to art, precious little drawing is done there. Instead, pompous exercises with mysterious, inflated meanings are conducted in the manner of seances by coolly weary, relentlessly picturesque graduate students.

I was therefore not surprised on entering the classroom not long ago to find the paper towels had been removed from the sink and arranged in rotating columns about the room. I had previously seen the drawing tables stacked in rhythmic patterns and Dixie cups arranged in regiments.

A girl in the corner near my studio was arranging raisins. I asked her if a class was scheduled for the coming hour. "Yes," she said. "Are you doing any drawing?" I asked. "Oh, no," she said. "What do you do?" "Oh," she said, "you know, like design." "Is that what you're doing with the raisins?" I asked. "Mmm-hmm," said she, "we're working with—um—modular things. Each raisin is a module." "And," I asked, "what are you doing with these modules?" "Well," she said, "I'm designing them." "For what purpose?" Now with a hint of exasperation, "To be effective." "Effective for what?" "Visually effective," said she. I left her to her raisins and disappeared into my studio.

When I emerged later I found her still there along with the rest of the class. "Boy, you sure put me on," said she, "asking all those questions. I thought you were a maintenance man." "I am," I said. "As best I can I maintain the culture and I maintain the lines of communication between the living and the dead." "I mean," she said, "asking me all those questions like you didn't know." "You think," said I, "that I was teasing you and that of course I knew what you were talking about. Well I wasn't teasing; and I don't know what you were talking about; and I had only hoped to reveal to you that you don't know what you are talking about yourself."

Lack of communication is more important today than ever before because mass communication and extended education have made more people aware of the differences in our society. Information is doubling every ten years. Eighty percent of the scientists who ever lived are alive today and 80 to 90% of the discoveries that will be well known in 45 years will be made during the professional careers of this year's college graduates. Hence, the obsolescence of ideas and methods of communication is more rapid than ever. Solving the problem begins with people, individually, being interested in and willing to communicate with others who speak through different values and different experiences. This involves people marketing themselves as individuals who are interested in communicating.

Some Forms and Symptoms of Change[2]

Present predictions of gross national product, capital spending, and family income for the next decade all indicate a period of rapid expansion for our economy. By

---

[2]Much of the statistical information in this section comes from a speech by Richard M. Paget, "Changes and Challenges in the 70's," presented to the Allied Chemical Corporation, June 16, 1970.

1980 the gross national product may be $1.5 trillion in today's dollars and $2 trillion in terms of 1980 dollars. This large increase will have at least two causes. First, it is estimated that there will be a 21% increase in man-hours during the decade. Almost 100 million people will be working in 1980 versus approximately 80 million persons today. Second, this large increase in gross national product assumes a continuation of an annual increase in productivity of 3%. This magnitude of growth indicates that our society has the economic potential to resolve many of the problems we face if we choose to focus sufficient resources on these problems.

In addition to the large expected change in gross national product, capital spending will continue on a high level and will increase from $80 billion in 1970 to $115 billion in 1980, in terms of 1970 dollars. Hopefully, an appropriate proportion of this investment will be directed toward improving the quality of our lives and our environment.

By 1980 about 30 cents out of every investment dollar will be spent for automated machines and equipment compared with 20 cents out of every investment dollar in the 1960's. This expected increase in investment illustrates the continuing emphasis our industrial society is placing on rapid change. For example, General Motors has recently invested in a highly automated assembly line for producing low-priced automobiles. A year ago, an assembly line of 48,000 workers was able to produce 60 cars per hour. Today, with extensive automation, that assembly line produces 100 cars per hour with the same number of workers. Hopefully, further progress of this kind will result in lower prices and will enable more people to enjoy the convenience of products already available to most Americans today.

A third variable, which also illustrates the magnitude of expected growth of our economy during the 1970's, is output. Economists are predicting a minimum increase in real output of 70% during the decade, and there are some analysts who believe the economy could grow between 4 and 5% per year. At present, the median family income in the United States is about $8,000. By 1980, we shall be approaching $13,000. With planning and a clear definition of priorities, this increase could contribute greatly to the elimination of poverty in our society.

Product life cycles will continue to shorten, and product introductions will continue to proliferate. In overall terms, 60% of the products sold by manufacturing in 1980 will not have been produced prior to 1970. Product obsolescence will be one third again as rapid in the 1970's as in the 1960's.

In addition, by 1980 research and development expenditures will almost be double 1970's level of $27 billion. This again illustrates the potential of our economy to improve the quality of products and services as well as to correct pollution externalities which threaten human population in major cities as well as wild life in rural regions.

The issue is: What priorities will we choose? Where will we direct the economic power that will be available during the next decade? Government and industry seem to be undergoing a general shift in priorities. It appears that the federal government is evolving toward a modified role in the world community. Also, there appears to be an effort to incorporate our own resources into new foreign aid programs that give recipient nations a greater opportunity to assume the responsibility for developing and protecting their own sovereignty. Hopefully, this will result in greater individual motivation within these nations.

The recently recommended revision of our welfare program is also a positive step toward using personal motivation to resolve some of the causes of poverty in our country. A major question that remains about the welfare program is: Does it go far enough?

The greatest single source of change in the next decade may come from the inescapable involvement of corporations in bringing about social change. Increasing numbers of business leaders, teachers, and analysts of business trends agree that if our society is to change, corporations and their management must play a significant role in bringing this about.

This is not the view of a few radicals. This view is supported by the CED, by respected scholars, and most recently by Henry Ford, who in a speech in late 1969 said:

> Now that public expectations are exploding in all directions, we can no longer regard profit and service to society as separate and competing goals, even in the short run. The company that sacrifices more and more short run profit to keep up with constantly rising public expectation will soon find itself with no long run to worry about. On the other hand, the company that seeks to conserve its profits by minimizing response to changing expectations will soon find itself in conflict with all the publics on which its profits depend.... We have to ask ourselves, what do people want that they didn't want before and how can we get a competitive edge by giving them more of what they really want?

A crisis is sometimes necessary to focus attention on the crucial problems a society faces. Poverty, discrimination, the war, and pollution have all been described as crises, and it has appeared recently that the louder, more frequent and more violent the complaint, the greater the possibility of remedial action. Actually, all of this protest is marketing. Some may dislike the form of the effort, but there should be no question that it is marketing and that these efforts in some cases have achieved a portion of their objectives. The effectiveness of these individual and group efforts points out the opportunity and need for constructive solutions to crucial problems.

It has been the purpose of the preceding material to suggest that our nation possesses the economic and social resources to solve many current problems. The following materials in this book point out additional problems and directions and hopefully demonstrate that the most needed element is constructive action by each of us. That is where the greatest opportunity for improvement lies.

A. *Some Indications of Change*

3. *The Future of the Industrial System*

JOHN KENNETH GALBRAITH

The two questions most asked about an economic system are whether it serves man's physical needs and whether it is consistent with his liberty. There is little doubt as to the ability of our industrial system to serve man's needs. It is able to manage them only because it serves them abundantly. It requires a mechanism for making men want what it provides. But this mechanism would not work—wants would not be subject to manipulation—had not these wants been dulled by sufficiency.

The prospects for liberty involve far more interesting questions. It has always been imagined that to associate all, or a large part, of economic activity with the state is to endanger freedom. The individual and his preferences, in one way or another, will be sacrificed to the needs and conveniences of the apparatus created ostensibly to serve him. As the industrial system evolves into a penumbra of the state, the question of its relation to liberty thus arises in urgent form. In recent years, in the Soviet-type economies, there has been an ill-concealed conflict between the state and the intellectuals. In essence, this has been a conflict between those for whom the needs of the government, including above all its needs as economic planner and producer of goods, are pre-eminent and those who assert the high but inconvenient claims of uninhibited intellectual and artistic expression. Is this a warning?

SOURCE. From *The New Industrial State* by John Kenneth Galbraith. Copyright © 1967 by John Kenneth Galbraith. Reprinted by permission of the publisher, Houghton Mifflin Company.

The instinct which warns of dangers in this association of economic and public power is sound. But conservatives have looked in the wrong direction for the danger. They have feared that the state might reach out and destroy the vigorous, money-making entrepreneur. They have not noticed that, all the while, the successsors to the entrepreneur were uniting themselves ever more closely with the state and rejoicing in the result. They were also, and with enthusiasm, accepting abridgement of their freedom. Part of this is implicit in the subordination of individual personality to the needs of organization. Some of it is in the exact pattern of the classical business expectation. The president of Republic Aviation is not much more likely in public to speak critically, or even candidly, of the Air Force than is the head of a Soviet *combinat* of the ministry to which he reports. No modern head of the Ford Motor Company will ever react with the same pristine vigor to the presumed foolishness of Washington as did its founder. No head of Montgomery Ward will ever again breathe defiance of a President as did Sewell Avery. Manners may be involved. But it would also be conceded that "too much is at stake."

The problem, however, is not the freedom of the businessman. Business orators have spoken much about freedom in the past. But it can be laid down as a rule that those who speak most of liberty are least inclined to use it. The high executive who speaks fulsomely of personal freedom carefully submits his speeches on the subject for review and elimination of controversial words, phrases and ideas, as befits a good organization man. The general who tells his troops, and the world, that they are in the forefront of the fight for freedom is a man who has always submitted happily to army discipline. The high State Department official, who adverts feelingly to the values of the free world extravagantly admires the orthodoxy of his own views.

The danger to liberty lies in the subordination of belief to the needs of the industrial system. In this the state and the industrial system will be partners. This threat has already been assessed, as also the means for minimizing it.

If we continue to believe that the goals of the industrial system—the expansion of output, the companion increase in consumption, technological advance, the public images that sustain it—are coordinate with life, then all of our lives will be in the service of these goals. What is consistent with these ends we shall have or be allowed; all else will be off limits. Our wants will be managed in accordance with the needs of the industrial system; the policies of the state will be subject to similar influence; education will be adapted to industrial need; the disciplines required by the industrial system will be the conventional morality of the community. All other goals will be made to seem precious, unimportant or antisocial. We will be bound to the ends of the industrial system. The state will add its moral, and perhaps some of its legal, power to their enforcement. What will eventuate, on the whole, will be the benign servitude of the household retainer who is taught to love her mistress and see her interests as her own, and not the compelled servitude of the field hand. But it will not be freedom.

If, on the other hand, the industrial system is only a part, and relatively a diminishing part, of life, there is much less occasion for concern. Aesthetic goals will have pride of place; those who serve them will not be subject to the goals of the industrial system; the industrial system itself will be subordinate to the claims of these dimensions of life. Intellectual preparation will be for its own sake and not for the better service to the industrial system. Men will not be entrapped by the belief that apart from the goals of the industrial system—apart from the production of goods and income by progressively more advanced technical methods—there is nothing important in life.

The foregoing being so, we may, over time, come to see the industrial system in fitting light as an essentially technical arrangement for providing convenient goods and services in adequate volume. Those who rise through its bureaucracy will so see themselves. And the public consequences will be in keeping, for if economic goals are the only goals of the society it is natural that the industrial system should dominate the state and the state should serve its ends. If other goals are strongly asserted, the industrial system will fall into its place as a detached and autonomous arm of the state, but responsive to the larger purposes of the society.

We have seen wherein the chance for salvation lies. The industrial system, in contrast with its economic antecedents, is intellectually demanding. It brings into existence, to serve its intellectual and scientific needs, the community that, hopefully, will reject its monopoly of social purpose.

4. *Management's New Role*

PETER F. DRUCKER

The major assumptions on which both the theory and the practice of management have been based these past fifty years are rapidly becoming inappropriate.

To a considerable extent the obsolescence and inadequacy of these assumed verities of management reflect management's own success. For management has been the success story par excellence of these last fifty years—more so even than science. But to an even greater extent, the traditional assumptions of management scholar and management practitioner are being outmoded by independent—or at least only partially dependent—developments in society, in economy, and in the world view of our age, especially in the developed countries. To a large extent objective reality is changing around the manager—and fast.

The Old Assumptions

Six assumptions may have formed the foundation of the theory and practice of management this last half century. Few practitioners of management have, of course, ever been conscious of them. Even the management scholars have, as a rule, rarely stated them explicitly.

SOURCE. Abridgement of Chapter 2 "Management's New Role," from *Technology, Management and Society* by Peter F. Drucker. Copyright © 1969 by Peter F. Drucker. By permission of Harper & Row, Publishers, Inc.

These assumptions deal with

The scope
The task
The position, and
The nature of management.

Assumption one: Management is management of business, and business is unique and the exception in society.

Assumption two: "Social responsibilities" of management, that is, concerns that cannot be encompassed within an economic calculus, are restraints and limitations imposed on management rather than management objectives and tasks. They are to be discharged largely without the enterprise and outside of management's normal working day. At the same time and because business is assumed to be the one exception, only business has social responsibilities; indeed, the common phrase is "the social responsibilities of business." University, hospital, or government agencies are clearly not assumed, in the traditional view, to have any social responsibilities.

Assumption three: The primary, perhaps the only, task of management is to mobilize the energies of the business organization for the accomplishment of known and defined tasks. The tests are efficiency in doing what is already being done, and adaptation to changes outside. Entrepreneurship and innovation—other than systematic research—lie outside the management scope.

Assumption four: It is the manual worker—skilled or unskilled—who is management's concern as resource, as a cost center, and as a social and individual problem.

Assumption five: Management is a "science" or at least a "discipline," that is, it is as independent of cultural values and individual beliefs as are the elementary operations of arithmetic, the laws of physics, or the stress tables of the engineer. But all management is being practiced within one distinct national environment and imbedded in one national culture, circumscribed by one legal code and part of one national economy.

Assumption six: Management is the result of economic development.

I fully realize that I have oversimplified—grossly so. But I do not believe that I have misrepresented our traditional assumptions. Nor do I believe that I am mistaken that these assumptions, in one form or another, still underlie both the theory and the practice of management, especially in the industrially developed nations.

—And the New Realities

Today, however, we need quite different assumptions. They, too, of course, oversimplify—and grossly, too. But they are far closer to today's realities than the assumptions on which theory and practice of management have been basing themselves these past fifty years.

Here is a first attempt to formulate assumptions that correspond to the management realities of our time.

Assumption one: Every major task of developed society is being carried out in and through an organized and managed institution. Business enterprise was only the first of those and, therefore, became the prototype by historical accident. But while it has a specific job—the production and distribution of economic goods and services—it is neither the exception nor unique. Large-scale organization is the rule rather than the exception. Our society is one of pluralist organizations rather than a diffusion of family units. And management, rather than the isolated peculiarity of one unique exception, the business enterprise, is generic and the central social function in our society.

Assumption two: Because our society is rapidly becoming a society of organizations, all institutions, including business, will have to hold themselves accountable for the "quality of life" and will have to make fulfillment of basic social values, beliefs, and purposes a major objective of their continuing normal activities rather than a "social responsibility" that restrains or that lies outside of their normal main functions. They will have to learn to make the "quality of life" into an opportunity for their own main tasks. In the business enterprise, this means that the attainment of the "quality of life" increasingly will have to be considered a business opportunity and will have to be converted by management into profitable business.

Assumption three: Entrepreneurial innovation will be as important to management as the managerial function, both in the developed and in the developing countries. Indeed, entrepreneurial innovation may be more important in the years to come. Unlike the nineteenth century, however, entrepreneurial innovation will increasingly have to be carried out in and by existing institutions such as existing businesses. It will, therefore, no longer be possible to consider it as lying outside of management or even as peripheral to management. Entrepreneurial innovation will have to become the very heart and core of management.

Innovation will increasingly have to be channeled in and through existing businesses, if only because the tax laws in every developed country make the existing business the center of capital accumulation. And innovation is capital-intensive, especially in the two crucial phases, the development phase and the market introduction of new products, processes, or services. We will, therefore, increasingly have to learn to make existing organizations capable of rapid and continuing innovation. How far we are still from this is shown by the fact that management still worries about "resistance to change." What existing organizations will have to learn is to reach out for change as an opportunity and to resist continuity.

Assumption four: A primary task of management in the developed countries in the decades ahead will increasingly be to make knowledge productive. The manual worker is "yesterday"—and all we can fight on that front is a rearguard action. The basic capital resource, the fundamental investment, but also the cost center of a developed economy, is the knowledge worker who puts to work what he has learned in systematic education, that is, concepts, ideas, and theories, rather than the man who puts to work manual skill or muscle.

Assumption five: There are management tools and techniques. There are management concepts and principles. There is a common language of management. And there may even be a universal "discipline" of management. Certainly there is a worldwide generic function which we call management and which serves the same purpose in any and all developed societies. But management is also a culture and a system of values and beliefs. It is also the means through which a given society makes productive its own values and beliefs. Indeed, management may well be considered the bridge between a "civilization" that is rapidly becoming worldwide, and a "culture" which expresses divergent tradition, values, beliefs, and heritages. Management must, indeed, become the instrument through which cultural diversity can be made to serve the common purposes of mankind. At the same time, management increasingly is not being practiced within the confines of one national culture, law, or sovereignty but "multinationally." Indeed, management increasingly is becoming an institution—so far, the only one—of a genuine world economy.

Assumption six: Management creates economic and social development. Economic and social development is the *result* of management.

All our experience in economic development proves this. Wherever we have only contributed the economic "factors of production," especially capital, we have not achieved development. In the few cases where we have been able to generate management energies (e.g., in the Cauca Valley in Colombia) we have generated rapid development. Development, in other words, is a matter of human energies rather than of economic wealth. And the generation and direction of human energies is the task of management.

* * *

Admittedly, these new assumptions oversimplify; they are meant to. But I submit that they are better guides to effective management in the developed countries today, let alone tomorrow, than the assumptions on which we have based our theories as well as our practice these last fifty years. We are not going to abandon the old tasks. We still, obviously, have to manage the going enterprise and have to create internal order and organization. We still have to manage the manual worker and make him productive. And no one who knows the reality of management is likely to assert that we know everything in these and similar areas that we need to know; far from it. But the big jobs waiting for management today, the big tasks requiring both new theory and new practice, arise out of the new realities and demand different assumptions and different approaches.

More important even than the new tasks, however, may be management's new role. Management is fast becoming the central resource of the developed countries and the basic need of the developing ones. From being the specific concern of one, the economic institutions of society, management and managers are becoming the generic, the distinctive, the constitutive organ of developed society. What management is and what managers do will, therefore—and properly—become increasingly a matter of public concern rather than a matter for the "experts." Management will increasingly be concerned as much with the expression of basic beliefs and values as with the accomplishment of measurable results. It will increasingly stand for the quality of life of a society as much as for its standard of living.

The task of the next generation is to make productive for individual, community, and society the new organized institutions of our New Pluralism. And that is, above all, the task of management.

5. *J. Irwin Miller: The Revolutionary Role of Business*

WILLIAM D. PATTERSON

The Social violence of the times is clearly challenging the capacity of our basic institutions—government, business, education, labor, the church, and the press—to offer a creative response. The discontent demand, and deserve, more from the Establishment than police action if the essential fabric of our democratic society is to be preserved.

It seems clear that the socioeconomic transformation of the U.S. will confront the coming generation of business leaders with historic changes in their responsibilities and their opportunities. This confrontation has already begun for today's business leadership and will continue to accelerate for the new generation of highly educated, trained executives.

This era of turbulence and flux has not gone unobserved. It has, in fact, been anticipated with a rare kind of prescience by J. Irwin Miller, the chairman of the board and chief executive officer of the Cummins Engine Company, Inc. In Mr. Miller's tall, angular, unassuming person there is at first little clue to the valuable public services he has rendered his community and nation while building a small family manufacturing enterprise, which was deficit-ridden when he took it over thirty-three years ago, into a solid, successful, diversified corporation with world-wide sales of $331 million.

SOURCE. Reprinted by permission from *Saturday Review,* January 13, 1968. Copyright 1968 Saturday Review, Inc.

The quiet, consummate skill with which he has woven together the varied strands of his private corporate and public service interests since graduating from Yale (1931) and Oxford (1933) Universities dramatically exemplifies *Saturday Review's* conviction that in our complex socioeconomic system the modern executive must embody a personal commitment to the good society as well as a sound economy in order to make our system work. Today's stresses and strains in the U.S. social order underscore this conviction, which motivated *Saturday Review* to establish its annual Businessman of the Year award twelve years ago. The 1968 citation goes to Mr. Miller.

Mr. Miller is very much a man of his times in the arenas of business, banking, education, government, the arts, and the church.

Mr. Miller regards a scholarly interest in the past as only a necessary resource on which one must draw to understand the present and perceive the future. While his view of the role of the businessman in America is a highly moral one, his approach to today's problems in our rapidly changing social and economic situation is not only philosophical but pragmatic. He has a "Main Street" view not only of the affairs of his town, but of the state of the nation.

"It is ridiculous ever to forget that you and your business are each implanted in the society of the moment and influenced by the forces of history, and will flourish according as that society is healthy and those historical forces are channeled in propitious directions. We cannot ignore the world of our time. We had better understand it.

"History is full of persons who didn't understand the world in which they lived. We Americans are a part of history. No man can ignore that we are the result of the forces of history, and that these forces are at work upon us today.

"Those who rightly interpret the direction of the changes, and who respond to them—such persons in history have mostly flourished. Those who remained the same—they perished, thinking they were holding to the old virtues, which an irresponsible generation had abandoned. For the most part they perished because their minds had become like the body of the dinosaur, unfit for the new climate of the world. Our world also is changing, and few disagree that we are changing to a degree and with a speed that has scarcely ever been recorded."

It is a dialogue on change in this country that brings out Mr. Miller's deep concern for a creative response by business, education, and government. This response should not be one of resistance to change, he argues, but of acceptance of the forces for change in our society and our economy.

As a trustee of the Ford Foundation, as a member of the Business Council—the elite group of U.S. business leaders through whom much of industry's cooperation with the federal government are channeled—as a chairman of various Presidential commissions, and as an active leader in the World Council of Churches, Mr. Miller has been an influential spokesman for flexible positive programs to cope with the accelerating currents of restlessness and challenge both in America and abroad. He has said:

"There have been many times of discontent in history. The discontented of colonial America were less the isolated farmers than the educated Jefferson, Adams, Franklin, and a whole host of schoolmasters, parsons, and merchants who had an idea of what they wanted. The discontented of nineteenth-century Russia were in part the peasants—but very intensely more the intellectuals, the professionals, those who had a window on the world.

"Today is also a day of discontent. One can look at Africa, South America, Asia—at our own youth in America—and conclude that the more education an individual possesses the harder it is to keep him in his place. In past times this group of persons has been only the smallest fragment of the total population of a nation; yet, when it has felt like it, the fragment has been able to stir up a very great deal of trouble. Never has so large a share of population been the recipient of considerable education. We cannot expect this large, new group among us to be docile. Whether discontented or happy with their state of life, educated persons have wanted a say in what happened to them, and have quite often been effective in getting that say. Today we see students wanting a say in the conduct of the universities; labor wanting a say in management decisions; the poor wanting a say in the conduct of the programs devised to help them; Negroes wanting not relief or charity, but much more—a say in the whole of the society.

"There is a new word being heard in the world. The word is addressed to the powerful and it goes like this: 'You in the Establishment seem to make most of the decisions which affect us. We want to share in those decisions and in the ones which affect you, too.' Now this word may be the wrong word, but it is still an important new fact. It is one which can no more be ignored than surprisingly similar words spoken by the weak American Colonials to the powerful Mother Country, and I think it is the natural response of men who possess more education, more confidence in their judgments that did their simpler forebears.

"We are a more educated and a wealthier people. We are also very obviously a more numerous people—with traffic jams, cities springing up overnight. We are being crowded together uncomfortably and faster than we like. By 1980 80 per cent of us will live in cities, and the strip city—Boston to Washington, Los Angeles to San Diego—will have made its appearance. Why go through this catalogue about the kind of world that is just ahead, for it is well known to us? Dr. Johnson once said, 'It is often more important to remind than to inform.' And I think we need reminding. We are strapped down to this society, and there is no escape from it—no western lands toward which to flee. We must stay and make a go of it. And I am not at all sure we shall make a go of it.

"I say this not because of external threats or the menace of Communism. In respect to these, we appear to be doing rather well. The storm signals of greatest import seem to me to have appeared on the domestic horizon."

One of the storm signals that has most actively involved Mr. Miller is the explosive Negro protest. As the first lay president of the National Council of the Churches of Christ in the U.S.A. (1960-63), he sponsored the formation of an active Council committee on civil rights in defense of the Negro's struggle against discrimination and oppression and otherwise spurred the direct concern of the nation's Protestant churches in ameliorating what he regards as one of the most dangerous issues facing the country. His views are eloquent and compelling:

"Today in this country the per capita wealth of all segments is growing astonishingly. But more significant to our future may well be the disturbing fact that the growth is not taking place evenly—and that some racial or national groups, notably the Negroes, are falling behind; that the disparity in income between them and comparable segments of the non-Negro population is growing greater. There is little point in asking whose fault it is. As we like to assert, it may be in large part 'their own fault.' It matters not; as the disparity grows so does the likelihood of explosion.

"The American Negro knows better than any of us why the United States is not among the leading nations in eliminating infant mortality. The American Negro knows better than any of us who it is that composes most of our current unemployment figure. The American Negro knows what his relative odds are for being drafted.

"The American Negro has seen hopeful legislation enacted by his federal government and little change in his neighborhood or opportunities. He interprets 'progress' as defined by the white majority to mean it won't happen to him in his lifetime.

"And so last summer, in a tiny segment of this amazingly patient people we began to see a change. We began to see American citizens who quite simply have given up on America and the American system. I think this may turn out to have been something new. I doubt whether they were subverted by the Communists. I think they have changed simply because America hasn't worked for them. They see no hope for jobs, for equal treatment, for decent housing, and so they have said, 'The hell with it. Let's wreck the joint.' And in Watts and other cities they did wreck the joint—and not to any end or purpose. To our cry that they are not helping themselves, only stopping 'progress,' they answer—'What progress?'

"What means this small new cloud in the domestic sky? Nothing at the moment that can't be handled. But this is not simply crime, which will respond to vigorous and prompt law enforcement. There are two sides to this state of affairs. Violence and disobedience are wrong and constitute a danger to the fabric of society; but it is also very wrong, and illegal, to keep any segment of our people depressed and deprived—simply because the white majority has the power to do so. Of the two dangers, the latter has usually proved in history to be the more formidable.

"It is not hard to imagine a few summers hence our major cities brought to a halt by a hopeless, desperate few who see no escape from conditions of growing misery. Remember that the American Negro is only one highly volatile ingredient of a most explosive mixture. The mixture may very well ignite, and the explosion can, for practical purposes, destroy the nation. If such a destruction takes place, its locus will be the big city, and its time could be any time now.

"To each generation it has always seemed that it really can't happen here. I think it can, and if it does, it will be the explosive product of the anarchic cancerous growth of the big city acting upon the disadvantaged groups who most intensely feel its deprivation, and misery."

Mr. Miller was chairman of a special committe on U.S. trade with East European countries and the Soviet Union which strongly recommended expansion and normalization of East-West trade. Mr. Miller believes that out of a normal trade with the Soviet Union the elements of a stable, viable, peaceful Soviet-American collaboration for mutual progress may emerge. He now is a member of three Presidential commissions and just a few weeks ago he was named to the committee to organize the new Institute for Urban Development, which will bring the best brains available to bear on the plight of our cities. It will be organized as a private corporation to be financed by government contracts for research into the nation's welter of urban problems.

This kind of partnership in which government draws on the sources of private industry is not an alien phenomenon to Mr. Miller. But he believes that business must provide even more leadership than it ever has before in finding the solution to public problems in this country. For his own leadership in this broad area of public service collaboration he has received honorary degrees from eight leading colleges and universities.

On the subject of the role of business in helping our society cope with the complex problems troubling it, Mr. Miller has spoken out boldly:

"The real answer is to take the full dimension and complexity of our great problems—and solve them, while there is yet time. I shall not be so rash as to try to propose solutions, but I do think it is useful to consider what roles our descendants might wish business and businessmen had played in this particular decade of the nation's history.

"Consider how this world is lining up: West vs. East; Northern nations vs. Southern nations; and so on. It is our custom to simplify our description by saying it is the 'haves vs. the have-nots.' Perhaps a more useful simplification might be that it is the 'Establishment' side vs. the 'Revolution' side.

"We in business are clearly members of the Establishment side. We possess power to influence, power to acquire and to spend, to employ, to expand, to shape the young. But the powerful Establishment in history seldom plays a role other than that of 'King' in the child's game of 'King of the Hill.' The only purpose the 'King' can have is to stay on top on the hill, a purpose in which he always finally fails.

"I propose that in the judgment of future history the time is here when business should itself become the 'Revolution' side. Now nothing could really make us more uncomfortable than a thought like this. Reformers are nuts. But before we too quickly reject this notion, let us contemplate the following:

"First, there are signs of grave trouble within our society, and the solutions are not clearly in motion. Second, these troubles are surprisingly similar in kind to the troubles that have brought other societies down in the past. Third, in history some societies have solved their problems and survived. Great Britain in the eighteenth and nineteenth centuries is an example. Others have failed and have perished or grievously suffered. France and Russia in the same centuries are examples. Finally, more socieities fail than survive under such a test.

"You don't like the idea that business has anything to do with social reform, but your business and mine ultimately go under if society goes under, and societies have gone under. Whose business is it then to tackle troubles?

"No one is going to solve the problems of our time unless he is powerful and organized. Two great independent institutions exist in our society today which qualify for such a description. One is business. The other is the great university. Business understands the here and now, how to organize, how to respond to change.

"Who is to say that neighborhoods, communities, the states, the whole nation do not stand in need of such expertise—are not in need of the capacity for flexible response, and for intelligent and rapid change?

"Education has in its classrooms the future. As long as we remain an industrial society, and as long as education remains the important key to advancement in that society, the universities will have within their walls the Establishment of the next generation. These are the persons who will have the great leverage to move society. The influence of the university upon them is inescapably great.

"If, then, we ought to be reformers, what ought to be the character of our response to this uneasy role? To begin with, it seems clear to me that our response ought somehow to approach total response. Our concerned revolutionaries must include education, labor, business, and the church. Otherwise the task will fall to government alone, and the individual will suffer. Second, the response must be for change. Third, the response must be not only appropriate but as rapid as the changes which create the need. We no longer have forever. We no longer have other places to which to flee.

"Finally, the response must be made in self-interest, never in selfish interest. Not a one of us is free because he is surrounded by others who have some care for his freedom. Our true self-interest is always best sought by seeking equally the true interest of every other man. This has been true through history.

"The changes in attitude and action which are now called for may well be unprecedented in history. It is not clear that we shall make them in time. If we do, it will be because we in business made accurate appraisal of what is required of us, and led the reform."

This sense of commitment to the society around him is deeply imbedded in Mr. Miller because of his strong religious beliefs and his sense that business has a social responsibility.

This philosophy of the individual businessman's responsibility for the good society can be seen in action in Columbus where Mr. Miller inspired a sort of architectural revolution to make his town a more pleasant place in which to live. The town has become a showcase of some of the best in modern architecture. Just over thirteen years ago Mr. Miller set up the Cummins Engine Foundation to pay design costs if his fellow townspeople would agree to use top architects for new public buildings. The result has been a phenomenon that is a model and inspiration for other towns.

Through more than $2,000,000 in seed money from the foundation, master architects such as Eliel Saarinen and his son Ero, among many others, were brought in to design churches, schools, a library, a fire station, a country club for the town, and several office buildings as well. The impact on the town, its sense of well-being, its pride in its own esthetics, the awareness of emulation, have, in the opinion of most of Columbus's residents, made it a better place to live and enabled it to attract able, young, educated managers to work there—helping other local enterprises to obtain the talent needed to compete successfully in national and international markets.

The varied range of his personal and professional interests seems to be summed up in a pragmatic, ecumenical attitude toward the world around him which has influenced his service to his church, to his business, to the federal government, to his town, and to the good society in which he so strongly believes.

The public service accent of his life has also been influenced by the high value he has always set on the role of higher education in American life. Mr. Miller has invested much time and thought in strengthening the capacity of the university to play its fullest possible role.

Mr. Miller blends his private corporate interest and the public good in our economic democracy in a way that seems to promise that the resources of business will be mobilized in a revolutionary effort to help solve the grave problems besetting us, and thus make a lasting contribution not only to our progress, but to the survival of our society and our nation.

B. *The Role of Marketing*

6. *Broadening the Concept of Marketing*

PHILIP KOTLER AND SIDNEY J. LEVY

The term "marketing" connotes to most people a function peculiar to business firms. Marketing is seen as the task of finding and stimulating buyers for the firm's output. It involves product development, pricing, distribution, and communication; and in the more progressive firms, continuous attention to the changing needs of customers and the development of new products, with product modifications and services to meet these needs. But whether marketing is viewed in the old sense of "pushing" products or in the new sense of "customer satisfaction engineering," it is almost always viewed and discussed as a business activity.

It is the authors' contention that marketing is a pervasive societal activity that goes considerably beyond the selling of toothpaste, soap, and steel. Political contests remind us that candidates are marketed as well as soap; student recruitment by colleges reminds us that higher education is marketed; and fund raising reminds us that "causes" are marketed. Yet these areas of marketing are typically ignored by the student of marketing. Or they are treated cursorily as public relations or publicity activities. No attempt is made to incorporate these phenomena in the body proper of marketing thought and theory. No attempt is made to redefine the meaning of product development, pricing, distribution, and communication in these newer contexts to see if they have a useful meaning. No attempt is made to examine whether the principles of "good" marketing in

SOURCE. Reprinted from *Journal of Marketing,* published by the American Marketing Association, Vol. 33, January, 1969.

traditional product areas are transferable to the marketing of services, persons, and ideas.

The authors see a great opportunity for marketing people to expand their thinking and to apply their skills to an increasingly interesting range of social activity. The challenge depends on the attention given to it; marketing will either take on a broader social meaning or remain a narrowly defined business activity.

The Rise of Organizational Marketing

One of the most striking trends in the United States is the increasing amount of society's work being performed by organizations other than business firms. As a society moves beyond the stage where shortages of food, clothing, and shelter are the major problems, it begins to organize to meet other social needs that formerly had been put aside. Business enterprises remain a dominant type of organization, but other types of organizations gain in conspicuousness and in influence. Many of these organizations become enormous and require the same rarefied management skills as traditional business organizations. Managing the United Auto Workers, Defense Department, Ford Foundation, World Bank, Catholic Church, and University of California has become every bit as challenging as managing Procter and Gamble, General Motors, and General Electric. These nonbusiness organizations have an increasing range of influence, affect as many livelihoods, and occupy as much media prominence as major business firms.

All of these organizations perform the classic business functions. Every organization must perform a financial function insofar as money must be raised, managed, and budgeted according to sound business principles. Every organization must perform a production function in that it must conceive of the best way of arranging inputs to produce the outputs of the organization. Every organization must perform a personnel function in that people must be hired, trained, assigned, and promoted in the course of the organization's work. Every organization must perform a purchasing function in that it must acquire materials in an efficient way through comparing and selecting sources of supply.

When we come to the marketing function, it is also clear that every organization performs marketing-like activities whether or not they are recognized as such. Several examples can be given.

The police department of a major U.S. city, concerned with the poor image it has among an important segment of its population, developed a campaign to "win friends and influence people." One highlight of this campaign is a "visit your police station" day in which tours are conducted to show citizens the daily operations of the police department, including the crime laboratories, police lineups, and cells. The police department also sends officers to speak at public schools and carries out a number of other activities to improve its community relations.

Most museum directors interpret their primary responsibility as "the proper preservation of an artistic heritage for posterity." As a result, for many people museums are cold marble mausoleums that house miles of relics that soon give way to yawns and tired feet. Although museum attendance in the United States advances each year, a large number of citizens are uninterested in museums. Is this indifference due to failure in the manner of presenting what museums have to offer? This nagging question led the new director of the Metropolitan Museum of Art to broaden the museum's appeal through sponsoring contemporary art shows and "happenings." His marketing philosophy of museum management led to substantial increases in the Met's attendance.

Nations also resort to international marketing campaigns to get across important points about themselves to the citizens of other countries. The junta of Greek colonels who seized power in Greece in 1967 found the international publicity surrounding their cause to be extremely unfavorable and potentially disruptive of international recognition. They hired a major New York public relations firm and soon full-page newspaper ads appeared carrying the headline "Greece Was Saved From Communism," detailing in small print why the takeover was necessary for the stability of Greece and the world.

An anti-cigarette group in Canada is trying to press the Canadian legislature to ban cigarettes on the grounds that they are harmful to health. There is widespread support for this cause but the organization's funds are limited, particularly measured against the huge advertising resources of the cigarette industry. The group's problem is to find effective ways to make a little money go a long way in persuading influential legislators of the need for discouraging cigarette consumption. This group has come up with several ideas for marketing anti-smoking to Canadians, including television spots, a paperback book featuring pictures of cancer and heart disease patients, and legal research on company liability for the smoker's loss of health.

What concepts are common to these and many other possible illustrations of organizational marketing? All of these organizations are concerned about their "product" in the eyes of certain "consumers" and are seeking to find "tools" for furthering their acceptance. Let us consider each of these concepts in general organizational terms.

Products

Every organization produces a "product" of at least one of the following types:

Physical products. "Product" first brings to mind everyday items like soap, clothes, and food, and extends to cover millions of *tangible* items that have a market value and are available for purchase.

Services. Services are *intangible* goods that are subject to market transaction such as tours, insurance, consultation, hairdos, and banking.

Persons. Personal marketing is an endemic *human* activity, from the employee trying to impress his boss to the statesman trying to win the support of the public. With the advent of mass communications, the marketing of persons has been turned over to professionals. Hollywood stars have their press agents, political candidates their advertising agencies, and so on.

Organizations. Many organizations spend a great deal of time marketing themselves. The Republican Party has invested considerable thought and resources in trying to develop a modern look. The American Medical Association decided recently that it needed to launch a campaign to improve the image of the American doctor. Many charitable organizations and universities see selling their *organization* as their primary responsibility.

Ideas. Many organizations are mainly in the business of selling *ideas* to the larger society. Population organizations are trying to sell the idea of birth control, and the Women's Christian Temperance Union is still trying to sell the idea of prohibition.

Thus the "product" can take many forms, and this is the first crucial point in the case for broadening the concept of marketing.

Consumers

The second crucial point is that organizations must deal with many groups that are interested in their products and can make a difference in its success. It is vitally important to the organization's success that it be sensitive to, serve, and satisfy these groups. One set of groups can be called the *suppliers. Suppliers* are those who provide the management group with the inputs necessary to perform its work and develop its product effectively. Suppliers include employees, vendors of the materials, banks, advertising agencies, and consultants.

The other set of groups are the *consumers* of the organization's product, of which four sub-groups can be distinguished. The *clients* are those who are the immediate consumers of the organization's product. The clients of a business firm are its buyers and potential buyers; of a service organization those receiving the services, such as the needy (from the Salvation Army) of the sick (from County Hospital); and of a protective or a primary organization, the members themselves. The second group is the *trustees* or *directors,* those who are vested with the legal authority and responsibility for the organization, oversee the management, and enjoy a variety of benefits from the "product." The third group is the active *publics* that take a specific interest in the organization. For a business firm, the active publics include consumer rating groups, governmental agencies, and pressure groups of various kinds. For a university, the active publics include alumni and friends of the university, foundations, and city fathers. Finally, the fourth consumer group is the *general public.* These are all the people who might develop attitudes toward the organization that might affect its conduct in some way. Organizational marketing concerns the programs designed by management to create satisfactions and favorable attitudes in the organization's four consuming groups: clients, trustees, active publics, and general public.

Marketing Tools

Students of business firms spend much time studying the various tools under the firm's control that affect product acceptance: product improvement, pricing, distribution, and communication. All of these tools have counterpart applications to nonbusiness organizational activity.

Nonbusiness organizations to various degrees engage in product improvement, especially when they recognize the competition they face from other organizations. Thus, over the years churches have added a host of nonreligious activities to their basic religious activities to satisfy members seeking other bases of human fellowship. Universities keep updating their curricula and adding new student services in an attempt to make the educational experience relevant to the students. Where they have failed to do this, students have sometimes organized their own courses and publications, or have expressed their dissatisfaction in organized protest. Government agencies such as license bureaus, police forces, and taxing bodies are often not responsive to the public because of monopoly status; but even here citizens have shown an increasing readiness to protest mediocre services, and more alert bureaucracies have shown a growing interest in reading the user's needs and developing the required product services.

All organizations face the problem of pricing their products and services so that they cover costs. Churches charge dues, universities charge tuition, governmental agencies charge fees, fund-raising organizations send out bills. Very often specific product charges are not sufficient to meet the organization's budget, and it must rely on gifts and surcharges to make up the difference. Opinions vary as to how much the users should be charged for the individual services and how much should be made up through general collection. If the university increases its tuition, it will have to face losing some students and putting more students on scholarship. If the hospital raises its charges to cover rising costs and additional services, it may provoke a reaction from the community. All organizations face complex pricing issues although not all of them understand good pricing practice.

Distribution is a central concern to the manufacturer seeking to make his goods conveniently accessible to buyers. Distribution also can be an important marketing decision area for nonbusiness organizations. A city's public library has to consider the best means of making its books available to the public. Should it establish one large library with an extensive collection of books, or several neighborhood branch libraries with duplication of books? Should it use bookmobiles that bring the books to the customers instead of relying exclusively on the customers coming to the books? Should it distribute through school libraries? Similarly the police department of a city must think through the problem of distributing its protective services efficiently through the community. It has to determine how much protective service to allocate to different neighborhoods; the respective merits of squad cars, motorcycles, and foot patrolmen; and the positioning of emergency phones.

Customer communication is an essential activity of all organizations although many nonmarketing organizations often fail to accord it the importance it deserves. Managements of many organizations think they have fully met their communication responsibilities by setting up advertising and/or public relations departments. They fail to realize that *everything about an organization talks*. Customers form impressions of an organization from its physical facilities, employees, officers, stationery, and a hundred other company surrogates. Only when this is appreciated do the members of the organization recognize that they all are in marketing, whatever else they do. With this understanding they can assess realistically the impact of their activities on the consumers.

Is Organizational Marketing a Socially Useful Activity?

Modern marketing has two different meanings in the minds of people who use the term. One meaning of marketing conjures up the terms selling, influencing, persuading. Marketing is seen as a huge and increasingly dangerous technology, making it possible to sell persons on buying things, propositions, and causes they either do not want or which are bad for them. This was the indictment in Vance Packard's *Hidden Persuaders* and numerous other social criticisms, with the net effect that a large number of persons think of marketing as immoral or entirely self-seeking in its fundamental premises. They can be counted on to resist the idea of organizational marketing as so much "Madison Avenue."

The other meaning of marketing unfortunately is weaker in the public mind; it is the concept of sensitively *serving and satisfying human needs*. This was the great contribution of the marketing concept that was promulgated in the 1950s, and that concept now counts many business firms as its practitioners. The marketing concept holds that the problem of all business firms in an age of abundance is to develop customer loyalties and satisfaction, and the key to this problem is to focus on the customer's needs. Perhaps the short-run problem of business firms is to sell people on buying the existing products, but the long-run problem is clearly to create the products that people need. By this recognition that effective marketing requires a consumer orientation instead of a product orientation, marketing has taken a new lease on life and tied its economic activity to a higher social purpose.

It is this second side of marketing that provides a useful concept for all organizations. All organizations are formed to serve the interest of particular groups: hospitals serve the sick, schools serve the students, governments serve the citizens, and labor unions serve the members. In the course of evolving, many organizations lose sight of their original mandate, grow hard, and become self-serving. The bureaucratic mentality begins to dominate the original service mentality. Hospitals may become perfunctory in their handling of patients, schools treat their students as nuisances, city bureaucrats behave like petty tyrants toward the citizens, and labor unions try to run instead of serve their members. All of these actions tend to build frustration in the consuming groups. As a result some withdraw meekly from these organizations, accept frustration as part of their condition, and find their satisfactions elsewhere. This used to be the common reaction of ghetto Negroes and college students in the face of indifferent city and university bureaucracies. But new possibilities have arisen, and now the same consumers refuse to withdraw so readily. Organized dissent and protest are seen to be an answer, and many organizations thinking of themselves as responsible have been stunned into recognizing that they have lost touch with their constituencies. They had grown unresponsive.

Where does marketing fit into this picture? Marketing is that function of the organization that can keep in constant touch with the organization's consumers, read their needs, develop "products" that meet these needs, and build a program of communications to express the organization's purposes. Certainly selling and influencing will be large parts of organizational marketing; but, properly seen, selling follows rather than precedes the organization's drive to create products to satisfy its consumers.

Conclusion

It has been argued here that the modern marketing concept serves very naturally to describe an important facet of all organizational activity. All organizations must develop appropriate products to serve their sundry consuming groups and must use modern tools of communication to reach their consuming publics. The business heritage of marketing provides a useful set of concepts for guiding all organizations.

The choice facing those who manage nonbusiness organizations is not whether to market or not to market, for no organization can avoid marketing. The choice is whether to do it well or poorly, and on this necessity the case for organizational marketing is basically founded.

7. The Growing Responsibilities of Marketing ROBERT J. LAVIDGE

Areas of Growing Responsibility

Marketing is being widely criticized for its failure to contribute more to the solution of social as well as economic problems.

As a result of changes in both marketing and its environment, it is likely that marketing people will have an expanding opportunity, *and responsibility,* to serve society during the 1970s. Examples relate to:

1. Consumerism.
2. The struggle of the poor for subsistence.
3. The marketing of social and cultural services.
4. The day-to-day functioning of the economy.
5. The use and pollution of society's resources.

Efficiency and Social Justice

Marketing has a key role to play in the drive for increased efficiency within our economy. It also has an opportunity to play a significant role in the drive for social justice which is replacing the drive for security or affluence among many members of our society. There is a need for more vigorous action in both of these areas, efficiency and social justice.

SOURCE. Reprinted from *Journal of Marketing,* published by the American Marketing Association, Vol. 34, January, 1970.

Consumerism

The "social concerns" of marketing men and women have been focused primarily on sins of commission—especially on fraudulent or deceptive advertising, packaging, pricing, and credit practices. Although some progress is being made, marketing leaders must do a more effective job, during the next decade, of identifying and reducing these practices. Moreover, history suggests that standards will be raised. Some practices which today are generally considered acceptable will gradually be viewed as unethical, then immoral, and will eventually be made illegal. Rather than resisting such changes, marketing leaders have a responsibility to provide intelligent guidance in bringing them about. But that is not enough.

The Struggle for Subsistence

For much of the United States' population the struggle for material subsistence no longer provides direction. But the subsistence struggle will continue during the 1970s throughout most of the world. Socially concerned marketing men and women will not be content with their role in satisfying other needs while a large share of the world's population struggles with hunger and starvation. With vastly improved communications and increased education, we will become increasingly conscious of the unsatisfied needs of people in the economically underdeveloped nations of the world and in the poverty areas of the United States. Marketing people must work simultaneously in cultures of affluence and of poverty during the 1970s. The dual culture problem will pose difficulties because actions appropriate for one culture could be very inappropriate for the other.

More than a decade ago, Peter Drucker noted marketing's opportunity in connection with the ". . . race between the promise of economic development and the threat of international world-wide class war. The economic development is the opportunity of this age. The class war is the danger. . . . And whether we shall realize the opportunity or succumb to danger will largely decide not only the economic future of this world—it may largely decide its spiritual, its intellectual, its political and its social future. Marketing is central in this new situation. For marketing is one of our most potent levers to convert the danger into the opportunity."

Walt Rostow, while serving as chairman of the Policy Planning Council of the Department of State, told the members of the American Marketing Association: "I can tell you—without flattery—that I believe the skills this organization commands and represents are going to prove critical in the generation ahead to the development of countries and regions which contain a clear majority of the world's population." The opportunity and the challenge about which Drucker and Rostow spoke remain to be met in the 1970s.

Social and Cultural Services

The coming decade also will witness an expansion of the role of marketing in connection with "... markets based on social concern, markets of the mind, and markets concerned with the development of people to the fullest extent of their capabilities." Kotler and Levy have pointed out that the work of marketing people is contributing to the enrichment of human life through improved marketing of educational, health and religious services, better utilization of natural resources, and enjoyment of the fine arts. Marketing people are helping the institutions which provide such social and cultural services to improve the tailoring of their services to their "customers" and to improve the "distribution," "pricing," and "promotion" of them.

The Day-to-day Functioning of the Economy

During the coming decade, marketing people will be responsible for helping bring material rewards to more members of society. Ethical, creative, efficient day-to-day marketing activities help the economy function more effectively to serve mankind. And, as William Lazer noted in a recent *Journal of Marketing* article (see p. 322) "... it is clear that when abundance prevails individuals and nations can afford to, and do, exercise increasing social concern." It is when basic needs are met that men can turn attention to other needs and values, to the higher aspirations of mankind. Nevertheless, it is likely that marketing people will find themselves increasingly under fire and working in what seems to be a hostile environment during the coming decade. There are likely to be continued increases in the importance of noneconomic values with growing resistance to competitive activity and resultant attacks on marketing. The marketing leaders who truly serve society will be those who search for, seize, and act on opportunities for improvement rather than merely defend themselves or take popular actions in the name of social justice regardless of their impact on society.

The Use and Pollution of Society's Resources

During the 1970s, marketing men and women will become increasingly concerned with the pollution of our air, water, and land (by others as well as by business firms). In evaluating the opportunities for new products and services, for example, the role of marketing people heretofore has focused largely on the question: Can it be sold? During the 1970s there will be increasing attention to: *Should* it be sold? Is it worth its cost to society?

8. *The Mission of Marketing*

WROE ALDERSON

Marketing has a threefold mission—to find the shortest route to market for existing products, to bring new products to market, and to bring more people more fully into the market economy. The essential story of what marketing does can be related to this threefold mission. Each of the three will be discussed in turn.

The Shortest Path to Market

The concept of finding the shortest path to market can be expressed in terms of relative costs and efficiencies. It does not necessarily mean the shortest path in miles, and yet there are times in marketing when mileage is a controlling factor.

The decrease in the number of local mills, many hundreds of them having gone out of business since the turn of the century, meant simply *that they were no longer located on an efficient path to market*. Both the farmer and the consumer have gained a much wider range of choices as a result.

One of the most striking illustrations that mileage is most often not the controlling factor in efficient marketing can be drawn from foreign trade. In the days of the China Clippers, Canton and Shanghai could trade with New York more efficiently than they could with places 300 or 400 miles back in the interior over the mud roads of that day.

SOURCE. From Wroe Alderson and Michael H. Halbert, *Men, Motives, and Markets,* ©1968. Reprinted by permission of Prentice-Hall, Inc., Englewood Cliffs, New Jersey.

Marketing Channel Length

While "distance of market" is not measured by miles, neither can it be measured by the number of steps in the channel of distribution. The cost would be prohibitive for the Kellogg Company to sell its corn flakes directly to its millions of consumers across the country. Corn flakes and other grocery products typically pas^{..} through a long channel because it is more efficient for this type of product. The majority of food and grocery products are sold by food brokers to chain stores and wholesale grocers who in turn sell to retail grocers. Actually, most food products have by this time already been through an assembly operation of several steps and before that were collected from the farmer and brought to the manufacturer.

Channel Efficiency and Common Interests

The real test of determining the shortest path to market is *finding the most efficient way to match the supply of products available and consumer needs.* This is accomplished, when the typical consumer purchase is small, through an intricate system of sorting and resorting, with numerous transactions in between. If the product is of large unit value and of a complex nature involving a large flow of goods and services along with the product, however, the shortest path to market often requires the aid of only a single intermediary.

The existence of a series of intermediaries imposes some serious problems for the firm which is seeking the shortest route to market. At each step in the channel an intermediary buys the product for resale, mainly because he hopes to make a profit either on the product itself or on related products. The manufacturer, if he holds a dominant position in the channel, has the problem of motivating each of these intermediaries to give his product sales support or, at the very least, to refrain from putting obstacles in its path.

In some cases the manufacturer and his retailers have an understood common interest because they are both in essentially the same line of business at two different levels. Thus, automobiles are the main business of Ford and General Motors but they are also the main business of Ford dealers and General Motor dealers. The area of common interest is also relatively clear with specialized shoe stores, camera stores, and appliance dealers.

Conflict of Interests

The situation becomes even more complicated when there are other intermediaries such as wholesalers in the channel. The retailer's stock and the wholesaler's stock usually do not strictly correspond but overlap on only a few items.

There are many lines of goods in which glaring differences remain, and they may always be there. David Craig and Werner Gabler, writing some years ago, came up with an appropriate term for this phenomenon. They called it the *discrepancy of assortments.* While the discrepancy of assortments is not the sole cause of conflict and tension in marketing channels, it is probably the most basic. Because of the discrepancy of assortments and other factors, in many cases there is continuous pressure to decrease the number of steps in the channel. To drop out intermediaries might turn out to be unfortunate and cost-increasing for some classes of goods, namely those which are of small unit value, physically identical, and presold to the consumer through advertising.

Shortening the Channel

For other classes of goods there have been some rather remarkable cases of achieving greater efficiency through shortening the channel by eliminating steps. One well-publicized case is that of the Raytheon Company, which manufactures advanced electronic equipment and components. At one time Raytheon had its own warehouses scattered around the country to maintain stocks of these products. These inventories were quite expensive to maintain, because of both investment cost and the special warehouse skills required. Raytheon found that it could do away with its warehouses in most areas, using air freight to deliver its products to its customers, who were almost entirely in the industrial field. A substantial saving was achieved, since the cost of air freight was less than the cost of warehousing.

The Introduction of New Products

The second dynamic aspect in the mission of marketing is expressed through the introduction of new products. Today this process involves very large expenditures for research and development and a similar sum of money for advertising. Total advertising expenditures were about $13 billion in 1964, while expenditures for research and development have been growing faster than advertising expenditures and are now running somewhat ahead of advertising. While the term "research and development" has come to be used very widely, it is most often used to apply to *product* research and development. The corresponding concept, which is only beginning to receive some recognition, is that of *market* research and development. The idea that markets have to be developed no less than products is a part of what is embraced by the *marketing concept.*

There is a paradox underlying the matching of goods and people so far as new products are concerned: it is uncertain whether a market exists for a new product in a specific sense until the product has been created. In conflict with this situation is the need for producing the product at least in limited quantities so that it can be presented to consumers and the demand for it can begin to be established. New products were often carried up to the finished article with no attempt made to measure demand or to measure the difficulty of generating demand.

A marketing executive of a well-known tool company gave an example of how his engineers came up with a hammer for a specific purpose and made his tool superior to anything available for that purpose. Later attempts to develop the market disclosed one fatal flaw in the latter program—only three or four people in the whole United States wanted a tool of that kind.

The Development Process and Product Novelty

Work may begin on a new product idea years before the company is ready to settle for a specific design. There is a continuous process of balancing consumer-use possibilities and production-technology possibilities against each other.

For a product to be considered new it must serve some purpose for some group of users better than any other available product. A balance must somehow be struck between the degree of novelty and the range of demand. Somewhere in between the most marketable design for the product may be located. One method which is often helpful in picking this best design is to try to identify the model *which would achieve the largest dollar volume of sales.* Individuals will pay more for a product if it gives them greater value, but the other dimension of marketability is the number who will pay more. Thus it is at least an important guideline to search for the design which will maximize the product of price and number of users.

In a more general way it can be stated that a new product must do one of two things: it must either serve a present need at a lower cost or serve a need better than anything else available. There is no reason why consumers should give up their established preferences unless the product qualifies on one ground or the other.

As a general rule, a product is likely to get into the market faster if it is a better product rather than a cheaper one. One problem with trying to market a cheaper product is that there is considerable confusion in the market with respect to the prices of many products because of the varying policies of retailers and others concerned. Also, a cheaper product is likely to be regarded with some suspicion as an inferior substitute, and may require some time to prove itself as good.

What is New?

In any discussion of the introduction of new products, the question of what is new comes up in several ways.

The degree of newness in a new product depends on how great an adjustment in habitual patterns of behavior is brought about by use of the product. When a consumer buys his first new automobile, the resulting adjustment is certainly on the average far greater than when he shifts from one cigarette to another. Another aspect of the problem of newness is that a product may already be well established in the market but new to an individual consumer.

New Product Diffusion

In recent years market analysts have talked about the process of "diffusion," the way in which a new product or a new culture trait may originate.

Market analysts have also postulated that some people are likely to prefer a product just because it is new, while others prefer it because of an established tradition.

Japan and Great Britain are both examples of countries with traditions that are much longer than the United States', yet in both countries the acceptance of innovation sometimes takes place with breathtaking speed.

Once more the real test of how new the product is concerns *how much difference it makes in human behavior.* Some new materials or components can be adopted with only minor changes in the production process. Other pieces of production equipment may operate on such different principles that they require complete reorganization of plant activities. There are also new products that force entirely new methods of marketing, even though the product itself is used for a well-established purpose.

New Product Advertising

There are many related questions of advertising and product research involved in the development of new markets and new products. On the advertising side it can be said that a product which is really new is not in competition at all unless the idea embodied in the product is somehow being publicized. Differentiated products vie for a place in the mind as a means of influencing the pattern of human behavior. If the supplier fails to identify specific claims, such products are simply not in competition. However new a product is, it is always to some degree a replacement for something else.

An advertising campaign for a product can be considered in either defensive or offensive terms. Defensively, the supplier may try to advertise in such a way as to prevent the consumer from shifting away from his product to others of the same class. The offensive advertising campaign might apply pressure in the opposite direction and try to stimulate consumers to shift to his product.

A good deal of advertising is condemned on the ground that it is being used to promote old products rather than new ones. The critic suggests that "legitimate" advertising would merely announce once and for all that a new product was available. One trouble with this reasoning is that it overlooks the fact that new consumers are always growing up and coming into the market and that *all* products are *new* for new consumers. There is also the fact that the hazards of competition would be greatly aggravated if the supplier of a new product were permitted to advertise his product without limit while the supplier of what was judged to be an old product was told that he could not advertise.

New Market Generation

To complete this section we will take note of one of the most striking examples of new markets created to absorb new products even where the new product seems to run counter to basic consumer psychology. The "product" in this case is life insurance. There was a time when no one bought life insurance simply because no such product existed. The individual had to become convinced that he could provide for the future of his family and that this objective had a claim on a significant part of his current income.

The reason it ran counter to consumer psychology was because the company, in effect, was inviting the individual *to bet on his own early demise.* True, the company made an attempt to select only good risks, but in cold-blooded financial terms the only way the individual insured could "win" was to pass away after making a few payments.

Expanding the Market Economy

Today we as a nation are spending billions of dollars for financial and technical aid to underdeveloped countries. What this really means is that we are trying to bring into the market economy millions of people who today have no money income or very tiny ones indeed. There are many ideas about how this can be done, and many articles and books have been written on the subject. One thing that is well established is that a country cannot be industrialized merely by putting up plants. There is no assurance that anyone will ever go to work in the plant unless a thorough study has shown that there is a market for its products. There have been two suggestions as to where to start, from a marketing viewpoint, which may be mentioned as examples of the dominant role marketing must play in underdeveloped areas.

One is the viewpoint of Peter Drucker, the well-known management consultant, and reflects his various experiences in Latin America. Sears Roebuck put up department stores in Mexico, Peru, and several other countries, which led very quickly to drastic changes in both marketing and production. Prices tumbled in other stores until the established stores learned to take a reasonable margin and move in the direction of mass merchandising. What was still more remarkable was the stimulus to local production. Going into Mexico City, Sears had assumed that 85 per cent of the merchandise sold would have to be imported from the United States. After a few years this percentage was approximately reversed. This meant that hundreds of small businesses enjoyed a spurt in growth and many of them were established for the purpose of *serving* Sears Roebuck, which for the first time offered an assured market.

A second approach might be called that of "double search," in which an industry in an advanced country is eager to extend its markets and tries to find some resource in the underdeveloped country which it can export to pay for imports. Thomas Ware, head of International Minerals and Chemicals, provides an example of one who employs this kind of imaginative thinking with respect to

India. Fertilizers are vital to India if its standard of living is not to decline still further. But India needs to produce some bulk commodity which it can exchange for fertilizers. This persistent search in the vast subcontinent of India may still reveal some resource of this kind.

—*Future Prospects for the Market Economy*

Market forces today will continue to transform the manner of life around the world. More people will come into the market who are not in it at all. People who are part of the way in will come all the way in. Differences in standard of living will be moderated within countries and between countries. The wealth of the world can produce a better way of life for the people of the world. Progress in the volume of goods and services which people can enjoy *is closely tied to progress in marketing*.

The development of specialized skills based on division of labor promotes local trade. Basic differences in climate and national resources promote international trade. Marketing may offer the best hope today for meeting the threats posed by nuclear war and the population explosion. World trade without exploitation is the best foundation for peace. The best hope for voluntary limitation of population is through the achievement of a comfortable standard of living around the world. In India, for example, a large family is partly a form of social insurance that some child will survive to take care of the parents when they grow old. In America the market economy bears the dark stain of Negro slavery. But in the longer view, marketing is a potential beneficent force enabling everyone to draw on the market for his needs while engaging in the work he knows best.

9. *The Revolutionary Role of Marketing* JOHN WISH

As this book is being compiled, Nader's Raiders did it again. This ambush resulted in extensive damage to the public image of the Federal Drug Administration. The April 20, 1970 edition of *Time* told it this way:

> Nader's Raiders struck again last week. This time their target was the Federal Food and Drug Administration, which they tore apart in what may well be the most devastating critique of a U.S. Government agency ever issued.

> The attack took the form of a 293-page report called *The Chemical Feast.* It was based on a two-year study of the FDA by Consumer Watchdog Ralph Nader and 20 student volunteers.

> Well aware of the report's general contents for several weeks, the FDA made a swift response. Just two days after its release, the agency announced plans to revoke thousands of food additives previously declared safe under its old sanctioning procedures.

In short, Nader and his group do their homework. They bring to bear their specialties on potential problems and let the chips fall where they may. In essence, Nader is a constructive Revolutionary Marketer.

Yes, the key to Nader's success is marketing. He promoted ideas to the nation in *Death at Any Speed* and now he is continuing to use his reputation and his sense of social needs to identify, articulate, and resolve present problems in our society.

As you read the materials in this book you will probably ask the questions many times, "What can I do?" and "How do I go about it?"

If you want some answers, one of Nader's men, Harrison Wellford, has written an article "On How to Be a Constructive Nuisance" (Selection 58—pp. 369-373). He too illustrates the powerful potential of marketing techniques.

PART TWO *Foundations of Marketing*

INTRODUCTION *to part two*

The objective of this part is to provide the reader with a knowledge of important findings and models related to marketing including such areas as:

The economy and economics.
Ethics.
The behavioral sciences, including psychology, social psychology, sociology, and demography.
Technology and the future of organizations.

A. The Economy and Economics

This section discusses three topics. First, the relation between economics and marketing is clarified by Robert Heilbroner in "The Economic Problem." Next, Walt Rostow discusses aspects of the market system as they relate to economic development. Finally, Wilbur Thompson provides some interesting insight into prices and the price system in our society. As a unit these articles raise and discuss some very important economic issues and findings related to the marketing process.

B. Ethics

The lessening of pressure on humans to satisfy basic needs and an increasing concern for the quality of life (as against the quantity of life) is leading to an emphasis on the means to ends rather than only on ends themselves. Perhaps for the first time we can afford a new *ethic* or perhaps with the threatening continuation of pollution, the nuclear race, and despair, we cannot afford not to have a new ethic. More likely, it is both our growing economic affluence and the increasing challenges to the survival of our civilization that are contributing toward a new ethic. The articles in Section B provide a basis for developing a personal ethic as well as a broad background for understanding the ethics that one may confront in the 1970's.

C. Psychology, Sociology, and Demography

In the past twenty years the behavioral sciences have contributed more to our ability to effectively implement and carry out marketing processes than any other group of disciplines. The major contribution of psychology, sociology, and demography has been in the consumer behavior area.

Each article in this section describes a different perspective on how behavioral sciences contribute to our understanding of marketing systems and processes. An examination of each article will provide the reader with constructs from the behavioral sciences which will be valuable in resolving the major issues our society faces.

D. Technology and the Future of Organizations

The final group of articles concerns changing technology, which exerts an increasing influence on our lives, and the evolving form of organizations. Both present some important problems for marketers.

First, one of the authors of this book describes some of the relationships between marketing and our society's changing technologies. Next, Anthony Athos asks and partially answers the question, "Is the Corporation Next to Fall?" Yes, even the corporation, the cornerstone of our industrial society, must change or become obsolete for we live in times when even foundations must be a'changing.

A. *The Economy and Economics*

10. *The Economic Problem*

ROBERT L. HEILBRONER

Not many years ago, an Indian demographer made the chilling calculation that of one hundred Asian and one hundred American infants, more Americans would be alive at sixty-five than Indians at *five!* The statistics, not of life, but of premature death throughout most of the world are overwhelming and crushing.

For most Americans, this consideration is apt to seem tragic but remote. None of us is conscious of a struggle for existence to anything resembling a life-or-death degree. That it might be possible for us to experience severe want, that we might ever know in our own bodies the pangs of hunger experienced by an Indian villager or a Bolivian peon is a thought which it is nearly impossible for us to entertain seriously.

Short of a catastrophic war, it is highly unlikely that any of us ever will know the full meaning of the struggle for existence. Nonetheless, even in our prosperous and secure society, there remains, however unnoticed, an aspect of life's precarious-ness, a reminder of the underlying problem of survival. *This is our helplessness as economic individuals.*

It is a curious fact that as we leave the most impoverished peoples of the world, where the human being with his twenty calories of energy scratches out for himself a bare subsistence, we find the economic insecurity of the individual many times multiplied. The solitary Eskimo, Bushman, Indonesian, Nigerian, left to his own devices, will survive a considerable time. Living close to the soil or to their animal

SOURCE. From Robert L. Heilbroner, *The Making of Economic Society,* © 1962. Reprinted by permission of Prentice-Hall, Inc. Englewood Cliffs, New Jersey.

prey, the peoples with the lowest standards of living in the world can sustain their own lives, at least for a while, almost single-handed. With a community numbering only a few hundred, they can live indefinitely. Indeed, a very large percentage of the human race today lives in precisely such fashion—in small, virtually self-contained peasant communities which provide for their own survival with a minimum of contact with the outside world. This large majority of mankind suffers great poverty, but it also knows a certain economic independence. If it did not, it would have been wiped out centuries ago.

When we turn to the New Yorker or the Chicagoan, on the other hand, we are struck by exactly the opposite condition, by a prevailing ease of material life, coupled at the same time by an extreme *dependence* of the individual in his search for the means of existence. In the great metropolitan areas where most Americans live, we can no longer envisage the solitary individual or the small community surviving, short of looting warehouses or stores for food and necessities. The overwhelming majority of Americans have never grown food, caught game, raised meat, ground grain into flour, or even fashioned flour into bread. Faced with the challenge of clothing themselves or building their own homes, they would be hopelessly untrained and unprepared. Even to make minor repairs in the machines which surround them, they must call on other members of the community whose business it is to fix cars, or repair plumbing, or whatever. Paradoxically, perhaps, the richer the nation, the more apparent is this inability of its average inhabitant to survive unaided and alone.

We survive in rich nations because the tasks we cannot do ourselves are done for us by an army of others on whom we can call for help. If we cannot grow food, we can buy it; if we cannot provide for our needs ourselves, we can hire the services of someone who can. This enormous *division of labor* enhances our capacity a thousandfold, for it enables us to benefit from other men's skills as well as our own.

Along with the abundance of material existence as we know it goes a hidden vulnerability: our abundance is assured only insofar as the organized cooperation of huge armies of people is to be counted upon. Indeed, our continuing existence as a rich nation hinges on the tacit precondition that the mechanism of social organization will continue to function effectively. *We are rich, not as individuals, but as members of a rich society, and our easy assumption of material sufficiency is actually only as reliable as the bonds which forge us into a social whole.*

Strangely enough, then, we find that man, not nature, is the source of most of our economic problems. To be sure, the economic problem itself—that is, the need to struggle for existence—derives ultimately from the scarcity of nature. If there were no scarcity, goods would be as free as air, and economics, at least in one sense of the word, would cease to exist as a social preoccupation.

And yet if the scarcity of nature sets the stage for the economic problem, it does not impose the only strictures against which men must struggle. For scarcity, as a felt condition, is not solely the fault of nature. Instead, we find in America—and indeed in all industrial societies—that as the ability to increase nature's yield has risen, so has the reach of human wants. In fact, in societies such as ours, where relative social status is importantly connected with the possession of material goods, we often find that "scarcity" as a psychological experience and goad becomes more pronounced as we grow wealthier: our desires to possess the fruits of nature race out ahead of our mounting ability to produce goods.

Thus the "wants" that nature must satisfy are by no means fixed—while, for that matter, nature's yield itself is not a constant, but varies over a wide range, depending on the social application of human energy and skill. Scarcity is therefore not attributable to nature alone but to "human nature" as well; and economics is ultimately concerned not merely with the stinginess of the physical environment, but equally with the appetite of the human temperament.

Hence we must begin a systematic analysis of economics by singling out the functions which social organization must perform to bring human nature into social harness. And when we turn our attention to this fundamental problem, we can quickly see that it involves the solution of two related and yet separate elemental tasks:

1. A society must organize a system for producing the goods and services it needs for its own perpetuation.

2. It must arrange a distribution of the fruits of its production among its own members, so that more production can take place.

The Production Problem

What is the difficulty which the production problem poses? What are the obstacles which a society encounters in organizing a system to produce the goods and services it needs? *The basic problem of production is to devise social institutions which will mobilize human energy for productive purposes.*

This basic requirement is not always so easily accomplished. For example, in the United States in 1933, the energies of nearly thirteen million people—one quarter of our work force—were not directed into the production process. Although these unemployed men and women were eager to work, although empty factories were available for them to work in, despite the existence of pressing wants, somehow a terrible and mystifying breakdown short-circuited the production process, with the result that an entire third of our previous annual output of goods and services simply disappeared.

In the very poorest nations, where production is most desperately needed, we frequently find that unemployment is a chronic condition. The streets of the Asian cities are thronged with people who cannot find work. But this, too, is not a condition imposed by the scarcity of nature. There is, after all, an endless amount of work to be done, if only in cleaning the filthy streets or patching up the homes of the poor, building roads, or planting forests. Yet, what seems to be lacking is a social mechanism to put the unemployed to work.

Both these examples point out to us that the production problem is not solely, or perhaps even primarily, a physical and technical struggle with nature. On these "scarcity" aspects of the problem will depend the speed with which a nation may forge ahead and the level of well-being it can reach with a given effort. But the original mobilization of productive effort itself is a challenge to its social organization, and on the success or failure of that social organization will depend the volume of the human effort which can be directed to nature.

Putting men to work is only the first step in the solution of the production problem. Men must not only be put to work; they must be put to work *in the right places*. They must produce the goods and services which society needs. In addition to assuring a large enough quantity of social effort, the economic institutions of society must also assure the *proper allocation of that social effort.*

In a nation such as India or Brazil, where the great majority of the population is born in peasant villages and grows up to be peasant cultivators, the solution to this problem offers little to vex our understanding. The basic demands of society—food and fiber—are precisely the goods which its peasant population "naturally" produces. But in an industrial society, the proper allocation of effort becomes an enormously complicated task. People in the United States demand much more than bread and cotton. They need, for instance, such things as automobiles. Yet no one "naturally" produces an automobile. On the contrary, in order to produce one, an extraordinary spectrum of special tasks must be performed. Some people must make steel. Others must make rubber. Still others must coordinate the assembly process itself. And this is but a tiny sampling of the far from "natural" tasks which must be performed if an automobile is to be produced.

As with the mobilization of its total production effort, society does not always succeed in the proper allocation of its effort. It may, for instance, turn out too many cars or too few. Of greater importance, it may devote its energies to the production of luxuries while the majority of its people are starving. Or it may even court disaster by an inability to channel its productive effort into areas of critical importance. In the early 1950's, for instance, the British suffered a near economic collapse because they were unable to get enough of their workers to mine coal.

Such allocative failures may affect the production problem quite as seriously as a failure to mobilize an adequate quantity of effort, for a viable society must produce not only goods, but the *right* goods. And the allocative question alerts us to a still broader conclusion. It shows us that the act of production, in and of itself, does not fully answer the requirements for survival. Having produced enough of the right goods, society must now *distribute* those goods so that the production process can go on.

The Distribution Problem

Once again, in the case of the peasant who feeds himself and his family from his own crop, this requirement of adequate distribution may seem simple enough. But when we go beyond the most primitive society, the problem is not always so readily solved. In many of the poorest nations of the East and South, urban workers have often been unable to deliver their daily horsepower-hour of work because they have not been given enough of society's output to run their human engines to capacity. Worse yet, they have often languished on the job while granaries bulged with grain and the well-to-do complained of the ineradicable "laziness" of the masses. At the other side of the picture, the distribution mechanism may fail because the rewards it hands out do not succeed in persuading people to perform their necessary tasks. Shortly after the Russian Revolution some factories were organized into communes in which managers and janitors pooled their pay, and from which all drew equal allotments. The results was a rash of absenteeism on the part of the previously better-paid workers and a threatened breakdown in industrial production. Not until the old unequal wage payments were reinstituted did production resume its former course.

As was the case with failures in the production process, distributive failures need not entail a total economic collapse. Societies can exist—and indeed, in the majority of cases, do exist—with badly distorted productive and distributive efforts. It is only rarely, as in the instances above, that maldistribution actively interferes with the actual ability of a society to staff its production posts. More frequently, an inadequate solution to the distribution problem reveals itself in social and political unrest or even in revolution.

Yet this, too, is an aspect of the total economic problem. For if society is to insure its steady material replenishment, it must parcel out its production in a fashion that will maintain not only the capacity but the willingness to go on working. And thus again we find the focus of economic inquiry directed to the study of human institutions. For a viable economic society, we can now see, is not only one which can overcome the stringencies of nature, but one which can contain and control the intransigence of human nature.

The Three Solutions to the Economic Problem

Man has succeeded in solving the production and distribution problems in but three ways. That is, within the enormous diversity of the actual social institutions which guide and shape the economic process, the economist divines but three overarching *types* of systems which separately or in combination enable humankind to solve its economic challenge. These great systemic types can be called economies run by Tradition, economies run by Command, and economies run by the Market. Let us briefly see what is characteristic of each.

Tradition

Perhaps the oldest and, until a very few years ago, by far the most generally prevalent way of solving the economic challenge has been tradition. It has been a mode of social organization in which both production and distribution were based on procedures devised in the distant past and rigidified as the outcome of a long process of historic trial and error.

Societies based on tradition solve the economic problems very manageably. First, they deal with the production problem—the problem of assuring that the needful tasks will be done—by assigning the jobs of fathers to their sons. And it was not merely in antiquity that tradition preserved a productive orderliness within society. In our own Western culture, until the fifteenth or sixteenth centuries, the hereditary allocation of tasks was also the main stabilizing force within society. Although there was some movement from country to town and from occupation to occupation, birth usually determined one's role in life. One was born to the soil or to a trade; and on the soil or within the trade, one followed in the footsteps of one's forebears.

Tradition not only provides a solution to the production problem of society, but it also regulates the distribution problem. Take, for example, the Bushmen of the Kalahari Desert in South Africa who depend for their livelihood on hunting prowess. Elizabeth Marshall Thomas, a sensitive observer of these peoples, reports on the manner in which tradition solves the problem of distributing their kill.

> The gemsbok has vanished ... Gai owned two hind legs and a front leg, Tsetchwe had meat from the back, Ukwane had the other front leg, his wife had one of the feet and the stomach, the young boys had lengths of intestine. Twikwe had received the head and Dasina the udder.

> It seems very unequal when you watch Bushmen divide the kill, yet it is their system, and in the end no person eats more than any other. That day Ukwane gave Gai still another piece because Gai was his relation, Gai gave meat to Dasina because she was his wife's mother ... No one, of course, contested Gai's large share, because he had been the hunter and by their law that much belonged to him. No one doubted that he would share his large amount with others, and they were not wrong, of course; he did.

Even in our own society, tradition continues to play a role in solving the economic problem. It plays its smallest role in determining the distribution of our own social output, although the persistence of such traditional payments as tips to waiters, allowances to minors, or bonuses based on length of service are all vestiges of old traditional ways of distributing goods, as is the differential between men's and women's pay for equal work.

More important is the place which tradition continues to hold, even in America, as a means of solving the production problem—that is, in allocating the performance of tasks. Much of the actual process of selecting an employment in our society is heavily influenced by tradition. We are all familiar with families in which sons follow their fathers into a profession or a business. On a somewhat broader scale, tradition also dissuades us from certain employments. Sons of American middle-class families, for example, do not usually seek factory work, even though factory jobs may pay better than office jobs, because "bluecollar employment" is not in the middle-class tradition.

Even in our society, which is clearly not a "traditional" one, custom provides an important mechanism for solving the economic problem. But now we must note one very important consequence of the mechanism of tradition. *Its solution to production and distribution is a static one.* A society which follows the path of tradition in its regulation of economic affairs does so at the expense of large-scale rapid social and economic change. Tradition solves the economic problem, but it does so at the cost of economic progress.

Command

A second manner of solving the problem of economic continuity also displays an ancient lineage. This is the method of imposed authority, of economic command. It is a solution based not so much on the perpetuation of a viable system by the changeless reproduction of its ways, as on the organization of a system according to the orders of an economic commander-in-chief.

Not infrequently we find this authoritarian method of economic control super-imposed upon a traditional social base. Thus the Pharaohs of Egypt exerted their economic dictates above the timeless cycle of traditional agricultural practice on which the Egyptian economy was based.

Economic command, like tradition, offers solutions to the twin problems of production and distribution. In times of crises, such as war or famine, it may be the only way in which a society can organize its manpower or distribute its goods effectively. Even in America, we commonly declare martial law when an area has been devastated by a great natural disaster. On such occasions we may press people into service, requisition homes, impose curbs on the use of private property such as cars, or even limit the amount of food a family may consume.

Quite aside from its obvious utility in meeting emergencies, command has a further usefulness in solving the economic problem. Unlike tradition, the exercise of command has no inherent effect of slowing down economic change. Indeed, the exercise of authority is the most powerful instrument society has for *enforcing economic change.* One example is, of course, the radical alterations in the systems of production and distribution which authority has effected in modern China or Russia. But again, even in our own society, it is sometimes necessary for economic authority to intervene into the normal flow of economic life to speed up or bring about change. The government may, for instance, utilize its tax receipts to lay down a network of roads which brings a backwater community into the flux of active economic life. It may undertake an irrigation system which will dramatically change the economic life of a vast region. It may very considerably affect the distribution of income among social classes.

Clearly, command can be an instrument of a democratic as well as a totalitarian will. There is no implicit moral judgment to be passed on this second of the great mechanisms of economic control. Rather, it is important to note that no society—certainly no modern society—is without its elements of command, just as none is devoid of the influence of tradition. If tradition is the great brake on social and economic change, so economic command can be the great spur to change. As mechanisms for assuring the successful solution to the economic problem, both serve their purposes, both have their uses and their drawbacks. Between them, tradition and command have accounted for most of the long history of man's economic efforts to cope with his environment and with himself. The fact that human society *has* survived is testimony to their effectiveness.

The Market

There is also a third solution to the economic problem—that is, a third solution to the problem of maintaining socially viable patterns of production and distribution. This is the *market organization of society,* an organization which, in truly remarkable fashion, allows society to insure its own provisioning with a minimum of recourse either to tradition or command.

Because we live in a market-run society, we are apt to take for granted the puzzling—indeed, almost paradoxical—nature of the market solution to the economic problem. But assume for a moment that we could act as economic advisers to a society which had not yet decided on its mode of economic organization. Suppose, for instance, that we were called on to act as consultants to one of the new nations emerging from the continent of Africa.

We could imagine the leaders of such a nation saying, "We have always experienced a highly tradition-bound way of life. Our men hunt and cultivate the fields and perform their tasks as they are brought up to do by the force of example and the instruction of their elders. We know, too, something of what can be done by economic command. We are prepared, if necessary, to sign an edict making it compulsory for many of our men to work on community projects for our national development. Tell us, is there any other way we can organize our society so that it will function successfully—or better yet, more successfully?"

Suppose we answered, "Yes, there is another way. Organize your society along the lines of a market economy."

"Very well," say the leaders. "What do we then tell people to do? How do we assign them to their various tasks?"

"That's the very point," we would answer. "In a market economy no one is assigned to any task. The very idea of a market society is that each person is allowed to decide for himself what to do."

There is consternation among the leaders. "You mean there is *no* assignment of some men to mining and others to cattle raising? No manner of selecting some for transportation and others for cloth weaving? You leave this to people to decide for themselves? But what happens if they do not decide correctly? What happens if no one volunteers to go into the mines, or if no one offers himself as a railway engineer?"

"You may rest assured," we tell the leaders, "none of that will happen. In a market society, all the jobs will be filled because it will be to people's advantage to fill them."

Our respondents accept this with uncertain expressions. "Now look," one of them finally says, "let us suppose that we take your advice and let our people do as they please. Now let's talk about something important, like cloth production. Just how do we fix the right level of cloth output in this 'market society' of yours?"

"But you don't," we reply.

"We don't! Then how do we know there will be enough cloth produced?"

"There will be," we tell him. "The market will see to that."

"Then how do we know there won't be *too much* cloth produced?" he asks triumphantly.

"Ah, but the market will see to that too!"

"But what *is* this market that will do all these wonderful things? Who runs it?"

"Oh, nobody runs the market," we answer. "It runs itself. In fact there really isn't any such *thing* as 'the market.' It's just a word we use to describe the way people behave."

"But I thought people behaved the way they wanted to!"

"And so they do," we say. "But never fear. They will want to behave the way you want them to behave."

"I am afraid," says the chief of the delegation, "that we are wasting our time. We thought you had in mind a serious proposal. But what you suggest is madness. It is inconceivable. Good day, sir." And with great dignity the delegation takes its leave.

Could we seriously suggest to such an emergent nation that it entrust itself to a market solution of the economic problem? The very perplexity which the market idea would rouse in the mind of someone unacquainted with it may serve to increase our own wonderment at this most sophisticated and interesting of all economic mechanisms. How *does* the market system assure us that our mines will find miners, our factories workers? How does it take care of cloth production? How does it happen that in a market-run nation each person can indeed do as he wishes and, withal, fulfill the needs which society as a whole presents?

Economics and the Market System

Economics, as we commonly conceive it, is primarily concerned with these very problems. Societies which rely primarily on tradition to solve their economic problems are of less interest to the professional economist than to the cultural anthropologist or the sociologist. Societies which solve their economic problems primarily by the exercise of command present interesting economic questions, but here the study of economics is necessarily subservient to the study of politics and the exercise of power.

It is a society which solves its economic problems by the market process that presents an aspect especially interesting to the economist. For here economics truly plays a unique role. Unlike the case with tradition and command, where we quickly grasp the nature of the economic mechanism of society, when we turn to a market society we are lost without a knowledge of economics. For in a market society it is not at all clear that the problems of production and distribution will be solved by the free interplay of individuals without guidance from tradition or command.

11. *The Concept of a National Market and its Economics Growth Implications* WALT W. ROSTOW

With a few exceptions, the developing nations of Asia, the Middle East, Africa, and Latin America began their first purposeful stage of modernization by concentrating their efforts in two areas: the production of manufactured goods in substitution for consumer goods imports and the creation of basic infrastructure; that is, roads, electric power, ports, education, etc. Agriculture and the modernization of rural life were systematically neglected, yielding now a dangerous decline in per capita food production in some major regions.

There was a certain legitimacy in these initial priorities. The development of an economy, at its core, consists in the progressive diffusion of the fruits of modern science and technology. Industry is the most dramatic form which modern science and technology assumes; and basic infrastructure is directly required for industrialization.

But there was also an element of irrationality. Agriculture was associated with the period of colonialism and/or with excessive dependence on export markets in industrial countries. It appeared to be second order—and, even, faintly humiliating business, as compared to industrialization.

The combination of these two factors—rational and irrational—has led to a phase of development concentrated largely in a few cities, centered around a few industries, and, as I say, to a systematic neglect of what agriculture could and must

SOURCE. From *Marketing and Economic Development,* Chicago: American Marketing Association, Fall 1965, pp. 126-135.

contribute by way of food, industrial raw materials, foreign exchange, and enlarged domestic markets.

The start of industrialization varied in time as among the developing countries of the contemporary world. The Latin American countries generally began just before or during the Second World War, while many others began seriously only in the years after 1945. Some, indeed, have not yet launched their first phase of sustained industrialization. Nevertheless, it is broadly true that we have come to the end or are coming to the end of the phase when the initial, narrow postwar strategy for development can be regarded as viable.

In one developing country after another the perception is spreading that the next phase of development must be based on a systematic diffusion of the modern skills, now largely concentrated in urban areas, out into the countryside; on the making of efficient national markets; and, from this widened basis, on the generation of new lines of diversified exports which alone promise to earn the foreign exchange which the developing countries will need in the years ahead. Only this pattern of widened domestic markets and diversified exports promises to provide the foundation for that deepening of the industrial structure (from consumer goods down to capital goods and the heavy industry sectors) which a modern industrial society requires.

If I may be permitted to use a somewhat private vocabulary, it can be said that during the past generation we have had in many parts of the world a take-off in which the leading sectors have been import-substitution industries in consumer goods fields; and for these nations to move on into the drive to industrial maturity requires that they convert their somewhat isolated urban industrial concentrations into active, dynamic centers which purposefully diffuse the process of modernization out across the nation, while they generate the capacity, on this wider market foundation, to pay their way as they move to full industrialization of their societies.

This is a shorthand approximation of the task for the next generation that lies before the nations within the Free World, which contain most of the population of Asia, the Middle East, Africa, and Latin America; and it is also the problem which must be solved if a modern industrialized China is really going to emerge.

The next stage of development in the Soviet Union and Eastern Europe must, evidently, be based not merely on a correction of agricultural inefficiency but upon the turning of their relatively mature industrial complexes to supply the things which people want when average income levels reach the point at which they now stand in these countries. Also, I would say that, just as most of the developing world is in a process of adjustment from take-off to the drive to technological maturity, the Soviet Union and Eastern Europe are in a process of adjustment from their own version of the drive to technological maturity to the age of high-mass consumption.

And here, of course, is where marketing comes in.

The modernization of the countryside in the developing countries evidently has many dimensions. We now know enough from practical experience to be able to say that, assuming roads and minimum basic education and assuming, also a certain backlog of relevant agricultural science, there are four necessary and sufficient conditions for an agricultural revolution.

First, the farmer must receive a reliable and fair price for his product.

Second, credit must be available at reasonable rates for him to make the change in the character of his output or the shift in productivity desired.

Third, there must be available on the spot technical assistance that is relevant to his soil, his weather conditions, and his change in either output or in productivity.

Finally, there must be available at reasonable rates two types of industrial products: inputs such as chemical fertilizers, insecticides, and farm tools; and incentive goods—that is, the consumer goods of good quality he and his family would purchase in greater quantity or work harder to get if they were cheaper or if his income were higher.

The modernization of rural life demands new and effective ways of getting to the farmer both the things he needs to increase productivity and incentive goods.

With respect to chemical fertilizers, insecticides, seeds, and farm machinery, there is a role, beyond conventional marketing, to be undertaken by the salesman. It may be regarded as sacrilege by some, but it has generally proved true that the most powerful agent in the diffusion of new agricultural technology has been the commercial firm rather than public institutions set up for technical assistance purposes. I would not for a moment denigrate the role in the United States of the county agent nor of those who have followed in his tradition in the developing areas; but it is simply a fact that there are not enough county agents out working in the villages to do the job in contemporary developing areas. Among other reasons, too many trained agricultural technologists are to be found working in government offices in the capital city rather than in grass roots jobs. A good, pragmatic performance in the diffusion of technical knowledge can be and is being done in many parts of the world by those who have a straight commercial interest in selling their products. The salesman knows he must spend his time with potential customers.

With respect to incentive goods, we must begin by accepting the fact that people in the rural areas of the developing world are poor. Until their income rises, they may not be able to buy a great deal more than they are buying. On the other hand, it is also true that what they can buy in their villages by way of manufactured goods is often shoddy and expensive. We know from the history of rural areas in the United States—even the quite recent experience of the Tennessee Valley area— that the availability of attractive and inexpensive consumer goods can be an important stimulus to production and productivity. Lower prices can yield more purchases in the short run; lower prices and the availability of incentive goods of good quality can yield more output, income, and purchases in the longer run. The same lesson can be observed in Mexico and other developing areas where efforts to increase productivity on the supply side are combined with such incentives.

The technical marketing problem from the city to the countryside consists in finding ways to lower the unit cost of distribution under circumstances where rural markets are scattered and the volume of any one commodity to be sold at any one point is low. The most successful solution in developing countries is, of course, the marketing of beer and soft drinks. The volume of sales, however, is sufficient in this case to support regular truck deliveries even at low levels of rural income. What appears to be required is the development of unified marketing arrangements for a wide range of consumer goods so that the overhead distribution costs for each commodity are reduced.

As I have seen soft drink trucks roll into distant villages, I have often wished they had a trailer attached containing textiles, shoes, household equipment, flashlights, transistor radios, books and the other things the villagers would buy if prices were lower.

Producers' cooperatives, food processing plants, and other substantial institutions in rural areas can often serve as centers for the efficient assembly and distribution of such incentive goods, as well as the fertilizers, insecticides, etc., needed to increase productivity.

The making of national markets through the more effective linking of urban and rural areas bears directly on the other great task of the developing countries in the years ahead; namely, their need to generate diversified exports. A whole range of special skills and special efforts is needed to market new products abroad. Potential markets must be studied with careful attention to local tastes; distribution channels must be established; regular and reliable flows of supplies must be moved and financed; quality controls must be built up; and efficient production must be generated if the exports are to be competitive.

Thus in facing now the tasks of widening the market, both in the developing areas and in the Soviet Union and in Eastern Europe, governments must overcome that most insidious of pressures; that is, the pressures created by the sometimes unconscious acceptance of ideas from the past that obscure the character and priority of current problems.

If I am correct that men must, in the generation ahead, diffuse the process of modernization out over long neglected rural regions, creating new efficient networks of distribution, we shall see not merely new and challenging tasks for those who command the skills of distribution but a new theoretical respect and appreciation for the art of that widening of the market which, for so long, was taken for granted.

12. *The City as a Distorted Price System*

WILBUR THOMPSON

The failure to use price—as an *explicit* system—in the public sector of the metropolis is at the root of many, if not most, of our urban problems. Price, serving its historic functions, might be used to ration the use of existing facilities, to signal the desired directions of new public investment, to guide the distribution of income, to enlarge the range of public choice and to change tastes and behavior. Price performs such functions in the private marketplace, but it has been virtually eliminated from the public sector. We say "virtually eliminated" because it does exist but in an implicit, subtle, distorted sense that is rarely seen or acknowledged by even close students of the city, much less by public managers. Not surprisingly, this implicit price system results in bad economics.

We think of the property tax as a source of public revenue, but it can be re-interpreted as a price. Most often, the property tax is rationalized on "ability-to-pay" grounds with real property serving as a proxy for income. When the correlation between income and real property is challenged, the apologist for the property tax shifts ground and rationalizes it as a "benefit" tax. The tax then becomes a "price" which the property owner pays for benefits received—fire protection, for example. But this implicit "price" for fire services is hardly a model of either efficiency or equity. Put in a new furnace and fireproof your building (reduce the likelihood of having a fire) and your property tax (fire service premium) goes up; let your property deteriorate and become a firetrap and your

SOURCE. Reprinted from *Psychology Today* Magazine, August, 1968. Copyright ©
Communications/Research/Machines/Inc.

fire protection premium goes down! One bright note is New York City's one-year tax abatement on new pollution-control equipment; a timid step but in the right direction.

Often "urban sprawl" is little more than a color word which reflects (betrays?) the speaker's bias in favor of high population density and heavy interpersonal interaction—his "urbanity." Still, typically, the price of using urban fringe space has been set too low—well below the full costs of running pipes, wires, police cars and fire engines farther than would be necessary if building lots were smaller. Residential developers are, moreover, seldom discouraged (penalized by price) from "leap frogging" over the contiguous, expensive vacant land to build on the remote, cheaper parcels. Ordinarily, a flat price is charged for extending water or sewers to a new household regardless of whether the house is placed near to or far from existing pumping stations.

Again, the motorist is subject to the same license fees and tolls, if any, for the extremely expensive system of streets, bridges, tunnels and traffic controls he enjoys, regardless of whether he chooses to drive downtown at the rush hour and thereby pushes against peak capacity or at off-peak times when it costs little or nothing to serve him. To compound this distortion of prices, we usually set the toll at zero. And when we do charge tolls, we quite perversely cut the commuter (rush-hour) rate below the off-peak rate.

It is not enough to point out that the motorist supports road-building through the gasoline tax. The social costs of noise, air pollution, traffic control and general loss of urban amenities are borne by the general taxpayer. In addition, drivers during off-peak hours overpay and subsidize rush-hour drivers. Four lanes of expressway or bridge capacity are needed in the morning and evening rush hours where two lanes would have served if movements had been random in time and direction; that is, near constant in average volume. The peak-hour motorists probably should share the cost of the first two lanes and bear the full cost of the other two that they alone require. It is best to begin by carefully distinguishing where market tests are possible and where they are not. Otherwise, the case for applying the principles of price is misunderstood; either the too-ardent advocate overstates his case or the potential convert projects too much. In either case, a "disenchantment" sets in that is hard to reverse.

Much of the economics of the city is "public economics," and the pricing of urban public services poses some very difficult and even insurmountable problems. Economists have, in fact, erected a very elegant rationalization of the public economy almost wholly on the *non*-marketability of public goods and services. While economists have perhaps oversold the inapplicability of price in the public sector, let us begin with what we are *not* talking about.

The public economy supplies "collectively consumed" goods, those produced and consumed in one big indivisible lump. Everyone has to be counted in the system, there is no choice of *in* or *out*. We cannot identify individual benefits, therefore we cannot exact a *quid pro quo*. We cannot exclude those who would not pay voluntarily; therefore we must turn to compulsory payments: taxes. Justice and air-pollution control are good examples of collectively consumed public services.

A second function of the public economy is to supply "merit goods." Sometimes the majority of us become a little paternalistic and decide that we know what is best for all of us. We believe some goods are especially meritorious, like education, and we fear that others might not fully appreciate this truth. Therefore, we produce these merit goods, at considerable cost, but offer them at a zero price. Unlike the first case of collectively consumed goods, we could sell these merit goods. A school-room's doors can be closed to those who do not pay, *quite unlike justice.* But we choose to open the doors wide to ensure that no one will turn away from the service because of its cost, and then we finance the service with compulsory payments. Merit goods are a case of the majority playing God, and "coercing" the minority by the use of bribes to change their behavior.

A third classic function of government is the redistribution of income. Here we wish to perform a service for one group and charge another group the cost of that service. Welfare payments are a clear case. Again, any kind of a private market or pricing mechanism is totally inappropriate: we obviously do not expect welfare recipients to return their payments. Again, we turn to compulsory payments: taxes. In sum, the private market may not be able to process certain goods and services (pure "public goods"), or it may give the "wrong" prices ("merit goods"), or we simply do not want the consumer to pay (income-redistributive services).

But the virtual elimination of price from the public sector is an extreme and highly simplistic response to the special requirements of the public sector. Merit goods may be subsidized without going all of the way to zero prices. Few would argue for full-cost admission prices to museums, but a good case can be made for moderate prices that cover, say, their daily operating costs (*e.g.*, salaries of guards and janitors, heat and light).

Unfortunately, as we have given local government more to do, we have almost unthinkingly extended the tradition of "free" public services to every new under-taking, despite the clear trend in local government toward the assumption of more and more functions that do not fit the neat schema above. The provision of free public facilities for automobile movement in the crowded cores of our urban areas can hardly be defended on the grounds that: (a) motorists could not be excluded from the expressways if they refused to pay the toll, or (b) the privately operated motor vehicle is an especially meritorious way to move through densely populated areas, or (c) the motorists cannot afford to pay their own way and that the general (property) taxpayers should subsidize them. And all this applies with a vengeance to municipal marinas and golf courses.

We need to understand better the rationing function of price as it manifests itself in the urban public sector: how the demand for a temporarily (or permanently) fixed stock of a public good or service can be adjusted to the supply. At any given time the supply of street, bridge and parking space is fixed; "congestion" on the streeets and a "shortage" of parking space express demand greater than supply at a zero price, a not too surprising phenomenon. Applying the market solution, the shortage of street space at peak hours ("congestion") could have been temporarily relieved (rationalized) by introducing a short-run rationing price to divert some motorists to other hours of movement, some to other modes of transportation, and some to other activities.

Public goods last a long time and therefore current additions to the stock are too small to relieve shortages quickly and easily. *The rationing function of price is probably more important in the public sector where it is customarily ignored than in the private sector where it is faithfully expressed.*

Rationing need not always be achieved with money, as when a motorist circles the block over and over looking for a place to park. The motorist who is not willing to "spend time" waiting and drives away forfeits the scarce space to one who will spend time (luck averaging out). The parking "problem" may be re-interpreted as an implicit decision to keep the money price artificially low (zero or a nickel an hour in a meter) and supplement it with a waiting cost or time price. The problem is that we did not clearly understand and explicitly agree to do just that.

The central role of price is to allocate—across the board—scarce resources among competing ends to the point where the value of another unit of any good or service is equal to the incremental cost of producing that unit. Expressed loosely, in the long run we turn from using prices to dampen demand to fit a fixed supply to adjusting the supply to fit the quantity demanded, at a price which reflects the production costs.

Prices which ration also serve to signal desired new directions in which to reallocate resources. If the rationing price exceeds those costs of production which the user is expected to bear directly, more resources should ordinarily be allocated to that activity. And symmetrically a rationing price below the relevant costs indicates an *uneconomic* provision of that service in the current amounts. Rationing prices reveal the intensity of the users' demands. How much is it really worth to drive into the heart of town at rush hour or launch a boat? In the long run, motorists and boaters should be free to choose, in rough measure, the amount of street and dock space they want and for which they are willing to pay. But, as in the private sector of our economy, free choice would carry with it full (financial) responsibility for that choice.

We need also to extend our price strategy to "factor prices"; we need a sophisticated wage policy for local public employees. Perhaps the key decision in urban development pertains to the recruiting and assignment of elementary- and secondary-school teachers. The more able and experienced teachers have the greater range of choice in post and quite naturally they choose the newer schools in the better neighborhoods, after serving the required apprenticeship in the older schools in the poorer neighborhoods. Such a pattern of migration certainly cannot implement a policy of equality of opportunity.

This author argued six years ago that

> Egalitarianism in the public school system has been overdone; even the army recognizes the role of price when it awards extra "jump pay" to paratroopers, only a slightly more hazardous occupation than teaching behind the lines. Besides, it is male teachers whom we need to attract to slum schools, both to serve as father figures where there are few males at home and to serve quite literally as disciplinarians. It is bad economics to insist on equal pay for teachers everywhere throughout the urban area when males have a higher productivity in some areas and when males have better employment opportunities outside teaching—higher "opportunity costs" that raise their supply price. It is downright silly to argue that "equal pay for equal work" is achieved by paying the same money wage in the slums as in the suburbs.

About a year ago, on being offered premium salaries for service in ghetto schools, the teachers rejected, by name and with obvious distaste, any form of "jump pay." One facile argument offered was that they must protect the slum child from the stigma of being harder to teach, a nicety surely lost on the parents and outside observers. One suspects that the real reason for advoiding salary differentials between the "slums and suburbs" is that the teachers seek to escape the hard choice between the higher pay and the better working conditions. *But that is precisely what the price system is supposed to do: equalize sacrifice.*

A much wider application of tolls, fees, fines and other "prices" would also confer greater control over the distribution of income for two distinct reasons. First, the taxes currently used to finance a given public service create *implicit* and *unplanned* redistribution of income. Second, this drain on our limited supply of tax money prevents local government from undertaking other programs with more *explicit* and *planned* redistributional effects.

More specifically, if upper-middle- and upper-income motorists, golfers and boaters use subsidized public streets, golf links and marinas more than in proportion to their share of local tax payments from which the subsidy is paid, then these public activities redistribute income toward greater inequality. Even if these "semi-proprietary" public activities were found to be neutral with respect to the distribution of income, public provision of these discretionary services comes at the expense of a roughly equivalent expenditure on the more classic public services: protection, education, public health and welfare.

Self-supporting public golf courses are so common and marinas are such an easy extension of the same principle that it is much more instructive to test the faith by considering the much harder case of the public museum: "Culture." Again, we must recall that it is the middle- and upper-income classes who typically visit museums, so that free admission becomes, in effect, redistribution toward greater inequality, to the extent that the lower-income nonusers pay local taxes (*e.g.,* property taxes directly or indirectly through rent, local sales taxes). The low prices contemplated are not, moreover, likely to discourage attendance significantly and the resolution of special cases (*e.g.,* student passes) seems well within our competence.

Unfortunately, it is not obvious that "free" public marinas and tennis courts pose foregone alternatives—"opportunity costs." If we had to discharge a teacher or policeman every time we built another boat dock or tennis court, we would see the real cost of these public services. But in a growing economy, we need only not hire another teacher or policeman and that is not so obvious. In general, then, given a binding local budget constraint—scarce tax money—to undertake a local public service that is unequalizing or even neutral in income redistribution is to deny funds to programs that have the desired distributional effect, and is to lose control over equity.

Typically, in oral presentations at question time, it is necessary to reinforce this point by rejoining: "No, I would not put turnstiles in the playgrounds in poor neighborhoods, rather it is only because we do put turnstiles at the entrance to the playgrounds for the middle- and upper-income-groups that we will be able to 'afford' playgrounds for the poor."

But there is more at stake in the contemporary chaos of hidden and unplanned prices than "merely" efficiency and equity. *There is no urban goal on which consensus is more easily gained than the pursuit of great variety and choice—"pluralism."* The great rural to urban migration was prompted as much by the search for variety as by the decline of agriculture and rise of manufacturing. Wide choice is seen as the saving grace of bigness by even the sharpest critics of the metropolis. Why, then, do we tolerate far less variety in our big cities than we could have? We have lapsed into a state of tyranny by the majority, in matters of both taste and choice.

In urban transportation the issue is not, in the final analysis, whether users of core-area street space at peak hours should or should not be required to pay their own way in full. The problem is, rather, that by not forcing a direct *quid pro quo* in money, we implicitly substitute a new means of payment—time—in the transportation services "market." The peak-hour motorist does pay in full, through congestion and time delay. But *implicit choices* blur issues and confuse decision-making.

Say we were carefully to establish how many more dollars would have to be paid in for the additional capacity needed to save a given number of hours spent commuting. The *majority* of urban motorists perhaps would still choose the present combination of "under-investment" in highway, bridge and parking facilities, with a compensatory heavy investment of time in slow movement over these crowded facilities. Even so, a substantial minority of motorists do prefer a different combination of money and time cost. A more affluent, long-distance commuter could well see the current level of traffic congestion as a real problem and much prefer to spend more money to save time. If economies of scale are so substantial that only one motorway to town can be supported, or if some naturally scarce factor (*e.g.,* bridge or tunnel sites) prevents parallel transportation facilities of different quality and price, then the preferences of the minority must be sacrificed to the majority interest and we do have a real "problem." But, ordinarily, in large urban areas there are a number of near parallel routes to town, and an unsatisfied minority group large enough to justify significant differentiation of one or more of these streets and its diversion to their use. Greater choice through greater scale is, in fact, what bigness is all about.

The simple act of imposing a toll, at peak hours, on one of these routes would reduce its use, assuming that nearby routes are still available without user charges, thereby speeding movement of the motorists who remain and pay. The toll could be raised only to the point where some combination of moderately rapid movement and high physical output were jointly optimized. Otherwise the outcry might be raised that the public transportation authority was so elitist as to gratify the desire of a few very wealthy motorists for very rapid movement, heavily overloading the "free" routes. It is, moreover, quite possible, even probable, that the newly-converted, rapid-flow, toll-route would handle as many vehicles as it did previously as a congested street and not therefore spin-off any extra load on the free routes.

Our cities cater, at best, to the taste patterns of the middle-income class, as well they should, *but not so exclusively.* This group has chosen, indirectly through clumsy and insensitive tax-and-expenditure decisions and ambiguous political processes, to move about town flexibly and cheaply, but slowly, in private vehicles. Often, and almost invariably in the larger urban areas, we would not have to encroach much on this choice to accommodate also those who would prefer to spend more money and less time, in urban movement. In general, we should permit urban residents to pay in their most readily available "currency"—time or money.

Majority rule by the middle class in urban transportation has not only disenfranchised the affluent commuter, but more seriously it has debilitated the low-fare, mass transit system on which the poor depend. The effect of widespread automobile ownership and use on the mass transportation system is an oft-told tale: falling bus and rail patronage leads to less frequent service and higher overhead costs per trip and often higher fares which further reduce demand and service schedules. Perhaps two-thirds or more of the urban residents will tolerate and may even prefer slow, cheap automobile movement. But the poor are left without access to many places of work—the suburbanizing factories in particular—and they face much reduced opportunities for comparative shopping, and highly constrained participation in the community life in general. A truly wide range of choice in urban transportation would allow the rich to pay for fast movement with money, the middle-income class to pay for the privacy and convenience of the automobile with time, and the poor to economize by giving up (paying with) privacy.

A more sophisticated price policy would expand choice in other directions. Opinions differ as to the gravity of the water-pollution problem near large urban areas. The minimum level of dissolved oxygen in the water that is needed to meet the standards of different users differs greatly, as does the incremental cost that must be incurred to bring the dissolved oxygen levels up to successively higher standards. The boater accepts a relatively low level of "cleanliness" acquired at relatively little cost. Swimmers have higher standards attained only at much higher cost. Fish and fisherman can thrive only with very high levels of dissolved oxygen acquired only at the highest cost. Finally, one can imagine an elderly convalescent or an impoverished slum dweller or a confirmed landlubber who is not at all interested in the nearby river. What, then, constitutes "clean?"

A majority rule decision, whether borne by the citizen directly in higher taxes or levied on the industrial polluters and then shifted on to the consumer in higher product prices, is sure to create a "problem." If the pollution program is a compromise—a halfway measure—the fisherman will be disappointed because the river is still not clean enough for his purposes and the landlubbers will be disgruntled because the program is for "special interests" and he can think of better uses for his limited income. Surely, we can assemble the managerial skills in the local public sector needed to devise and administer a structure of user charges that would extend choice in outdoor recreation, consistent with financial responsibility, with lower charges for boat licenses and higher charges for fishing licenses.

Perhaps the most fundamental error we have committed in the development of our large cities is that we have too often subjected the more affluent residents to petty irritations which serve no great social purpose, then turned right around and permitted this same group to avoid responsibilities which have the most critical and pervasive social ramifications. It is a travesty and a social tragedy that we have prevented the rich from buying their way out of annoying traffic congestion—or at least not helped those who are long on money and short on time arrange such an accommodation. Rather, we have permitted them, through political fragmentation and flight to tax havens, to evade their financial and leadership responsibilities for the poor of the central cities. That easily struck goal, "pluralism and choice," will require much more managerial sophistication in the local public sector than we have shown to date.

Urban managerial economies will probably also come to deal especially with "developmental pricing" analogous to "promotional pricing" in business. Prices below cost may be used for a limited period to create a market for a presumed "merit good." The hope would be that the artificially low price would stimulate consumption and that an altered *expenditure pattern* (practice) would lead in time to an altered *taste pattern* (preference), as experience with the new service led to a fuller appreciation of it. Ultimately, the subsidy would be withdrawn, whether or not tastes changed sufficiently to make the new service self-supporting—provided, of course, that no permanent redistribution of income was intended.

For example, our national parks had to be subsidized in the beginning and this subsidy could be continued indefinitely on the grounds that these are "merit goods" that serve a broad social interest. But long experience with outdoor recreation has so shifted tastes that a large part of the costs of these parks could now be paid for by a much higher set of park fees.

It is difficult, moreover, to argue that poor people show up at the gates of Yellowstone Park, or even the much nearer metropolitan area regional parks, in significant number, so that a subsidy is needed to continue provision of this service for the poor. A careful study of the users and the incidence of the taxes raised to finance our parks may even show a slight redistribution of income toward greater inequality.

Clearly, this is not the place for an economist to pontificate on the psychology of prices but a number of very interesting phenomena that seem to fall under this general heading deserve brief mention. A few simple examples of how charging a price changes behavior are offered, but left for others to classify.

In a recent study of depressed areas, the case was cited of a community-industrial-development commission that extended its fund-raising efforts from large business contributors to the general public in a supplementary "nickel and dime" campaign. They hoped to enlist the active support of the community at large, more for reasons of public policy than for finance. But even a trivial financial stake was seen as a means to create broad and strong public identification with the local industrial development programs and to gain their political support.

Again, social-work agencies have found that even a nominal charge for what was previously a free service enhances both the self-respect of the recipient and his respect for the usefulness of the service. Paradoxically, we might experiment with higher public assistance payments coupled to *nominal* prices for selected public health and family services, personal counseling and surplus foods.

To bring a lot of this together now in a programmatic way, we can imagine a very sophisticated urban public management beginning with below-cost prices on, say, the new rapid mass transit facility during the promotional period of luring motorists from their automobiles and of "educating" them on the advantages of a carefree journey to work. Later, if and when the new facility becomes crowded during rush hours and after a taste for this new transportation mode has become well established, the "city economist" might devise a three-price structure of fares: the lowest fare for regular off-peak use, the middle fare for regular peak use (tickets for commuters) and the highest fare for the occasional peak-time user. Such a schedule would reflect each class's contribution to the cost of having to carry standby capacity.

If the venture more than covered its costs of operation, the construction of additional facilities would begin. Added social benefits in the form of a cleaner, quieter city or reduced social costs of traffic control and accidents could be included in the cost accounting ("cost-benefit analysis") underlying the fare structure. But below-cost fares, taking care to count social as well as private costs, would not be continued indefinitely except for merit goods or when a clear income-redistribution end is in mind. And, even then, not without careful comparison of the relative efficiency of using the subsidy money in alternative redistributive programs. We need, it would seem, not only a knowledge of the economy of the city, but some very knowledgeable city economists as well.

B. *Ethics*

13. *Ethics and Business: An Economist's View* KENNETH BOULDING

If we are to talk about the ethical principles of a part of a society and of an aspect of human behavior, we must be able to see these in the framework of a larger ethical system. Even though I can claim only amateur status as a moral philosopher, I feel it is necessary to say something about ethical principles in general before I can begin to apply them to a business society.

The first principle of my ethical theory is that all individual human behavior of any kind is guided by a value system; that is, by some system of preferences. In this sense everybody has a personal ethical system. No one could live, move, or act without one. We can distinguish between what might be called the "real" personal ethic, which might be deduced from a person's actual behavior, and the "verbal" ethic, which would be derived from his statements. We find it a common—indeed, almost a universal—phenomenon that a person will give lip service to one set of ethical principles, but that in his behavior he will follow another set of values. Without a set of values of some kind, however, his behavior is inexplicable.

It is clear that merely to say that everyone behaves according to a personal ethic or value system does not solve the problem of ethical theory, the major perplexity of which is to develop a rule of choice among possible personal value systems. The individual is faced not only with images of the world which are ranked according to a particular value system, he is faced with a number of different value systems

SOURCE. From *Beyond Economics,* copyright 1969 by The University of Michigan Press, Ann Arbor, Mich. Reprinted by permission.

according to which the world may be ranked. It is assumed that out of all possible ways of choosing—that is, out of all possible value systems—only one is "right" or "best." This is the ethical value system.

By way of illustration, let us imagine an individual who is at a point of time where he faces three possible futures: A, B, and C. If he chooses A, he will be a little richer, and other people will be richer too. If he chooses B, he will be greatly richer, and nobody else will be worse off. If he chooses C, he will be a little poorer, but other people will be a lot poorer. Which he chooses, of course, depends on his value system; that is, on his personal ethic. If he has an altruistic personal ethic, in which he enjoys the riches of others as if they were his own, he will probably choose A. If he has a selfish personal ethic, in which he places a high value on his own riches but is indifferent to the condition of others, he is likely to choose B. If he has a malevolent personal ethic, in which he takes a positive satisfaction in the misfortunes of others, he is likely to choose C. Thus, any choice is possible depending on the personal ethic of the individual making the choice.

My third principle is that no a priori proof is possible in any proposition of ethical theory; that is, we cannot arrive at a rule of choice which will always give us the best personal ethic by a process involving pure logic, without reference to the world of experience. This does not mean, however, that ethical problems are in principle insoluble. The problem here is essentially one of limiting the field of choice among personal ethical systems. Suppose we had a society in which the prevailing personal ethic involved killing all children at birth. It is clear that a society of this kind would not persist beyond a generation and its prevailing personal ethic would die with it. Thus, even though we may not wish to set up survival value as an absolute standard for the choice of personal ethical systems, it is clear that survival value strongly limits the choices which may in practice be made.

I am not suggesting that survival is the only test of validity. I am suggesting that it narrows the field of choice. It does not necessarily narrow the field to a single position. Within cultures that have survival value there are still better or worse cultures by other criteria. A culture, for instance, may have survival value and yet be extremely disagreeable for the individuals to live in. The more we limit the field of choice, however, the harder it becomes to resolve the arguments about how to limit it further. Some, for instance, may not wish to exclude those value systems which lead to unhappiness if by excluding them we also exclude certain aspects of nobility and creativity. The solution which seems to be working itself out is one in which we have a number of different cultures, each embodying a different ethical principle. Within a complex society there is room for many such subcultures and many ethical systems, ranging from the Amish to the Zoroastrians. It is one of the great virtues of the division of labor, as Durkheim pointed out, that it permits a diversity of subcultures and therefore a diversity of ethical systems within the framework of a larger society; it is not necessary to impose a single ethical system on the whole society.

My fourth proposition is that corresponding to every culture or subculture there is an ethical system which both creates it and is created by it. In other words, any ethical system is embodied in a social system of which it is an essential part. Changes in ethical systems inevitably produce changes in the social system, and changes in the social system likewise react upon the ethical system. Sometimes a change in the ethical system is embodied in explicit form, in the shape, for instance, of a Bible, a Koran, or a Book of Mormon, around which a subculture is then built. Sometimes the ethical system exists in an almost unconscious set of rules of behavior and norms of conduct (as in the development of mercantile capitalism) which never become embodied in sacred writings or achieve any charismatic power, yet which profoundly affect human conduct and are transmitted from generation to generation.

Threat Exchange and Love

Before going on to apply these principles to the ethical problems of a business society, we must take a brief look at the nature of social systems in general, for we must be able to see a business society as a special case among possible social systems. I define a business society as a social system which is organized primarily through the institution of exchange. Exchange, however, is not the only organizer of social systems and is not the only organizer even in a business society. A social system consists essentially of relationships among persons. If we want to be more exact we might even define it as a system of relationships among roles, for very often it is not the whole person that is significant but the person acting in a role, and one person may occupy many roles in the course of a lifetime. The conflict of roles within the person would then be regarded as essentially a problem of the social system. There are, of course, a great many relationships which are possible between persons and among roles. However, most of these can be classified into three major categories. The first of these is the threat system, in which one says to another, "You do something nice to me or I will do something nasty to you." A threat system, however, is intrinsically unstable. It tends to pass over from the unilateral threat system, which is a powerful organizer if unchallenged, into a bilateral threat system of deterrence: "If you do something nasty to me I will do something nasty to you." Deterrence is an inherently unstable social system because of the fact that the threat is only capable of being an organizer as long as it is credible, and it is only credible if it is occasionally carried out. A system of deterrence, therefore, always involves the eventual carrying out of mutual threats, and when this happens everybody is worse off. The threat system then becomes a negative-sum game, like the "prisoners' dilemma" of game theory, in which the dynamics of the system leads everybody into positions where everybody is worse off.

By contrast, the exchange system, which may be regarded as peculiarly characteristic of a business society, is a positive-sum game and is a much more successful organizer. Exchange is the relationship whereby one says to another, "You do something nice to me and I will do something nice to you." An exchange system, therefore, is based upon promises rather than threats, and a business society especially is built upon what Harry Scherman once called "the promises men live by." The great advantage of a promise system over a threat system is that when the promises are carried out, as they have to be if they are to be effective in organizing behavior, everybody is better off rather than worse off.

There is another set of relationships among persons and roles which may be called generally the integrative system. This is a rather heterogeneous category which includes persuasion, teaching, and love: "What you want, I want." All social systems and subsystems are based on mixtures of these three major elements, in varying proportions. Thus, in an authoritarian state or in a military organization, the threat system is dominant, but exchange is still present. The member of the organization gets something for what he puts into it. The integrative system likewise must be present; otherwise generals and dictators would not have to make speeches. At the other extreme we have the family or the larger utopian community, in which the integrative system is dominant, and in which people do what they do because of persuasion, teaching, or love. Even in the family or in the integrative community, however, there must be some exchange; there must be some sense in which the individual gets something for what he gives up, and there is likewise at least the remains of the threat system, for even in the most loving community there is the underlying threat of expulsion or of the withdrawal of love. One suspects that the stability of a social system depends upon the proportion in which the three main organizers are employed. A system which tries to rely too much on any single one of them is likely to be unstable.

Ethics in Business Society

It is now high time to get past the preliminaries and begin to apply these principles to the ethics of a business society. We should notice first that no society is a pure business society. No society, that is, has ever organized itself around the institutions of exchange alone. Every society has a government which organizes the threat system and every society has integrative institutions in the family, the church, the school, the club, and so on. Furthermore, business institutions themselves, such as the corporation, the bank, the organized commodity or security exchanges, and the labor union, are not organized solely by exchange. There are coercive or threat system elements in the threat of cutting off exchange, the withdrawal of custom, quitting, firing, and so on. There may be internal threat systems in the shape of industrial discipline, and there are also extensive integrative systems in the attempt to build morale, loyalty, the corporate image, systems of authority and instruction, and so on.

Again the first thing to note is that there are certain individual value systems which undermine the institutions of exchange and are, therefore, extremely threatening to a business system. An exchange system, for instance, cannot flourish in the absence of a minimum of simple honesty because an exchange system is an exchange of promises, and honesty is the fulfillment of promises. Thus, if capitalism is to work successfully, there must be defenses in the society against dishonesty. These defenses may lie in part in the threat system; that is, in the system of law and police. But I suspect that a good part of the burden must also be carried by the integrative system in the internalization of these moral standards in the individual. This is done in the home, in the church, and in the school, but it is also done, of course, by the example of those around the individual and especially the example of his peer group.

The second set of problems relates to the political images, value systems, and institutions which provide the framework for a market-oriented economy. Because exchange is not sufficient to organize society by itself, even in a society which is organized mainly by exchange, there must be a minimum governmental framework. The success of the market economy of the United States, for instance, can be attributed in large part to the fact that there has been no hesitation in using the instruments of government for economic purposes where this has seemed to be desirable. An exchange economy, for instance, may pass over into a degree of monopolistic organization which undermines it. Hence, we have antitrust and related legislation.

The third ethical problem of a business society arises out of the fact that the institutions of exchange in themselves do not develop enough of the integrative system. Exchange is a highly abstract relationship. It is something, indeed, which can be done just as well by a machine as by a person in many cases, as the rise of vending machines indicates. At some points in the society, however, there must be personal relationships which are richer than those of the exchange relationship if the society and its activities are to have meaning and significance for the individuals. In spite of the success of a business society in increasing productivity and in providing for human wants, it has a tendency to undermine itself because of its inability to generate affection. It is a positive-sum game in which everybody benefits, but in which the game itself is apparently so lacking in emotional effect that it does not produce loyalty, love, and self-sacrifice. Very few people have ever died for a Federal Reserve Bank, and nobody suggests that they should. Consequently when the institutions of a business society come under attack from those who are emotionally committed to another way of organizing economic life, they often fail to generate in their own supporters the same degree of emotional commitment. The situation is, indeed, even worse than I have suggested, for when business institutions, such as corporations, attempt to develop emotional commitment and try to develop welfare capitalism, baseball teams, company songs, and the school spirit, the overall effect is likely to be slightly ridiculous, like that of a good solid workhorse putting on wings and trying to set up in business as a Pegasus.

Thus, we face this dilemma: if a business society is to survive it must develop an integrative system and integrative institutions, but the peculiar institutions of a business society (such as markets, corporations, banks, and so on), because they are essentially instrumental in character, are not capable of developing a powerful integrative system in themselves. If market institutions are to survive, therefore, they must be supplemented by a matrix of integrative institutions, such as the family, the church, the school, and the nation, which develop individual value systems based on love, self-sacrifice, identification with goals outside the person, and altruism.

Unless these integrative institutions exist, there is grave danger that the market institutions may develop a personal ethic which is inimical to their survival in the individuals who operate them. The exchange system almost inevitably provides opportunities for individuals to make personal gains by the sacrifice of moral principles because the institutions of exchange, in themselves, provide neither the policing nor the internalization—that is, neither the threat system nor the integrative system—by which these moral values can be sustained. A society which devotes a disproportionate amount of its life and energy to the exchange system may find this system eventually undermined. On the other hand it is equally true that when coercive systems, such as the state or the military, or integrative institutions, such as the church or the school, attempt to go into trade—that is, into the exchange system—they are apt to be very unsuccessful. The problem of society, like so many other problems, is a problem of finding the right proportions. Disproportionate emphasis on either the coercive systems, the market system, or the integrative system is likely to result in a corruption of the moral life and the eventual disintegration of the society. These considerations may help to illuminate what is undoubtedly one of the most complex problems of our day: the ideological struggle between socialism and capitalism. The ethical appeal of socialism is primarily to the integrative system. The exchange system is despised as being somehow a low and unworthy form of human activity, and in a sense the ultimate ideal of the socialist is a society in which all things are done for love and not for money. In practice, unfortunately, the attempt to abolish exchange as a major organizer of society and in particular to abolish the institution of private property in commodities (which is, of course, an essential condition of exchange, for we cannot exchange what we do not have) results not in the replacement of exchange by love as the major organizer of the system but rather in the replacement of exchange by coercion and by threats.

Much of the moral appeal of communism, however, rests precisely on its appeal to the altruism of the individual and to the desire we all have, in greater or lesser degrees, to identify ourselves with a larger body and to work for "others." We must make it quite clear to ourselves and to the world that altruism is in no way inconsistent with the institutions of the market or with the organization of society through exchange. There is nothing in a profit system which requires a narrow selfishness and a lack of identification with mankind on the part of the profit maker. This confusion between the profit system, as an organizer of economic life, and the "profit motive," in the bad sense of unadulterated lust for selfish gain, is responsible for a great deal of confusion in social thought. We can, indeed, argue that the profit system will operate successfully only if the profit motive is constantly tempered by altruism, by a sense of public responsibility, and by the sense of identification of the individual with the larger community. Here again, however, the problem of balance is crucial. Pure altruism is no more desirable than pure selfishness. It is one of the great advantages of a system of private property that it clearly limits the responsibilities of the individual to that which is immediate to him. Protestations of general love for mankind are apt to sound hollow from a person who neglects his immediate responsibility to his own children, his own neighbors, and those who are his partners in the complex of exchange relationships.

The challenge of socialism to an absolutely pure market economy, unrestrained by coercion and unmodified by love, would be a very severe one. We can, however, assert with some confidence that in what might be called the North Atlantic Community the challenge of socialism has been profitably met. We need not hesitate to admit that in large part it has been the socialist challenge which has enabled us to modify the market economy in the direction of a better balance among the three organizing elements. If we admit this, we can challenge the socialist world also to achieve a better balance, to make more use of the market as an organizer where this is more effective, and to abandon its undue reliance on the coercive system without abandoning its very proper appeal to the integrative system and to the identification, at some levels, of the individual with the great society of mankind.

14. *Which Ethic for Marketers?*

HENRY O. PRUDEN

Many an individual who holds a position in a marketing organization finds that he must compromise his personal code of ethics in favor of an organizational code of ethics or forego the income and the status of career success. As a citizen he is supposed to follow his individual conception of ethics, which for most individuals has its roots in a Judeo-Christian culture. But as an employee he is expected to follow the organizational conception of ethics which in many ways resembles the bluffing strategies of a poker game. Yet the prevailing organizational ethic and those marketers who thrive by it may contain within them the seeds of their own demise. The organizational ethic breeds self-agrandizement, intolerance of dissent, resistance to change, and unresponsiveness to consumerism, all of which may be hastening the day when corporate marketing will become a quasi public-utility.

How can the ethical dilemma of the individual and the drift toward public control of organized marketing be corrected? The legal remedy stands close at hand. Another alternative is to rely upon the individual marketer's personal code of ethics. But through the eyes of the individual, the organizational world might appear as a vast Leviathan holding forth status and security in exchange for loyalty to its system of authority. To withdraw from the organizational system or rebel against it and be thrown out, leaves one to live strictly by his own ethic; it would place a man in a Hobbesian state of nature where the life of his career would be "nasty, brutish, and short." The individual solution is exercised by few, though for all it is the ultimate recourse.

Adherence to a professional ethic can be a way out of the individual dilemma and the organizational predicament of marketing. A professional ethic could offer

the individual marketer a third basis of authority, one in addition to his individual ethic and the organizational ethic. A professional ethic could also provide marketing organizations with a new rationale, one geared to future social, intellectual and technological demands. A professional ethic would embrace a process of professionalization for formulating an ethic reflecting rapidly developing knowledge, education and the application of skills, and an ideal of service to clients. A professional ethic in marketing could earn community sanction for the collective actions of the professional marketing group through whom the norms of the profession would be developed, disseminated, inculcated, and upheld.

The purpose of this article is to present three ideal types of ethics: an individual ethic, an organizational ethic, and a professional ethic. The paper offers a model proposing some relationships among the individual, organizational, and professional ethics. It will be argued that the professional ethic is the most appropriate for marketers in view of mounting social demands and radically changing technology, and that its development is the responsibility of the American Marketing Association.

Three Ethics

Figure 1, the model, (p. 100) presents the individual, organizational, and professional ethics as ideal types and suggests some interrelationships among them. The model seeks to increase the number of options or ethical dimensions open to the individual marketer. Rather than the choice of conforming to the organizational ethic or rebelling and withdrawing according to the dictates of one's individual ethic, a third option is open—the professional ethic. The model further rests upon the notion of power: the power of organizational rewards and punishments supporting authority, the power of an individual to withdraw his essential services, and finally the power of a profession to exercise sanctions through the collective action of the professional group. A marketer's business behavior would probably be guided by an ideology which was the synthesis of these three ethics. This synthesis, however, would likely be a dynamic balance since there are liable to be fundamental points of conflict among the three ethics. If one of the ethics should become overbearing, the individual has recourse to either one or a combination of the other two.

The concepts of "ethics" and "ethical behavior" are given broad interpretation in this article. More formally, the dictionary defines ethics as "a set of moral principles or values; a theory or system of moral values; the principles of conduct governing an individual or a group." Kenneth Boulding in *The Organizational Revolution* defines "ethical conduct" in this manner: "It seems not unreasonable to regard ethical conduct as that which is motivated by the larger and more objective interest as against the smaller and more personal interest. This is one meaning of the

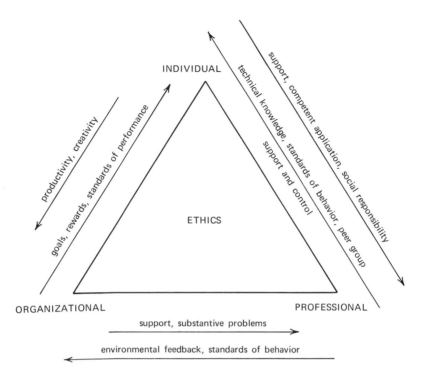

FIGURE 1. Three ethical frames of reference for the marketer.

injunction to love our neighbor as ourselves; that we should see ourselves as we really are, and should act in the interest of the 'whole.' Action in the general interest is the heart of ethical conduct."

Individual Ethic

By individual ethic the author means that a marketer is "his own man, that he is independent." This is what Alan B. Schoonmaker seems to have in mind with the concept of "individualism" in America: "We believe in independence; we believe in individualism; they are a part, an inescapable part, of the basic American ideology. We believe that we should be free to make our own decisions, that we should control our own lives and our own destinies, that our fate should be in our own hands rather than in someone else's."

The individual ethic is wrapped with the traditional American dream of individualism and independence. The traditional dream stressed rugged individualism and entrepreneurship in business combined with religious principles in private life.

In the first case it was felt that one could open his own store, start a factory, or homestead a small farm. In the second case it was a personal code of telling the truth and following the golden rule. This traditional view of the individual ethic can be contrasted to a more modern notion of individualism appropriate for a world of large organizations. The traditional view of the individual ethic saw the individual living a life outside of the big organization. The ethic stressed self-fulfillment through independence. It valued for the person the freedom to seek his own interests, make his own decisions, and control his own destiny. It did not provide that someone should submit to the decisions of others whose authority was based upon their positions in organizations.

The modern view of an individual ethic views individuals operating within the large organization. This modern view of individual ethics has several common fronts with the management creed based upon industrial humanism. The modern ethic stresses individual autonomy, self-realization, equality of opportunity, freedom of thought and expression—and a number of other democratic humanistic values.

This modern individual ethic frequently comes into conflict with the organizational ethic. Presthus has observed that large organizations act as miniature societies which place authority, status, and small group pressures on the individual. Many of these come into conflict with the goals of self-fulfillment and autonomy suggested by the individual ethic. As a consequence some individuals may conform to the organizational ethic and be rewarded with upward mobility. Others may be indifferent to the organization and seek their self-fulfillment in off-work activities. Another type of individual may seek some accommodation between the organization and another reference group such as his professional peers. Schoonmaker also underscores the fact that there is an inescapable and irreconcilable conflict between individuals and the organization.

Organizational Ethic

Robert Presthus portrays an organization ethic where the organizational goals of profit, growth, and survival override the self realization of the individual. Accomplishment of goals within large organizations requires standardization, routinization, and specialization, with the consequent narrowing of individual responsibility for organized actions. Thus the individual is given narrow, specialized tasks which he is to perform and to which his responsbility is limited. The group interests of functional departments within organizations tend to reinforce the specialized and myopic view of their members.

Individual resistance to this organizational control is difficult. The top-most members of the organization compose an oligarchy which controls the power to distribute rewards. This power is used to reinforce hierarchical authority with the promise of promotion and status to loyal subordinates. This control is furthered by a common need to be liked and a deference to authority among individuals. An individual who resists the organization's ends or means risks both career and social isolation.

There are mixed views as to whether the organizational ethic provides for the responsiveness of an organization to its clients (customers). A negative view is that the organization as a bureaucracy is basically insensitive and indifferent to the aspirations of its clients. A positive view is that the organization is customer-oriented and its rewards are primarily a consequence of service to its customers, commonly known as the "marketing concept."

Although the "marketing concept" does offer a customer-centered philosophy to guide business activities, there are limits to its efficacy. John Douglas has observed a striking parallel between the newer theory Y concept of management and the newer customer-oriented approach of marketing. Both approaches call for more participation in management decision-making by subordinates and by customers to enhance the goals of the organization and the goals of the individual. Douglas feared a drift toward an irresponsible, stultifying redistribution of power into the hands of subordinates and customers who reflect mass values. William G. Scott does not believe that the newer management-employee participation relations and by extension the newer management-customer relations are really new. Despite the rhetoric, the old management-centered, production-centered and the newer participation forms of employee and customer relations with management are of the same cloth. Namely, they both endorse sustaining management's prerogatives by eliminating the causes of subordinate discontent through participation in decision-making, at management's discretion, without a major redistribution of power to employees and customers.

The functionality of the organizational ethic involves the problem of whether it recognizes the legitimate individualized claims of the men employed and whether it responds to the external demands for service and change. The power and authority of management are the key variables in this problem. Hence, the resolution of the problem rests upon whether marketing organizations in the future are guided by authority based upon hierarchy or authority based upon the specialist's knowledge of professionals.

Professional Ethic

The professional ethic provides a frame of reference to guide the behavior of marketers. Presthus believes that the ". . . professional ethic centers on individual independence, on the free exchange of information, and on rigorous disavowal of authority as a basis for truth." Kenneth R. Andrews feels that an occupation may be judged a profession according to how well it meets the five criteria of knowledge, competent application, social responsibility, self-control, and community sanction. The professional ethic can be seen to operate both on the level of ideology and in the behavior of professional men. It differs from the individual ethic in that it emphasizes the collective consensus and actions of a group of professional peers. It differs from the organizational ethic in that it stresses the norms of the profession as a basis for authority rather than the organizational basis of authority.

The professional man is frequently found ambivalent with respect to his position in an organization. They are among those who frequently feel an ethical conflict between their professional standards and their requisites of organizational success. The loyalty of professional men is apt to be to the professional peers who are engaged in similar activities and are scattered throughout a number of separate organizations. Valuing work—the problems to be solved—rather than rising in a bureaucracy, the professional tends to emphasize knowledge and technique. He also tends to be change-oriented. When aware that the fruits of their actions have detrimental effects on a client system, professionals are typically led toward collective concern for the limitation and correction of their activities.

A professional ethic in marketing would be built upon scientifically substantiated knowledge and would look to the validation of this knowledge by the professional peer group. The professional group could then disseminate new technical knowledge concerning the profession, foster individual attitudes of service to customers, and provide feedback from a monitoring of consequences upon the customer system. The professional association could exercise disciplinary action on those individuals who are not competent or who deviate from professional standards. The association should be able to judge performance both with respect to the functions of individuals and the consequences to clients. In the wake of these efforts would come public sanction for the profession.

For the individual marketer the standards of a profession and the support of a professional peer group would be a source of power. The additional knowledge would enhance his ability to carry out important work functions. The professional peer association through its collective sanction could tend to counter balance the exclusive power and authority of an organization.

Relating Individual, Organizational, and Professional Ethics

The model (Figure 1) reveals an arrangement of expectations and exchanges. There are expectations associated with each ethic and exchanges among organizational and professional groups and individuals. A marketer could subscribe to any of several combinations of ethics.

The interface between the individual pole and the organizational pole can be seen as an exchange between the person and the organization. The individual contracts to be productive and creative within an organization. In exchange the organization provides the individual with supportive rewards and it demands goal directed behavior and particular standards of performance from the individual.

The individual-professional linkage calls for financial and other support and the performance of professionally competent, socially responsible behavior by the individual. In return, technical knowledge and behavioral standards emanate from the profession. The individual marketer through his professional membership is also subject to support or control from his peers in the association.

The organizational-professional interface also calls for the support, financially and otherwise, of the professional marketing association. In addition, the organization would be expected to provide professionals with problems and research opportunities in order to advance the state of the art. It would be proper for the professional association to provide the organization with data and its interpretation regarding the reaction of customers, governmental and private groups to the actions of particular categories of organizations. The profession should also inform the organization of professionally acceptable standards of behavior.

Viability of Individual and Organizational Ethics

The individual and organizational ethics furnish the marketer with vital methods for checks and balances. A drawback of rampant professionalism is that it leads to the narrow specialized perspective on the part of its membership. This could lead to an ethical sense of members' limited responsibility over the consequences of their actions and a trained incapacity to respond to new ideas and opposing viewpoints, made more troublesome by a self-centered sense of superiority. The ethic of the organization, derived from its need to adapt in order to profit, grow, and survive, would act as a check against overzealous professionalism. Also the individual frame of reference would be an effective counter against overbearing professional and/or organizational control by balancing one against the other or ultimately withdrawal from both.

Summary

In summary, three ethical frames of reference are open to the individual marketer. The individual will influence and be influenced by each of these ethics. He may view the professional ethic as a countervailing force to the now dominant organizational ethic, and the organizational ethic as a future countervailing force to the professional ethic. His individual ethic is an ultimate countervailing force to either autocratic organizational or autocratic professional control. To bring about this system of countervailing forces will require the development of a professional ethic derived from a professional approach to marketing.

15. *Is Business Bluffing Ethical?*

ALBERT Z. CARR

A respected businessman with whom I discussed the theme of this article remarked with some heat, "You mean to say you're going to encourage men to bluff? Why, bluffing is nothing more than a form of lying! You're advising them to lie!"

I agreed that the basis of private morality is a respect for truth and that the closer a businessman comes to the truth, the more he deserves respect. At the same time, I suggested that most bluffing in business might be regarded simply as game strategy—much like bluffing in poker, which does not reflect on the morality of the bluffer.

I quoted Henry Taylor, the British statesman who pointed out that "falsehood ceases to be falsehood when it is understood on all sides that the truth is not expected to be spoken"—an exact description of bluffing in poker, diplomacy, and business. I cited the analogy of the criminal court, where the criminal is not expected to tell the truth when he pleads "not guilty." Everyone from the judge down takes it for granted that the job of the defendant's attorney is to get his client off, not to reveal the truth; and this is considered ethical practice. I mentioned Representative Omar Burleson, the Democrat from Texas, who was quoted as saying, in regard to the ethics of Congress, "Ethics is a barrel of worms"—a pungent summing up of the problem of deciding who is ethical in politics.

SOURCE. Albert Z. Carr, "Is Business Bluffing Ethical?" *Harvard Business Review,* January-February 1968 © 1968 by the President and Fellows of Harvard College; all rights reserved. Adapted from *Business as a Game,* New American Library, 1968.

I reminded my friend that millions of businessmen feel constrained every day to say *yes* to their bosses when they secretly believe *no* and that this is generally accepted as permissible strategy when the alternative might be the loss of a job. The essential point, I said, is that the ethics of business are game ethics, different from the ethics of religion.

He remained unconvinced. Referring to the company of which he is president, he declared: "Maybe that's good enough for some businessmen, but I can tell you that we pride ourselves on our ethics. In 30 years not one customer has ever questioned my word or asked to check our figures. We're loyal to our customers and fair to our suppliers. I regard my handshake on a deal as a contract. I've never entered into price-fixing schemes with my competitors. I've never allowed my salesmen to spread injurious rumors about other companies. Our union contract is the best in our industry. And, if I do say so myself, our ethical standards are of the highest!"

He really was saying, without realizing it, that he was living up to the ethical standards of the business game—which are a far cry from those of private life. Like a gentlemanly poker player, he did not play in cahoots with others at the table, try to smear their reputations, or hold back chips he owed them.

But this same fine man, at the very time, was allowing one of his products to be advertised in a way that made it sound a great deal better than it actually was. Another item in his product line was notorious among dealers for its "built-in obsolescence." He was holding back from the market a much-improved product because he did not want it to interfere with sales of the inferior item it would have replaced. He had joined with certain of his competitors in hiring a lobbyist to push a state legislature, by methods that he preferred not to know too much about, into amending a bill then being enacted.

In his view these things had nothing to do with ethics; they were merely normal business practice. He himself undoubtedly avoided outright falsehoods—never lied in so many words. But the entire organization that he ruled was deeply involved in numerous strategies of deception.

Discard the Golden Rule

This view of business is especially worrisome to people without much business experience. A minister of my acquaintance once protested that business cannot possibly function in our society unless it is based on the Judeo-Christian system of ethics. He told me:

I know some businessmen have supplied call girls to customers, but there are always a few rotten apples in every barrel. That doesn't mean the rest of the fruit isn't sound. Surely the vast majority of businessmen are ethical. I myself am acquainted with many who adhere to strict codes of ethics based fundamentally on religious teachings. They contribute to good causes. They participate in community activities. They cooperate with other companies to improve working conditions in their industries. Certainly they are not indifferent to ethics.

That most businessmen are not indifferent to ethics in their private lives, everyone will agree. My point is that in their office lives they cease to be private citizens; they become game players who must be guided by a somewhat different set of ethical standards.

The point was forcefully made to me by a Midwestern executive who has given a good deal of thought to the question:

So long as a businessman complies with the laws of the land and avoids telling malicious lies, he's ethical. If the law as written gives a man a wide-open chance to make a killing, he'd be a fool not to take advantage of it. If he doesn't, somebody else will. There's no obligation on him to stop and consider who is going to get hurt. If the law says he can do it, that's all the justification he needs. There's nothing unethical about that. It's just plain business sense.

This executive (call him Robbins) took the stand that even industrial espionage, which is frowned on by some businessmen, ought not to be considered unethical. He recalled a recent meeting of the National Industrial Conference Board where an authority on marketing made a speech in which he deplored the employment of spies by business organizations. More and more companies, he pointed out, find it cheaper to penetrate the secrets of competitors with concealed cameras and microphones or by bribing employees than to set up costly research and design departments of their own. A whole branch of the electronics industry has grown up with this trend, he continued, providing equipment to make industrial espionage easier.

Disturbing? The marketing expert found it so. But when it came to a remedy, he could only appeal to "respect for the golden rule." Robbins thought this a confession of defeat, believing that the golden rule, for all its value as an ideal for society, is simply not feasible as a guide for business. A good part of the time the businessman is trying to do unto others as he hopes others will *not* do unto him. Robbins continued:

Espionage of one kind or another has become so common in business that it's like taking a drink during Prohibition—it's not considered sinful. And we don't even have Prohibition where espionage is concerned; the law is very tolerant in this area. There's no more shame for a business that uses secret agents than there is for a nation. Bear in mind that there already is at least one large corporation—you can buy its stock over the counter—that makes millions by providing counterespionage service to industrial firms. Espionage in business is not an ethical problem; it's an established technique of business competition.

"We don't Make the Laws"

Wherever we turn in business, we can perceive the sharp distinction between its ethical standards and those of the churches. Newspapers abound with sensational stories growing out of this distinction:

We read one day that Senator Philip A. Hart of Michigan has attacked food processors for deceptive packaging of numerous products.

The next day there is a Congressional to-do over Ralph Nader's book, *Unsafe At Any Speed,* which demonstrates that automobile companies for years have neglected the safety of car-owning families.

Then another Senator, Lee Metcalf of Montana, and journalist Vic Reinemer show in their book, *Overcharge,* the methods by which utility companies elude regulating government bodies to extract unduly large payments from users of electricity.

These are merely dramatic instances of a prevailing condition; there is hardly a major industry at which a similar attack could not be aimed. Critics of business regard such behavior as unethical, but the companies concerned know that they are merely playing the business game.

Among the most respected of our business institutions are the insurance companies. A group of insurance executives meeting recently in New England was startled when their guest speaker, social critic Daniel Patrick Moynihan, roundly berated them for "unethical" practices. They had been guilty, Moynihan alleged, of using outdated actuarial tables to obtain unfairly high premiums. They habitually delayed the hearings of lawsuits against them in order to tire out the plaintiffs and win cheap settlements. In their employment policies they used ingenious devices to discriminate against minority groups.

It was difficult for the audience to deny the validity of these charges. But these men were business game players. Their reaction to Moynihan's attack was much the same as that of the automobile manufacturers to Nader, of the utilities to Senator Metcalf, and of the food processors to Senator Hart. If the laws governing their businesses change, or if public opinion becomes clamorous, they will make the necessary adjustments. But morally they have in their view done nothing wrong. As long as they comply with the letter of the law, they are within their rights to operate their businesses as they see fit.

The small business is in the same position as the great corporation in this respect. For example:

In 1967 a key manufacturer was accused of providing master keys for automobiles to mailorder customers, although it was obvious that some of the purchasers might be automobile thieves. His defense was plain and straightforward. If there was nothing in the law to prevent him from selling his keys to anyone who ordered them, it was not up to him to inquire as to his customers' motives. Why was it any worse, he insisted, for him to sell car keys by mail, than for mail-order houses to sell guns that might be used for murder? Until the law was changed, the key manufacturer could regard himself as being just as ethical as any other business-man by the rules of the business game.

Violations of the ethical ideals of society are common in business, but they are not necessarily violations of business principles. Each year the Federal Trade Commission orders hundreds of companies, many of them of the first magnitude, to "cease and desist" from practices which, judged by ordinary standards, are of questionable morality but which are stoutly defended by the companies concerned.

In one case, a firm manufacturing a well-known mouthwash was accused of using a cheap form of alchohol possibly deleterious to health. The company's chief executive, after testifying in Washington, made this comment privately:

"We broke no law. We're in a highly competitive industry. If we're going to stay in business, we have to look for profit wherever the law permits. We don't make the laws. We obey them. Then why do we have to put up with this 'holier than thou' talk about ethics? It's sheer hypocrisy. We're not in business to promote ethics. Look at the cigarette companies, for God's sake! If the ethics aren't embodied in the laws by the men who made them, you can't expect businessmen to fill the lack. Why, a sudden submission to Christian ethics by businessmen would bring about the greatest economic upheaval in history!"

It may be noted that the government failed to prove its case against him.

The Individual and the Game

An individual within a company often finds it difficult to adjust to the require-ments of the business game. He tries to preserve his private ethical standards in situations that call for game strategy. When he is obliged to carry out company policies that challenge his conception of himself as an ethical man, he suffers.

It disturbs him when he is ordered, for instance, to deny a raise to a man who deserves it, to fire an employee of long standing, to prepare advertising that he believes to be misleading, to conceal facts that he feels customers are entitled to know, to cheapen the quality of materials used in the manufacture of an established product, to sell as a new product that he knows to be rebuilt, to exaggerate the curative powers of a medicinal preparation, or to coerce dealers.

There are some fortunate executives who, by the nature of their work and circumstances, never have to face problems of this kind. But in one form or another the ethical dilemma is felt sooner or later by most businessmen. Possibly the dilemma is most painful not when the company forces the action on the executive but when he originates it himself—that is, when he has taken or is contemplating a step which is in his own interest but which runs counter to his early moral conditioning. To illustrate:

The manager of an export department, eager to show rising sales, is pressed by a big customer to provide invoices which, while containing no overt falsehood that would violate a U.S. law, are so worded that the customer may be able to evade certain taxes in his homeland.

A company president finds that an aging executive, within a few years of retirement and his pension, is not as productive as formerly. Should he be kept on?

The produce manager of a supermarket debates with himself whether to get rid of a lot of half-rotten tomatoes by including one, with its good side exposed, in every tomato six-pack.

An accountant discovers that he has taken an improper deduction on his company's tax return and fears the consequences if he calls the matter to the president's attention, though he himself has done nothing illegal. Perhaps if he says nothing, no one will notice the error.

A chief executive officer is asked by his directors to comment on a rumor that he owns stock in another company with which he has placed large orders. He could deny it, for the stock is in the name of his son-in-law and he has earlier formally instructed his son-in-law to sell the holding.

Temptations of this kind constantly arise in business. If an executive allows himself to be torn between a decision based on business considerations and one based on his private ethical code, he exposes himself to a grave psychological strain.

This is not to say that sound business strategy necessarily runs counter to ethical ideals. They may frequently coincide; and when they do, everyone is gratified. But the major tests of every move in business, as in all games of strategy, are legality and profit. A man who intends to be a winner in the business game must have a game player's attitude.

The business strategist's decisions must be as impersonal as those of a surgeon performing an operation—concentrating on objective and technique, and subordinating personal feelings. If the chief executive admits that his son-in-law owns the stock, it is because he stands to lose more if the fact comes out later than if he states it boldly and at once. If the supermarket manager orders the rotten tomatoes to be discarded, he does so to avoid an increase in consumer complaints and a loss of goodwill. The company president decides not to fire the elderly executive in the belief that the negative reaction of other employees would in the long run cost the company more than it would lose in keeping him and paying his pension.

All sensible businessmen prefer to be truthful, but they seldom feel inclined to tell the *whole* truth. In the business game truth-telling usually has to be kept within narrow limits if trouble is to be avoided. The point was neatly made a long time ago (in 1888) by one of John D. Rockefeller's associates, Paul Babcock, to Standard Oil

Company executives who were about to testify before a government investigating committee: "Parry every question with answers which, while perfectly truthful, are evasive of *bottom* facts." This was, is, and probably always will be regarded as wise and permissible business strategy.

For Office Use Only

An executive's family life can easily be dislocated if he fails to make a sharp distinction between the ethical systems of the home and the office—or if his wife does not grasp that distinction. Many a businessman who has remarked to his wife, "I had to let Jones go today" or "I had to admit to the boss that Jim has been goofing off lately," has been met with an indignant protest. "How could you do a thing like that? You know Jones is over 50 and will have a lot of trouble getting another job." Or, "You did that to Jim? With his wife ill and all the worry she's been having with the kids?"

If the executive insists that he had no choice because the profits of the company and his own security were involved, he may see a certain cool and ominous reappraisal in his wife's eyes. Many wives are not prepared to accept the fact that business operates with a special code of ethics. An illuminating illustration of this comes from a Southern sales executive who related a conversation he had had with his wife at a time when a hotly contested political campaign was being waged in their state:

> "I made the mistake of telling her that I had had lunch with Colby, who gives me about half my business. Colby mentioned that his company had a stake in the election. Then he said, 'By the way, I'm treasurer of the citizens' committee for Lang. I'm collecting contributions. Can I count on you for a hundred dollars?'
>
> "Well, there I was. I was opposed to Lang, but I knew Colby. If he withdrew his business I could be in a bad spot. So I just smiled and wrote out a check then and there. He thanked me, and we started to talk about his next order. Maybe he thought I shared his political views. If so, I wasn't going to lose any sleep over it.
>
> "I should have had sense enough not to tell Mary about it. She hit the ceiling. She said she was disappointed in me. She said I hadn't acted like a man, that I should have stood up to Colby.
>
> "I said, 'Look, it was an either-or situation. I had to do it or risk losing the business.'
>
> "She came back at me with, 'I don't believe it. You could have been honest with him. You could have said that you didn't feel you ought to contribute to a campaign for a man you weren't going to vote for. I'm sure he would have understood.'
>
> "I said, 'Mary, you're a wonderful woman, but you're way off the track. Do you know what would have happened if I had said that? Colby would have smiled and said, "Oh, I didn't realize. Forget it." But in his eyes from that moment I would

be an oddball, maybe a bit of a radical. He would have listened to me talk about his order and would have promised to give it consideration. After that I wouldn't hear from him for a week. Then I would telephone and learn from his secretary that he wasn't yet ready to place the order. And in about a month I would hear through the grapevine that he was giving his business to another company. A month after that I'd be out of a job.'

"She was silent for a while. Then she said, 'Tom, something is wrong with business when a man is forced to choose between his family's security and his moral obligation to himself. It's easy for me to say you should have stood up to him—but if you had, you might have felt you were betraying me and the kids. I'm sorry that you did it, Tom, but I can't blame you. Something is wrong with business!' "

This wife saw the problem in terms of moral obligation as conceived in private life; her husband saw it as a matter of game strategy. As a player in a weak position, he felt that he could not afford to indulge an ethical sentiment that might have cost him his seat at the table.

Playing to Win

If a man plans to take a seat in the business game, he owes it to himself to master the principles by which the game is played, including its special ethical outlook. He can then hardly fail to recognize that an occasional bluff may well be justified in terms of the game's ethics and warranted in terms of economic necessity. Once he clears his mind on this point, he is in a good position to match his strategy against that of the other players. He can then determine objectively whether a bluff in a given situation has a good chance of succeeding and can decide when and how to bluff, without a feeling of ethical transgression.

To be a winner, a man must play to win. This does not mean that he must be ruthless, cruel, harsh, or treacherous. On the contrary, the better his reputation for integrity, honesty, and decency, the better his chances of victory will be in the long run. But from time to time every businessman, like every poker player, is offered a choice between certain loss or bluffing within the legal rules of the game. If he is not resigned to losing, if he wants to rise in his company and industry, then in such a crisis he will bluff—and bluff hard.

In the last third of the twentieth century even children are aware that if a man has become prosperous in business, he has sometimes departed from the strict truth in order to overcome obstacles or has practiced the more subtle deceptions of the half-truth or the misleading omission. Whatever the form of the bluff, it is an integral part of the game, and the executive who does not master its techniques is not likely to accumulate much money or power.

16. Consumerism — An Appraisal of Business Ethics

In the exercise of its traditional functions—producing, distributing and selling a vast variety of material goods—U.S. industry's unparalleled accomplishments are the envy of other countries.

In the process of developing the most efficient production and distribution systems in history, American business has contributed not only to national economic progress, but also to a richer, fuller, more diverse life for individual American citizens.

Yet, in the midst of affluence and economic progress, pressing social problems such as poverty and the urban crisis plague the nation. Within the vastly altered American environment, changes in cultural attitudes and social values have produced a new awareness of these problems and of the need to solve them.

In addition to material subsistence wants, the American consumer is increasingly placing emphasis on "human fulfillment" wants such as cleaner and safer cities, improved public transportation and housing, better health facilities, the elimination of poverty and suffering, and achieving a higher quality in life.

The generally higher aspirations of society underline another important dimension of consumerism, namely growing awareness of an alleged corporate indifference to ethics, aesthetics and social responsibilities.

SOURCE. "Consumerism—An Appraisal of Business Ethics," *Business and the Consumer—A Program for the Seventies,* Chamber of Commerce of the United States. Copyright 1970. Reprinted by permission.

Within certain top industry circles, consumerism is increasingly recognized as one dimension of a new corporate social responsibility. As a result, some industry efforts had been undertaken already to meet consumer needs through voluntary programs of self-regulation, new marketing strategies, and partnership efforts with government and consumer groups.

However, the unabated strength of the consumer movement with its pressure for more mandatory controls makes clear the need to understand the position of critics of business ethics and lack of aesthetics.

Vance Packard, in his book *The Waste Makers,* indicts business and particularly the mass media for turning consumers into wastemakers; and for initiating pressures for high production and consumption which lead to a "hyperthyroid" economy and to false values.

Packard describes the following business practices which he asserts have contributed to a commercialization of American life:

Marketing to induce each consumer to buy more of each product.
Marketing to induce the "throwaway spirit."
Marketing to achieve planned obsolescence.
Design of products to achieve style obsolescence.
Design of products for servicing complexity.
Pricing products to create confusion.
Fostering hedonism in the masses.

The tone of the "consumer era" as launched by President John F. Kennedy, has been summed up by Arthur Schlesinger, Jr. in his book, *A Thousand Days:*

... despite his support of economic growth and his concern over persisting privation, the thrust of his preoccupation was less with the economic machine and its quantitative results than with the quality of life in a society which, in the main, has achieved abundance.

Attacks on certain business practices and the tardiness of business in responding constructively have helped to foster a favorable climate for consumerism in the United States. Corporate strategies, particularly in marketing and advertising, need to be reexamined in the light of the changing social environment to reflect a greater awareness and sensitivity to the public's evolving ethical values and non-materialistic aspirations. Business will need to become more attuned to the changing values of a better-educated younger generation which is quite critical of orthodox business practices, such as product "puffing" in advertising.

The corporation must go beyond its traditional role of business enterprise and seek to anticipate and meet, rather than simply react to others' proposed solutions to social problems. This may require not only a changed "product" and new marketing strategies, but also a changed corporate structure capable of placing greater emphasis on the internal implications of consumerism.

C. *Psychology, Sociology, and Demography*

17. A Theory of Human Motivation

A. H. MASLOW

The Basic Needs

The "physiological" needs.—The needs that are usually taken as the starting point for motivation theory are the so-called physiological drives.

These physiological needs are the most prepotent of all needs. What this means specifically is that in the human being who is missing everything in life in an extreme fashion, it is most likely that the major motivation would be the physiological needs rather than any others. A person who is lacking food, safety, love, and esteem would most probably hunger for food more strongly than for anything else.

If all the needs are unsatisfied, and the organism is then dominated by the physiological needs, all other needs may become simply non-existent or be pushed into the background. It is then fair to characterize the whole organism by saying simply that it is hungry, for consciousness is almost completely preempted by hunger. All capacities are put into the service of hunger-satisfaction, and the organization of these capacities is almost entirely determined by the one purpose of satisfying hunger. The receptors and effectors, the intelligence, memory, habits, all may now be defined simply as hunger-gratifying tools. Capacities that are not useful for this purpose lie dormant, or are pushed into the background.

But what happens to man's desires when there *is* plenty of bread and when his belly is chronically filled?

SOURCE. Reprinted from *Psychological Review* by permission of the American Psychological Association.

At once other (and "higher") needs emerge and these, rather than physiological hungers, dominate the organism. And when these in turn are satisfied, again new (and still "higher") needs emerge and so on. This is what we mean by saying that the basic human needs are organized into a hierarchy of relative prepotency.

One main implication of this phrasing is that gratification becomes as important a concept as deprivation in motivation theory, for it releases the organism from the domination of a relatively more physiological need, permitting thereby the emergence of other more social goals. The physiological needs, along with their partial goals, when chronically gratified cease to exist as active determinants or organizers of behavior. They now exist only in a potential fashion in the sense that they may emerge again to dominate the organism if they are thwarted. But a want that is satisfied is no longer a want. The organism is dominated and its behavior organized only by unsatisfied needs. If hunger is satisfied, it becomes unimportant in the current dynamics of the individual.

The safety needs.—The healthy, normal, fortunate adult in our culture is largely satisfied in his safety needs. The peaceful, smoothly running "good" society ordinarily makes its members feel safe enough from wild animals, extremes of temperature, criminals, assault and murder, tyranny, etc. Therefore, in a very real sense, he no longer has any safety needs as active motivators. Just as a sated man no longer feels hungry, a safe man no longer feels endangered. If we wish to see these needs directly and clearly we must turn to neurotic or near-neurotic individuals, and to the economic and social underdogs. In between these extremes, we can perceive the expressions of safety needs only in such phenomena as, for instance, the common preference for a job with tenure and protection, the desire for a savings account, and for insurance of various kinds (medical, dental, unemployment, disability, old age).

Other broader aspects of the attempt to seek safety and stability in the world are seen in the very common preference for familiar rather than unfamiliar things, or for the known rather than the unknown. The tendency to have some religion or world-philosophy that organizes the universe and the men in it into some sort of satisfactorily coherent, meaningful whole is also in part motivated by safety-seeking.

Otherwise the need for safety is seen as an active and dominant mobilizer of the organism's resources only in emergencies, e.g., war, disease, natural catastrophes, crime waves, societal disorganization, neurosis, brain injury, chronically bad situation.

The love needs.—If both the physiological and the safety needs are fairly well gratified, then there will emerge the love and affection and belongingness needs, and the whole cycle already described will repeat itself with this new center. Now the person will feel keenly, as never before, the absence of friends, or a sweetheart, or a wife, or children. He will hunger for affectionate relations with people in general, namely, for a place in his group, and he will strive with great intensity to achieve this goal. He will want to attain such a place more than anything else in the world and may even forget that once, when he was hungry, he sneered at love.

The esteem needs.—All people in our society (with a few pathological exceptions) have a need or desire for a stable, firmly based, (usually) high evaluation of themselves, for self-respect, or self-esteem, and for the esteem of others. By firmly based self-esteem, we mean that which is soundly based upon real capacity, achievement and respect from others. These needs may be classified into two subsidiary sets. These are, first, the desire for strength, for achievement, for adequacy, for confidence in the face of the world, and for independence and freedom. Secondly, we have what we may call the desire for reputation or prestige (defining it as respect or esteem from other people), recognition, attention, importance or appreciation. These needs have been relatively stressed by Alfred Adler and his followers, and have been relatively neglected by Freud and the psychoanalysts. More and more today however there is appearing widespread appreciation of their central importance.

Satisfaction of the self-esteem need leads to feelings of self-confidence, worth, strength, capability and adequacy of being useful and necessary in the world. But thwarting of these needs produces feelings of inferiority, of weakness and of helplessness. These feelings in turn give rise to either basic discouragement or else compensatory or neurotic trends. An appreciation of the necessity of basic self-confidence and an understanding of how helpless people are without it, can be easily gained from a study of severe traumatic neurosis.

The need for self-actualization.—Even if all these needs are satisfied, we may still often (if not always) expect that a new discontent and restlessness will soon develop, unless the individual is doing what he is fitted for. This tendency might be phrased as the desire to become more and more what one is, to become everything that is capable of becoming.

The specific form that these needs will take will of course vary greatly from person to person. In one individual it may take the form of the desire to be an ideal mother, in another it may be expressed athletically, and in still another it may be expressed in painting pictures or in inventions. It is not necessarily a creative urge although in people who have any capacities for creation it will take this form.

The clear emergence of these needs rests upon prior satisfaction of the physiological, safety, love and esteem needs. We shall call people who are satisfied in these needs, basically satisfied people, and it is from these that we may expect the fullest (and healthiest) creativeness. Since, in our society, basically satisfied people are the exception, we do not know much about self-actualization, either experimentally or clinically. It remains a challenging problem for research.

Summary

1. There are at least five sets of goals which we may call basic needs. These are briefly physiological, safety, love, esteem, and self-actualization. In addition, we are motivated by the desire to achieve or maintain the various conditions upon which these basic satisfactions rest and by certain more intellectual desires.

2. These basic goals are related to each other, being arranged in a hierachy of prepotency. This means that the most prepotent goal will monopolize consciousness and will tend of itself to organize the recruitment of the various capacities of the organism. The less prepotent needs are minimized, even forgotten or denied. But when a need is fairly well satisfied, the next prepotent ("higher") need emerges, in turn to dominate the conscious life and to serve as the center of organization of behavior, since gratified needs are not active motivators.

Thus man is a perpetually wanting animal. Ordinarily the satisfaction of these wants is not altogether mutually exclusive, but only tends to be. The average member of our society is most often partially satisfied and partially unsatisfied in all of his wants. The hierarchy principle is usually empirically observed in terms of increasing percentages of non-satisfaction as we go up the hierarchy. Reversals of the average order of the hierarchy are sometimes observed. Also it has been observed that an individual may permanently lose the higher wants in the hierarchy under special conditions. There are not only ordinarily multiple motivations for usual behavior, but in addition many determinants other than motives.

18. Group Influence in Marketing and Public Relations FRANCIS S. BOURNE

Reference-group theory, as it has developed, has become broad enough to cover a wide range of social phenomena, both with respect to the relation of the individual to the group and with respect to the type of influence exerted upon the individual by the group in question.

Reference groups against which an individual evaluates his own status and behavior may be of several kinds:

1. They may be membership groups to which a person actually belongs and may involve either: (a) Small face-to-face groups in which actual association is the rule, such as families or organizations, whether business, social, religious, or political, or (b) groups in which actual membership is held but in which personal association is absent. (For example, membership in a political party, none of whose meetings are personally attended.) These groups may be of the same kinds as the former but differ only in the lack of face-to-face association with other members.

2. They may be groups or categories to which a person automatically belongs by virtue of age, sex, education, marital status and so on. This sort of reference-group relationship involves the concept of role. For example, before taking a certain action an individual might consider whether this action would be regarded as appropriate in his role as a man or husband or educated person or older person or a

SOURCE. From "Some Applications of Behavioural Research," 1957. By permission of UNESCO.

combination of all these roles. What is involved here is an individual's perception of what society—either in general or that part of it with which he has any contact—expects people of his age, sex, education or marital status to do in given circumstances.

3. They may be anticipatory rather than actual membership groups. Thus a person who aspires to membership in a group to which he does *not* belong may be more likely to refer to it or compare himself with its standards when making a decision than he is to refer to the standards of the group in which he actually belongs but would like to leave. This involves the concept of upward mobility. When such upward mobility is sought in the social or business world, it is ordinarily accompanied by a sensitivity to the attitudes of those in the groups to which one aspires, whether it involves the attitudes of country-club members in the eyes of the aspiring non-member or the attitudes of management in the eyes of the ambitious wage-earner or junior executive.

4. They may be negative, dissociative reference-groups. These constitute the opposite side of the coin from the anticipatory membership groups. Thus an individual sometimes avoids a certain action because it is associated with a group (to which the individual may or may not in fact belong) from which he would like to dissociate himself.

Reference-groups influence behavior in two main ways. First, they influence *aspiration levels,* and thus play a part in producing satisfaction or frustration. If the other members of one's reference-group (for example, the neighbors) are wealthier, more famous, better gardeners, etc., one may be dissatisfied with one's own achievements and may strive to do as well as the others.

Secondly, reference-groups influence *kinds* of behavior. They establish approved patterns of using one's wealth, of wearing one's fame, of designing one's garden. They also lay down taboos, and may have the power to apply actual sanctions (for example, exclusion from the group). They thus produce *conformity* as well as *contentment* (or discontent).

These two kinds of influence have, however, a good deal in common. Both imply certain perceptions on the part of the individual, who attributes to the reference-group characteristics it may or may not actually have. Both involve psychological rewards and punishment.

Different Kinds of Decisions and Reference-Group Influence

Marketing and Reference-Group Relevance

The conspicuousness of a product is perhaps the most general attribute bearing on its susceptibility to reference-group influence. Reference-groups may influence either (a) the purchase of a product, or (b) the choice of a particular brand or type, or (c) both.

The possible susceptibility of various product and brand-buying to reference-group influence is suggested in Figure 1. According to this classification, a

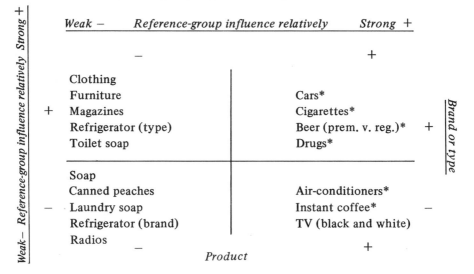

FIGURE 2. *Products and brands of consumer-goods may be classified by extent to which reference-groups influence their purchase[a]*

---

[a]The classification of all products marked with an asterisk (*) is based on actual experimental evidence. Other products in this table are classified speculatively on the basis of generalizations derived from the sum of research in this area and confirmed by the judgement of seminar participants.

particular item might be susceptible in reference-group influence in its purchase in three different ways, corresponding to three of the four cells in the above figure. Reference group influence may operate with respect to brand or type but not with respect to product (Brand + Product −) as in the upper left cell, or it may operate both with respect to brand and product (Brand + Product +) as in the upper right cell, or it may operate with respect to product but not brand (Brand − Product +) as in the lower right cell.

Only the "minus-minus" items of the kind illustrated (Brand − Product −) in the lower left cell are not likely to involve any significant reference-group influence in their purchase *at the present time.*

What are some of the characteristics that place an item in a given category, and what significance do such placements have for marketing and advertising policy?

"Product plus, Brand plus" Items. Cars are a case in which both the product and the brand are socially conspicuous. Whether or not a person buys a car, and also what particular brand he buys, is likely to be influenced by what others do.

"Product plus, Brand minus" Items. Instant coffee is one of the best examples of this class of item. The brand itself is not conspicuous or socially important and is a matter largely for individual choice. In the case of air-conditioners, it was found that little prestige is attached to the particular brand used, and reference-group influence related largely to the idea of purchasing the product itself.

"Product minus, Brand plus" Items. This group is essentially made up of products that all people or at least a very high proportion of people use, although differing as to type or brand.

Perhaps the leading example in this field is clothing. There could hardly be a more socially visible product than this, but the fact that everyone in our society wears clothing takes the *product* out of the area of reference-group influence. The *type* of clothing purchased is, however, very heavily influenced by reference-groups, with each subculture in the population (teenagers, zootsuiters, Ivy League Collegians, Western Collegians, workers, bankers, advertising men, etc.) setting its own standards and often prescribing, within fairly narrow limits, what those who feel related to these groups can wear.

"Product minus, Brand minus" Items. Purchasing behaviour in this class of items is governed by product attributes rather than by the nature of the presumed users. In this group, neither the products nor the brands tend to be socially conspicuous. This is not to say that personal influence cannot operate with respect to purchasing the kind of items included in this group. As with all products, some people tend to exert personal influence and others tend to be influenced by individual persons. Reference-groups as such, however, exert relatively little influence on buying behaviour in this class of items, examples of which are salt, canned peaches, laundry soap and radios. It is apparent that placement in this category is not *necessarily* inherent in the product itself and hence is not a static placement. Items can move in and out of this category.

Implications of Strong and Weak Reference-Group Influence for Advertising and Marketing

It should be stressed again that this scheme of analysis is introduced to show how reference-group influence might enter into purchasing behavior in certain cases. It cannot be regarded as generally applicable to marketing problems on all levels. There is still a need to know more precisely where many different products or brands fit into this scheme.

Assuming, however, that a product or brand has been correctly placed with respect to the part played by reference-groups in influencing its purchase, how can this help in marketing the product in question?

1. Where neither product nor brand appear to be associated strongly with reference-group influence, advertising should emphasize the product's attributes, intrinsic qualities, price, and advantages over competing products.

2. Where reference-group influence is operative, the advertiser should stress the kinds of people who buy the product, reinforcing and broadening where possible the existing stereotypes of users. The strategy of the advertiser should involve learning what the stereotypes are and what specific reference-groups enter into the picture, so that appeals can be "tailored" to each main group reached by the different media employed.

19. *The Significance of Social Stratification in Selling*

RICHARD P. COLEMAN

Dating back to the late 1940's, advertisers and marketers have alternately flirted with and cooled on the notion that W. Lloyd Warner's social class concept is an important analytic tool for their profession. The Warnerian idea that six social classes constitute the basic division of American Society has offered many attractions to marketing analysts when they have grown dissatisfied with simple income categories or census-type occupational categories and felt a need for more meaningful classifications, for categorizations of the citizenry which could prove more relevant to advertising and marketing problems.

It is the thesis of this writer that the role of social class has too often been misunderstood or oversimplified, and that if the concept is applied in a more sophisticated and realistic fashion, it will shed light on a great many problems to which, at first glance, it has not seemed particularly relevant.

The Warnerian Social Classes

Briefly characterized, the six classes are as follows, starting from the highest one and going down:

1. The Upper-Upper or "Social Register" Class is composed of locally prominent families, usually with at least second or third generation wealth. Almost

SOURCE. Richard P. Coleman, "The Significance of Social Stratification in Selling," Proceedings, American Marketing Association Conference, December, 1960.

inevitably, this is the smallest of the six classes—with probably no more than one-half of one percent of the population able to claim membership in this class. The basic values of these people might be summarized in these phrases: living graciously, upholding the family reputation, reflecting the excellence of one's breeding, and displaying a sense of community responsibility.

2. The Lower-Upper or "Nouveau Riche" Class is made up of the more recently arrived and never-quite-accepted wealthy families. Included in this class are members of each city's "executive elite," as well as founders of large businesses and the newly well-to-do doctors and lawyers. At best only one and one-half percent of Americans rank at this level—so that all told, no more than 2 percent of the population can be counted as belonging to one layer or the other of our Upper Class. The goals of people at this particular level are a blend of the Upper-Upper pursuit of gracious living and the Upper-Middle Class's drive for success.

3. In the Upper-Middle Class are moderately successful professional men and women, owners of medium-sized businesses and "organization men" at the managerial level; also included are those younger people in their twenties or very early thirties who are expected to arrive at this occupational status level—and possibly higher—by their middle or late thirties (that is, they are today's "junior executives" and "apprentice professionals" who grew up in such families and/or went to the "better" colleges). Ten percent of Americans are part of this social class and the great majority of them are college educated.

The motivating concerns of people in this class are success at career and taste-fully reflecting this success in social participation and home decor. Cultivating charm and polish, plus a broad range of interests are also goals of the people in this class, just as in the Lower-Upper. For most marketing and advertising purposes, this class and the two above it can be linked together into a single category of "upper status people." The major differences between them—particularly between the Upper-Middle and the Lower-Upper—are in degree of "success" and the extent to which this has been translated into gracious living.

4. At the top of the "Average Man World" is the Lower-Middle Class. Approximately 30 percent or 35 percent of our citizenry can be considered members of this social class. For the most part they are drawn from the ranks of non-managerial office workers, small business owners, and those highly-paid blue-collar families who are concerned with being accepted and respected in white-collar dominated clubs, churches, and neighborhoods. The key word in understanding the motivations and goals of this class is Respectability, and a second important word is Striving. The men of this class are continually striving, within their limitations, to "do a good job" at their work. Being "respectable" means that they live in well-maintained homes, neatly furnished, in neighborhoods which are more-or-less on the "right side of town." It also means that they will clothe themselves in coats, suits, and dresses from "nice stores" and save for a college education for their children.

5. At the lower half of the "Average Man World" is the Upper-Lower Class, sometimes referred to as "The Ordinary Working Class." Nearly 40 percent of all Americans are in this class, making it the biggest. The proto-typical member of this class is a semi-skilled worker on one of the nation's assembly lines. Many of these "Ordinary Working Class" people make very good money.

6. The Lower-Lower Class of unskilled workers, unassimilated ethnics, and the sporadically employed comprises about 15 percent of the population, but this class has less than 7 or 8 percent of the purchasing power, and will not concern us further here. Apathy, fatalism, and a point of view which justifies "getting your kicks whenever you can" characterize the approach toward life, and toward spending money, found among the people of this class.

Now, we do not mean to imply by these characterizations that the members of each class are always homogeneous in behavior. To suggest such would be to exaggerate greatly the meaning of social classes. To properly understand them, it must be recognized that there is a considerable variation in the way individual members of a class realize these class goals and express these values.

Social Class Versus Income

Let us proceed now to stating the basic significance of this class concept for people in the selling field. In the first place, it explains why income categories or divisions of Americans are quite often irrelevant in analyzing product markets, consumers' shopping habits and store preferences, and media consumption. For example, if you take three families, all earning around $8,000 a year, but each from a different social class, a radical difference in their ways of spending money will be observed.

An Upper-Middle Class family in this income bracket is apt to be found spending a relatively large share of its resources on housing (in a "prestige" neighborhood), on rather expensive pieces of furniture, on clothing from quality stores, and on cultural amusement or club memberships. Meanwhile, the Lower-Middle Class family—probably has a better house, but in not so fancy a neighborhood; it is apt to have as full a wardrobe though not so expensive, and probably more furniture though none by name designers. These people almost certainly have a much bigger savings account in the bank.

The significance to merchandisers and advertisers of these findings about motivational differences between classes is fairly obvious, the major idea being that for many products, advertising appeals and merchandising techniques must be differentially geared to the points of view reflected in these three main social classes. Advertising of brands or goods aimed at a specific class must take into account the motivations of that class, and not try to sell everything as if it were an Upper Class or Upper-Middle status symbol.

The "Overprivileged" as "Quality Market"

Within each social class group there are families and individuals whose incomes are above average for their class, overprivileged segments of each class. After they have met the basic expectations and standards of their group in the housing, food, furnishing, and clothing areas, they have quite a bit of money left over which is their equivalent of "discretionary income."

In much the same way, each class has its "underprivileged" members; in the Upper-Middle Class these are the younger couples who haven't made the managerial ranks yet, the college professors, the genteel professionals, and a few downwardly mobile people from high-status backgrounds who are trying to hang on to what fragment of status they have left.

In the middle of each class's income range are its "average" members, families who are neither underprivileged nor overprivileged by the standards of their class. A lot of people in the middle income range of their class see themselves as underprivileged because they are aspiring to become one of the "overprivileged" in their class or to move on up the ladder to a higher class.

The relevance of all this to the car market is that when you look at this particular market today, you find it is the "average" members of each class, whether Upper-Middle, Lower-Middle, or Upper-Lower, who constitute the heart of the Low-Priced Three's audience; these are the people who are buying Fords and Chevrolets this year and last, and probably next. No longer is the Ford and Chevrolet market just a lower-middle income market, or (in class terms) a Lower-Middle or a Lower Class market. Rather, it is recruited from the middle income group *within each* social class. Indeed, the $15,000-a-year Upper-Middle "organization man" is apt to choose a Ford or Chevy from the Impala-Galaxie level or else a top-price station wagon once he ventures into this market, whereas the average-income Lower-Middle man will settle for a middle-series Bel Air or Fairlane 500, and the "average income" Upper Lower guy either splurges for an Impala or "sensibly" contents himself with the spartan Biscayne.

Today, rich blue-collar workers are joining prosperous Lower-Middle Class salesmen and well-to-do Upper Middle Class business owners in buying Pontiacs, Buicks, Oldsmobiles, Chryslers and even Cadillacs. In fact, what there is left of big-car lust in our society is found at peak strength among the "overprivileged" Upper-Lowers or else among men who have achieved higher status, but grew up as kids in the Upper-Lower class and have not forgotten their wide-eyed envy of the big car owner.

Finally, as you may have guessed by now, the compact car market's heart is to be found in the "underprivileged" segments of each class (here we are speaking of the market for a compact as a first car). The overwhelming majority of Rambler purchasers, Falcon buyers, and foreign economy car owners come from this socio-economic territory. Thus, it is not the really poor who are buying these cheapest most economical cars—rather it is those who think of themselves as poor relative to their status aspirations and to their needs for a certain level of clothing, furniture and housing which they could not afford if they bought a more expensive car.

The market for compacts as second cars is somewhat more complicated in its socio-economic geography, being located in the middle range of the Upper-Middle Class, and the "overprivileged" segment of the Lower-Middle. The "overprivileged" Upper Middle may have one as a third car, but he prefers either a T-Bird, a foreign sports car, a Pontiac convertible, or a beat-up station wagon as his second car, while the "overprivileged" Upper Lower is apt to go for a used standard if he wants a second car.

In summary, today's market for quality goods and quality brands is not necessarily drawn from what has historically been described as the "Quality Market" of Upper-Middle and Upper Class people, nor even necessarily from the highest income categories. Rather, in many instances, it is drawn from those people within each social level who have the most discretionary income available for enjoying life's little extras above and beyond the requirements of their class. Every merchandiser and advertiser ought to take a good hard look at what he is selling and ask himself if it bears this particular relationship to the class and income picture. If his product does, and if his brand is one of the more expensive, then he should merchandise it not as if it were just for social climbers or for the upper classes, but rather as part of the Better Life, U.S.A. If, on the other hand, his brand is one of the least expensive, then he is not just selling to the poor, but rather to those in all classes who feel it is only sensible on their part to settle for a brand such as his and save the difference for other things which are more important in their statement of social class aspiration and identity.

Social Class Isn't Always Important

Now, to make the picture complete, it must be pointed out that Social Research, Inc., has found some products in which the income factor is all-important and the social class variable is relevant only to the extent that it is correlated with income. Perhaps the most perfect example of this is the market for air conditioners in Southeastern states. In this area the expensiveness of a family's air conditioning equipment—whether centrally installed or window units to the number of four, three, two, or one—is directly related with family income. It is not merely a function of discretionary income—as in our example about purchase of medium-priced cars—it is instead almost completely a function of total annual income. If homes of more Upper-Middles than Upper-Lowers are fully air-conditioned it is largely because more of them can afford to be; it is not because Upper-Middles as a group are placing higher priority on the air-conditioned existence.

In short, not only must the sophisticated marketer abandon social class in favor of income categories on occasion in his analysis and interpretation of a market, he must recognize that at times both income and class are superseded in importance by divisions of the public into brow levels, by divisions into "high mobiles" and "low mobiles," innovators and non-innovators, inner-directed and other-directed, urbanites, suburbanites, exurbanites, ruralites, and Floridians, or what have you.

As a final point, let it be noted that the way of life and the goals of people in each social class are in perpetual flux. Neither the "who" of each class nor "what motivates them" are constants to be assumed without continual re-evaluation. Right now, particularly, it is very clear that our society is changing. Every year the collar-color line is breaking down further.

In short, the form of our society and its division into social classes is not fixed as of Yankee City in 1931, Jonesville in 1944, Kansas City in 1952, or St. Louis in 1960. We won't be able to say exactly the same things about either the classes themselves or their relationships to specific markets by next year at this time. This fact about the American class structure, that it is not static, that it is in the process of change, is in itself important to merchandisers, to advertisers, to anyone in selling. Among other things, it means that undoubtedly they have played a part in past changes and can play a leading role in directing future changes. But of more direct concern here, to the marketing analyst it means that if he allows his stratification concept to become dated, his use of it will cease as of that moment to be sophisticated.

20. Demography and the Marketing Process S.H.GAMBLE AND J.H.SCHEIBELHUT

One noticeable trend in marketing in recent years has been toward an increased use of quantitative information and appropriate models for marketing decisions. This is not to say that the field of marketing is a science; however, decision making is becoming more objective when dealing with issues including repetitive processes and for this reason some marketers are becoming more systematic in their approach to decision making.

In problems containing human variables and unique decision situations the trend toward science over hueristics has been less pronounced. The effects to organize solutions to these behavioral problems have been numerous, but progress has been slow.

One major factor which has contributed to the increase in more systematic and fact-based problem solutions has been the application of models developed in numerous marketing related disciplines. Mathematics, statistics, economics, sociology, psychology, anthropology, and political science all have made valuable contributions to problem solutions related to marketing. Marketing in turn has made contributions integrating models from separate disciplines and providing financial resources on promising research areas.

Demography is one discipline which has recently contributed to a more objective application of marketing processes. Demography is one discipline which holds a great deal of potential for markets but its usefulness has only been exploited by a portion of the large number of researchers and practitioners who could benefit from demographic information and models.

There are several reasons why demographic information and expertise have not been fully utilized in solving problems related to marketing. These include the following reasons:

There is some unfamiliarity with what demography is.

There is a lack of understanding of how demographic information relates to marketing.

There is no compilation of demographic models and past studies demonstrating useful application of these models.

Sufficient consideration has not been given to present and future problems where demographic information and models could make a contribution.

The following three sections discuss these topics and attempt to provide useful insights into how demographic information and models can contribute to the solution of problems related to marketing.

A Definition of Demography

There has been some disagreement on precisely what types of information are included within the discipline of demography, even among demographers. One useful definition developed by Philip Hauser and Otis Duncan is the following:

Demography is the study of the size, territorial distribution and composition of population, changes therein, and the components of such changes, which may be identified as natality, mortality, territorial movement, and social mobility (change of status).

From this definition it is generally clear that demography concerns information about populations and more specifically human populations. This discipline includes information about the magnitude, location and movement in population groups. With one exception demography is generally a discrete body of information and area for study. The exception is social mobility, which overlaps with sociology.

Relation of Demography to the Marketing Progress

Demographic techniques and information provide marketing with systematic models and empirical data for defining, evaluating, and influencing groups.

The terms marketer and marketing process, as used by the authors, assume a broad definition of marketing such as that used by Kotler and Levy in their article (Selection 6), "Broadening the Concept of Marketing" (see p. 39). Marketing is not a discipline used exclusively by profit-motivated organizations. The marketer may be any person, group, or organization participating in a marketing process—

politicians must market their candidacies to the public and effectively communicate their ability to satisfy the needs of the consumers; the federal government must be concerned with marketing its policies if it hopes to maintain the support of the people; the American Cancer Society must sell its successes and potential value if it hopes to continue to receive contributions; and churches must constantly reevaluate and retailor their products to meet the dynamic demands of their consumers. Marketing processes, when conceived as a sequence of mental and physical activity which use available resources to convert consumer needs into flows of need-satisfying goods and services, are therefore important to every individual and group which wishes to have its diverse needs met in society. Demography has made some valuable contributions to the intelligent application of marketing techniques and processes. The major contribution of demography has been to provide marketing theorists and practitioners with more specific information describing characteristics of groups. In addition models have been developed suggesting relationships between patterns in demographic data and marketing strategies which may help solve important problems. The following section discusses some models and studies which demonstrate the value of demography.

Some Useful Demographic Models

The reason for the increasing value of demographic research during the past two decades comes from several sources. One major cause has been the additional financial resources available to private industry investigations and university research since 1950. In addition, current researchers have available a large quantity of historical data which provides valuable comparative statistics, and suggests directions for continuing investigations.

In the 1940's age was the most common demographic variable used to evaluate human behavior. Examples of consumer need differences based on age are numerous. However, the strongest and most consistent relationships have concerned the very young and very old. These two groups seem to have more homogenous needs than other groups. It seems that the consumption of these two groups (the very young and very old) are least influenced by additional factors such as multiple peer groups, the social significance of goods, and family life cycle stages.

In order to include more important demographic characteristics in a model, marital status and family size have also been used by demographers to identify differences in patterns of needs and consumption. In addition, an even more powerful and recently more common model has been the Family Life Cycle model. The FLC is a hybrid of demographic variables. It combines age, marital status, family size, age of children, and residence of children to provide a model which places family units into more homogeneous consuming groups than any of the above models for most types of consumption. Below is one example of the FLC model which provides useful division into life cycle stages:

Family Life Cycle Stages

1. Young singles.
2. Young marrieds without children.
3. Marrieds with youngest child under 6.
4. Marrieds with youngest child over 6 but under 13.
5. Marrieds with youngest child 13 or over.
6. Marrieds with children in launching period.
7. Marrieds with empty nests.
8. Solitary survivor.

Why do suburban mothers with children between the ages of 4 and 12 consume a relatively high amount of floor wax; why do young girls consume a great deal of shampoo; why do mothers spend such a large amount of their income on food; why do older adults with no children living at home tend to spend a large proportion of their income on travel; and why do parents with children who are adolescent or in their launching period frequently move into the nicest home in which they will ever live? The answer to each of these questions is *a need* of a group of consumers who have at least one characteristic in common—a particular stage in the Family Life Cycle Model.

An additional factor, related to life cycle stages, which is important to marketing, is the changing proportion of persons within particular life cycle stages. At present almost 50 per cent of the American population is under 25, and the proportion and income of persons over 65 is increasing, while recently the birth rate has been dropping. Recognition of trends within particular life cycle stages provides additional valuable information for forecasting the potential of a particular FLC stage market.

Occupation is another demographic construct which has been useful in marketing research. This variable has contributed information to marketing in two ways. First, occupation has been used to identify common consumption patterns of persons in similar types of occupations. In addition, occupational information combined with data on education, residence, community activities, family background and other variables helps to develop useful definitions of social cleavages referred to as social classes. Warner, Coleman, Glock and Nicosia, and many others have discussed the importance of social class information to marketing. Social class, probably more than any other single model, has been found useful as a method for grouping individuals who solve the problem of satisfying their needs in similar ways. Many of the problems the nation presently faces are closely related to social class. For example:

The problems of housing are partly related to a migration of lower classes to urban core areas, the willingness of these classes to accept substandard housing, the greed of middle class and upper class building owners and the lack of influence of lower classes with the economic and political forces within our nation.

The use of unethical selling practices seems to be concentrated in lower class urban areas where buyers are less likely to recognize and react to potentially illegal practices, where high pressure selling is more effective and where customers are less likely to have the money and influence to protect their rights.

Ethnic background, race, and religion have all been demonstrated to have a relationship to the consumption of specific types of goods and services. A common ideological position, which is the common characteristic of these three variables, has been shown to be closely related to consumption of particular types of food and birth control pills. Moreover as subculture identities have been emphasized in recent years, some total mixes of food, clothing, and social activities have become associated with particular groups. Equally important, some patterns in social demands are evident in ethnic, racial, and religious minority groups.

Two additional types of demographic constructs which have made valuable contributions to marketing are territorial mobility and place of residence. One out of every five Americans changes residence each year, and the direction of this movement has been toward the suburban belts around our major cities and toward the Pacific Coast and South Atlantic regions of our nation. Trends such as these cause shifts in the form of concentrations of particular consumer needs due to regional, rural, and urban problems. Information of this kind is valuable for developing more efficient satisfaction of needs for growing and changing market areas. One example of the problems resulting from this mobility is the economic plight of the small farmer. The flow of people from rural to urban areas has resulted in the rapid growth in a minority of farms owned by affluent urban dwellers. The economies of scale on large farms, the prices of produce, and the high prices of machinery have made life difficult for the rural dweller whose economic income has depended on the same plot of land for over 50 years. Marketers can contribute to the solution of this problematic symptom of social change by:

Developing more efficient systems of exchange which provide a higher proportion of final price to the original producer.

Examining the consumption habits of rural populations and considering new methods for distributing the goods they need.

Studying new ways for coordinating the needs and desires of rural populations with the skills and expertise possessed by farmers.

For those who believe that the problems of rural areas are not serious when compared to the complex problems of urban centers, one must at least agree that urban problems seem to be generally recognized as being more serious. However, it is revealing to note that in spite of the heavy populations and large ghettos in our major cities, 50 percent of all malnutrition in our nation exists in rural areas.

The only completely new demographic model to be developed in the past ten years is the Zip code, which was developed by the United States Post Office Department for use in mail delivery. Each Zip sectional center radiates from a transportation hub and tends to reflect the economic facts of life and cultural environment of the area, which in turn influences the ways in which persons satisfy their needs. Butcher and Tyler feel that for the organization that desires a control system which measures affectiveness of major marketing mix elements, the Zip system usually provides a better answer than trading areas by country.

Having briefly described some of the most important demographic models related to marketing, the next section describes some research studies which have involved demographic models.

Some Abstracts of Research Studies

Leo F. Schnore published research findings in 1963 in which he investigated the accuracy of the common belief that the socio-economic status of suburbia is higher than that of the central city.

He found that although analysis of the 1960 census data suggests that in larger and older areas suburbia does have a higher socio-economic status than the central city, smaller and newer cities tend to rank higher in income, education, and occupational status than their suburbs. The age of the city was the best predictor of the city-suburban differences in socio-economic status. In newer cities, modern transportation facilities have lessened the pressure on land use in central zones, resulting in a higher probability that new cities will be free of the historical patterns of deterioration because of an expanding central business district.

These conclusions have significant value because they identify a critical variable (transportation system) for city planning and distribution systems in the future, and point out that better systems of transporation are necessary for a reversal of the deterioration of present central cities. This study and others have resulted in increased resources being assigned to the integration of transportation, recreation, housing and other systems in new urban and suburban development efforts.

Lansing and Kish have reinforced other research findings that the stages of the Family Life Cycle are better predictors of group consumption than age classes. In order to reach this conclusion, Lansing and Kish compared the predictive power of Family Life Cycle stage and age of head of spending group for six economic characteristics which included: (1) own home, (2) have debts, (3) wife working, (4) income over $4,000, (5) bought new car, (6) bought TV. In each case, Family Life Cycle stage was a more powerful predictor. The reason for the superiority of the FLC's model is that it is generally more sensitive to the social role and the resulting consumption problems of the consuming unit. For instance, age as a predictor of wife working indicated that women tend to work indefinitely without interruption. In contrast, the FLC indicated that young wives with no children are more likely to work than young wives with children.

Age indicated that the proportion of consuming units owning homes increased with the passage of time, with a slight decrease for those over 65. FLC indicated a sharp drop in ownership by solitary survivors as compared to units where the husband and wife were still living. Even though Lansing and Kish investigated only six economic characteristics, they concluded that the FLC has greater explanatory power for many economic, social, political and psychological variables. Of course, in selecting the best variable, there is always a need for a basic understanding of the situation being investigated. A model which is usually a more powerful prediction may not be appropriate for some situations. For example, attitudes towards savings and loan institutions might be more accurately reflected by age classes than by stage in Family Life Cycle, since the historical experience of bank failures during the Great Depression affected the attitude of those living during the period. In addition age might prove to be an important variable in distinguishing between attitudes toward such things as resistance to change and support of group and national violence and war.

Fred C. Akers in 1965 published research findings indicating that race can be a valuable group consumption predictor for particular types of goods. Aker's study compared automobile ownership of blacks and whites. He concluded that blacks:

Tend to own higher priced automobiles than whites, regardless of make.
Tend to own higher priced models than whites.
Tend to own automobiles with more cylinders than whites.

In addition, using multivariate analysis, Akers also found that the race variable explains more of the variance among automobile owners than other demographic variables such as income, education, sex, age, and family size. This study provides additional insight into differences between consumer groups and a means to segmenting persons into groups which have relatively similar methods for satisfying their needs.

James E. Bell, Jr., in April of 1969 published research results demonstrating the importance of territorial mobility in market segmentation. His research revealed several interesting findings. For example:

Income, education, and occupational levels of the mobile household head are well above the national average.
Families with mobile household had a mobility rate nearly five times the national average.
Mobiles purchase furniture and appliances at a rate twice that of non-mobiles with similar incomes.

His general conclusion is that the mobile market segment has distinct character which can justify market cultivation for some organizations. One group of mobiles Bell didn't include in his study are the migratory workers of the South. One survey showed that they too have some interesting characteristics such as a median income below the Social Security Administration's poverty level. This is one more group, identifiable by demographic characteristics, that many benefits of our nation are not reaching. Better marketing can help.

Edward A. Suchman and Herbert Menzel used demographic and psychological models to study voting surveys. They combined the psychological variables, degree of identification with the demographic variables, religious demonination, and ethnic minority groups. The result was that:

Each minority group voted Democratic to a far greater extent than did the native-born white Protestants.

The Democratic vote was even stronger among the members of each minority group who were most deeply involved in the group.

Their most valuable finding was a cross-disciplinary model which was a more powerful predictor of a particular type of behavior than either the psychological or the demographic model alone. Of course many cross disciplinary models have been found useful.

Smith and Liefeld have done much work with a Life Style Matrix which combines social class and Family Life Cycle. They believe that this demo-sociographic model is a more powerful predictor of consumer needs than any other equally simple model.

One example of the value of their model was demonstrated when it was used in a consulting job for a company. They found a definite strong relationship between:

Volume of the product consumed and social class and Family Life Cycle relationship with volume of consumption.

Type of product consumed was also closely related to the groups within the matrix, however in the case of bread types, social class was the stronger predictor.

Using the information from the research they had done, Smith developed a promotional mix which communicated the advantages of the product tailored to the values and needs of the demo-sociographic market segments selected. Two years after the research was completed the company's sales had increased 50 percent. The company's owner, as well as Smith and Liefeld, are convinced that the research findings and resulting advertising efforts played a major role in this sales increase. Of course it is not clear that the increased sales of this product had any significant marginal value to society, but it does demonstrate the potential for using this model to communicate valuable ideas to groups facing particular problems.

One example where this method might be applied is in the efforts to persuade persons to continue their education or training. Since the values of many groups and the problems they confront are different, the reasons for continuing or return-ing to a training or development program may be quite different and the kind of program may vary widely. The identification of an effective way to communicate with these people and the identification of kinds of programs which can help meet their needs are tasks where marketing can make a contribution.

Several major magazines have initiated some potentially revealing market strate-gies by segmenting by Zip code area and occupation. They provide special advertising as well as article content to these segments. *Look* magazine, for example, presently publishes a special edition for 15 percent of their subscribers who live in Zip code areas which are relatively affluent. These issues contain some special advertising of products such as Chanel No. 5 and Seagrams Crown Royal which do not appear in other issues.

Time magazine uses occupation as the control variable. They send special issues to businessmen, doctors and students. *Reader's Digest* this summer will begin a special demographic edition aimed at its most economically affluent readers.

Probably the major motivation for demographic segmentation is the opportunity it offers for advertisers to more efficiently spend their promotional dollars. How-ever, some magazines have gone beyond just differences in advertising. *Farm Journal* and *Look* have offered special articles in editions aimed at particular occupational groups or Zip code areas. *Farm Journal,* for example, circulates special articles to meet the needs of hog farmers, dairy farmers, or cattle ranchers in particular regions.

Unfortunately, there is little evidence of the impact of these demographic segmentation efforts. Until such investigations are completed and the results are published, one must depend on the purposive strategies of such firms as Norman Craig and Kummel, the ad agency of Chanel. Before demographic segmentation, they never used *Look* as a media. Now, with demographic segmentation, *Look* accounts for a significant portion of Chanel's advertising effort in the printed media.

Hopefully this kind of segmentation will result, someday, in more desirable products of many kinds for all consumers.

The seven abstracts described above have illustrated briefly the breadth of research efforts in demography and the past, present and potential usefulness of demographic models. The next sections deal specifically with some problems related to marketing which demographic information and models can help alleviate.

Future Applications of Demography in Marketing Processes

The orientation of marketing is rapidly expanding from concern with managerial problems to a concern with marketing-related problems of any organization, group, or individual. The proliferation of information published by the government and elsewhere, the increased availability of financial resources for research, a growing volume of past findings which have provided a foundation for future efforts, and the increased number of useful models has provided a mix of tools which can help the marketer meet the problems he faces. For example:

The Family Life Cycle model can provide valuable information for grouping families in segments having relatively homogeneous needs.

Urban housing needs are one critical need which can be partially resolved by combining FLC information with social class information to determine what type of housing might satisfy basic as well as social needs of particular groups.

The FLC concept should be used to restratify our present welfare system. Admittedly this would add considerable complexity to the classification problem, however, the problems resulting from oversimplified and unrealistic groupings are even more costly to our society.

The American Negro and other racially cleaved groups are receiving increased attention in the labor force and the market place. In order to utilize the human resources in these groups and in order to take advantage of the buying power of these groups, demographers, anthropologists, and others must provide additional data which can assist marketers and others in bringing these persons closer to the central flow of inducements and contributions in our society.

Demographic models, especially the Family Life Cycle, may prove to be of increasing value as a means of stratifying our present welfare system. Age and family size are not sufficient criteria. FLC gives a more meaningful segmentation of welfare groups with common problems and needs.

Finally, demographers must continue to study shifts in age group proportions relative to the total population and to the rates of geographic mobility and directions of geographic mobility so that they can effectively assign and direct appropriate resources through present and new distribution systems. According to the Census Bureau, bith rates fell in 1969 to the lowest level since the depression. Our country will have 325 million people by 1985, and between 1965 and 1985, 80 percent of our population growth will be persons under 35. We must continue to use this information if we hope to remain knowledgeable about problems and potential problems related to consumer needs.

Of course, these are only a few opportunities for applying demographic information and models to problems related to marketing. The 1970 census information will provide major revisions in our present perceptions of some dimensions of our rapidly changing society. Mayor Lindsay's recent suggestion that a census be taken every five years by full-time census people should receive serious consideration. The potential usefulness of demographic data suggests that more current and accurate data is certainly worth the cost of more frequent and more professional data gathering.

D. Technology and the Future of Organizations

21. *Technology and Marketing*

S. H. GAMBLE

A European visitor walked up to a sailor in downtown Boston and asked why American ships were built to last only a short time. According to the visitor:

> The sailor answered without hesitation that the art of navigation is making such rapid progress that the finest ship would become obsolete if it lasted beyond a few years. In these words which fell accidentally from an uneducated man, I began to recognize the general and systematic idea upon which your great people direct all their concerns.

Almost 150 years have passed since Alexis de Tocqueville recognized this very important pattern in the way Americans direct their society. Today there is some question about whether Americans have control of the technology which is a prime mover of change within society, but there is no question that today's technologies can have even greater influences on our society than was true in the 1800's. Of course, the degree to which their influences are favorable or unfavorable remains to be determined.

The relationship between technology and marketing is important because marketing is concerned with the means society uses to direct its resources and capabilities to the satisfaction of consumer needs. Technology is one important determinant of a society's capability to meet the needs of consumers.

Categories of Technological Change

An understanding of the difficulty of dealing with technologies can be illustrated by signs of change which are evident today. To illustrate these difficulties, it is useful to identify two categories of change: (1) trends in technological change that are continuations from the past, and (2) change which represents or requires new technologies that represent discontinuities from previous experience.

The increasing rate of change is illustrated by the following trends and descriptions.

The volume of knowledge is expected to double during the 1970's, which represents the greatest increase in the volume of knowledge for any decade in history.

More than four out of five scientists who have ever lived will be alive in the 1970's. This again is a record volume.

By 1980 research and development expenditures will be almost twice the level of 1970 of $27 billion.

Product obsolescence will be one-third again as rapid in the 1970's as it was in the 1960's.

All of these examples are closely related to rapid continuing technological development. In addition to increasing rates of change, there will be greater discontinuities facing our society in the next decade than was evident in the 1950's and early 1960's. The following examples illustrate some of these changes.

Large quantities of scientists and R&D expenditures will be available in this decade to help provide revolutionary new technologies in such areas as metals, oceanography, energy, and circuiting. Much of this work will provide new ways for satisfying present needs.

There will be significant increases in the proportion of well-educated, highly trained workers in many organizations. This results from several factors including the fact that present employment in knowledge-producing occupations is growing twice as fast as that of the labor force in general. New forms of organizations and methods of management will be required to meet the needs of this proliferation of knowledge workers and this will represent a significant discontinuity from present forms and methods.

The socioeconomic priorities in our society are shifting from an emphasis on magnitude of gross national products and the volume of output to an emphasis on the quality of life, the quality of outputs, and the quality of our environment. This is a clear departure from past experience.

An additional discontinuity is a shift from a system where separate organizations will undertake to solve specific problems to a system where multiple organizations will work in a coordinated effort to solve complex problems. The aerospace and defense industries initially demonstrated the feasibility of multicompany coordination in solving difficult technological problems. In an era when complex social problems are a major challenge, there is a great need to apply this same new organizational technology to a broader range of problems.

The above illustrations are given to demonstrate that individuals and organizations must anticipate, prepare for and utilize the opportunities which these changes provide. The many indications of rapid change and discontinuous change suggest that the innovations of the 1970's will require a serious and concerted effort if we are to appreciate the potential benefits of new developments in our society. The following are some examples of how changing technologies can be utilized by marketing processes to better meet the future needs of consumers.

The Marketing System and Technological Change

Food distribution systems are one area where the United States is not using available technology to meet the food needs of many millions of persons. Today in the United States about 40 million persons are malnourished. In intercity areas where poverty exists in its most congested form, small food distributors selling food products at relatively high mark-ups contribute to an unfortunate situation—the poor pay more. Several factors contribute to this problem. The people in these areas do not shop for low price purchase opportunities, transportation to large supermarkets is unavailable or too expensive and credit interest rates raise effective prices of foods far above their shelf prices. A similar problem exists in rural areas. Fifty percent of the malnutrition in the United States is in rural areas. Presently the federal government provides food stamp programs as well as free food programs, however, many customers cannot afford the transportation costs necessary to obtain the free foods, and even fewer seem able to get to food stamp centers. Moreover, there have been insufficient efforts to combine government subsidies with the distribution capability of the private sector and thereby provide a multi-organizational solution to the food selling and distribution problem.

The solution to these problems involves new technologies including new combinations of existing resources which can better meet the needs of these people. For example, one alternative is home delivery food distribution. In urban areas, large-scale, highly mechanized home delivery systems which are government subsidized could provide necessary food items to welfare families. In rural areas, a home delivery system could provide necessary foods to families and help to eliminate present transportation expenses.

An obvious question is: What would be the cost of such a delivery system? Clearly the cost for a family in a rural area would be greater than the comparable costs in urban areas; however, the most important considerations are the opportunity costs of not having such a program. What is the cost of having 40 million persons malnourished in our society? What is the cost of having food inefficiently distributed by large numbers of very small retailers, who survive largely on credit payments from persons who cannot afford the interest rates? What is the cost of having individual families, many of whom do not have cars, transport themselves 10, 20, or 30 miles to food or food stamp distribution areas rather than having a single food distributor deliver food to families during one 50-mile food distribution circuit? Whatever the cost, it is too high, especially when one considers today's technology and marketing know-how. In 1970, technologies are available for home delivery food distribution. These include the highway system sufficient for rapid food transit, large trucks and panel trucks necessary for transporting goods, as well as the potential for computerized order listing and control systems and automated order gathering systems. Meanwhile, such technological developments as the touch tone data phone and picture phone will in the future make home delivery far more desirable to a much larger segment of the American population. And perhaps most important is the technical capability for several sections of our economy to work together to resolve important complex social problems. Food distribution is one such problem where technology should be directed.

A second area where technology has recently increased our ability to satisfy consumer needs is housing. Recent developments in materials and mass production of modular units have made possible the production of low-cost housing which can meet the needs of many American consumers. Unfortunately, at present much of this effort is being directed at the middle-class and upper-middle class housing market for second homes to be used as vacation and weekend family recreation centers. In addition to modular construction, new materials and architectural designs are creating new capabilities for lower cost housing. Again, however, much of this technology is being used for middle-class families.

The potential of these new capabilities is badly needed in areas congested with low-income families. One example of present conditions follows. One evening in August of 1970 while driving home, I noticed a five-story building, 25 percent of which had been demolished, apparently by explosives. We stopped and asked a policeman what had happened. He said a car had run into the building. The following day the Sunday *New York Times* front page carried a picture of a five-story brownstone building which had been demolished by one automobile. Apparently a run-away car had struck the building and had destroyed the walls, floors, and ceilings of a corner of the building. A mother and her young baby had fallen five stories from their apartment after the impact. Amazingly, neither was seriously injured. This example illustrates the quality of housing which presently exists in many parts of our major urban areas. Marketing can play an important role in communicating the unacceptable present conditions of this housing and encourage persons to demand that available and future technologies are better applied to meeting the housing needs in the United States.

In 1970 the solution to the pollution problem includes the application of present technologies as well as the development of new ones. Many journals have discussed present activities which companies are pursuing to reduce their pollution, particularly water pollution. For anyone who has recently walked on the banks of the Cuyahoga River, Lake Erie or the southern tip of Lake Michigan, the problem is obvious. Since some pertinent technology exists, part of this problem can be resolved by:

Persuading a sufficient number of people of the dangers of pollution so that they influence companies through law or other mediums to apply present technologies.

Causing companies to believe improved pollution reduction technologies will be profitable in the future so that new technologies are developed. Both processes require at least the marketing of ideas which can contribute to the implementation of both solutions.

Air pollution is a somewhat different problem because the large industrial firm is not the major polluter. The two most important contributions are the internal combustion engine and incinerators. Again, the problem will be solved when a sufficient number of Americans are willing to pay the price for pollution reducing technologies in their cars and in their apartments, homes, and offices. It is the task of marketing to clearly communicate to consumers the actual effect of the present environment on their health and happiness, and to assist in the planning development of new methods for solving this problem.

One discontinuity mentioned earlier, which must be applied more effectively if we are to overcome some complex social problems, is the application of multiorganizational capabilities to particular problems. Our education system, food distribution to the poor, housing, socialization by training of disadvantaged persons, pollution, and many other issues are highly complex. Each transcends the knowledge, legal, and geographic boundaries of any single public or private organization. A major problem of such consideration is that organizations are unwilling to make the necessary sacrifices to permit effective multiorganizational action. Individuals and groups must market the immediate need for such efforts if realistic solutions are to be developed.

Of course, the examples described above represent only a cross section of issues whereby marketing can contribute to a more effective use of our society's resources in meeting consumer needs. One important prerequisite for the continuing application of technology and marketing to existing problems is that each individual recognizes the character and potential of the system in which he lives. Robert Oppenheimer has characterized our time in the following words:

One thing that is new is the prevalence of newness, the changing scale and scope of change itself, so that the world alters as we walk on it, so that the years of man's life measure not some small growth or rearrangement or moderation of what he learned in childhood, but a great upheaval.

22. *Is the Corporation Next to Fall?*

ANTHONY G. ATHOS

"Within five years, a president of a major corporation will be locked out of his office by his junior executives," remarked George Koch, president of the Grocery Manufacturers Association, not long ago. The very idea would have seemed outrageous and impossible only a few years ago. But recent experience in other large organizations, notably in universities, makes it clear that the cigars of any chief executive could become public property before long.

This prediction of internal revolt gains credence when considered in the light of the present situation. There is the much-discussed antipathy of the young for all large organizations, and allegedly for large corporations in particular. This loss of acceptance and the potential long-run loss of manpower have been of concern to business—a concern heightened by recruiters' reports that it is already more difficult to attract sufficient numbers of highly qualified young men to corporate life, even from the graduate schools of business administration.

Then, the rapidly increasing attacks on the products and practices of corporations by individuals and groups (for instance, Ralph Nader and his raiders) have become such a serious problem that companies have undertaken vigorous joint efforts to contend with what has become known as "consumerism." Of course, the

SOURCE. Adapted from Anthony Athos, "Is the Corporation Next to Fall?" reprinted from Harvard Business Review, Jan.-Feb. 1970, Copyright © 1970 by the President and Fellows of Harvard College; all rights reserved.

deep suspicion of the military-industrial-educational complex focuses on corporations as a prime target.

Finally, the hints from recruiters that even MBAs are harder to hire are supported by impressions gained from professors that such students, like the crusading critics, are more openly questioning the products and practices of corporations and, like the young in general, are more doubtful of the values traditionally implicit in corporate life itself.

In short, the situation is rapidly becoming ripe for the kind of action Koch predicts.

So far, the corporate response seems neither fast enough nor thorough enough, largely because the implications of all the forces affecting business are so confusing that attention is directed toward the few young men who are radical in violent action rather than the many other young (and not so young) men who have become radical in perception. By better understanding these latter men, who are more closely related to the future of corporations, we can get an initial grasp of the problems that require skillful executive response.

Thus those with top responsibility in corporations not only must adjust themselves and their institutions in many ways to potential and present executives with "young" ideas, but must sense where they should *not* do so—rather, insisting and helping these talented men to appreciate better the extent to which they too must adjust. Such an understanding is not easy to come by; no simple conception of cause and effect, no single prescription, can be trusted.

This article is an attempt to provide some understanding. It will consider a number of significant changes of attitude in relatively moderate and very promising young men (whose ideas have already affected many of their seniors). It will explore how these changes are a threat to corporations, and suggest a framework for executive response.

How it Looks from Scarsdale

One of the most intellectually simple, but emotionally difficult, aspects to grasp in understanding these young men relates to the fact that many of them have lived all of their lives politically, socially, and financially secure. They simply have assumed that what they need will be available to them, and frequently that what they want in addition can be easily obtained.

One of the college juniors in the Program for Business Internship run at the Harvard Business School in the summer of 1967 was asked what he had learned from it. He searched the ceiling for a few seconds and said, "Well, I guess I could get at it by saying that I learned the garbage may not always be collected." He, like others, seemed bemused at the amount of resources and effort that goes into providing what he had previously taken for granted. So it is for many students in general.

While their fathers experienced the Depression, the Second World War, and often Korea, most of them were born after World War II, were too young even to have read about Korea, and grew up in the great economic boom of the 1950's in families that achieved relative affluence. Much as their fathers took the radio for granted, they take TV as given.

And, just as their fathers learned from economic and political uncertainty the potential for loss of luxuries and even life, they learned from economic growth and a relatively stable political situation that they could go on to *other* goals. It makes sense that they would assume as given what their fathers had earned, as their fathers had assumed before them; it was all each generation had experienced.

In a brilliantly insightful article, Kenneth Keniston pointed out, among other things, that the achievements of the United States in productivity have realized, for most of those who concern us here, the dreams of affluence and security which have animated much of American life since the country's founding. The rewards of this achievement were savored by the fathers who had wrought it, but were merely taken for granted by the sons who benefited from it. Then the sons discovered that what they had assumed as given was not available to all Americans, and it shocked them.

They were indignant that not everyone was rich enough to live and learn and choose as they were, and secure enough to seek new goals that become possible only when economic and social security exists. (In their suburban innocence they had believed in the American Dream, and it seemed especially flawed by their discovery of racial preduduce.) Not appreciating from personal experience the effort and time it took to achieve "wealth" for many, and the value their elders thus placed on "earning," they demanded that wealth be "given" to the others immediately.

And when the Viet Nam war threatened them with the disrupting and dangerous experience of their fathers, they were furious. A war questionable in conception was not likely to compel them easily to give up their assumption of peace.

Knowing only relative peace, wealth, and social acceptance, they demanded them for all Americans as rights, as bases from which new efforts might be made toward greater goals of human enhancement. And they demanded them NOW.

New Goals and Values

While these young men and women were attending to the nation's unresolved economic, racial, and social problems, and to the threat an unpopular war posed to them and others, they were also searching for those greater goals to replace the ones already largely achieved. These goals related more to what would allow them to be themselves than to doing what others wanted, and to experiencing themselves than achieving what others cared about. The means for accomplishing the goals related more to what has meaning for man as a human than to efficiency for organizations as economic units.

This search had proceeded far enough for them to begin to view the problems of poverty, race, and war through a looking glass ground by different values from those of their elders. Not valuing "earning" itself, as their parents did (actually *had to,* in order to accumulate wealth), they demanded we "give" wealth to the poor— that is, not sharing our experience and thus our values, they questioned our assumptions about the economic structures we had developed, especially those assumptions about the distribution of wealth.

Being concerned with meaning and man, they increasingly saw blacks as persons rather than vaguely as units of another race, and thus they could identify with the pain of individuals and feel a moral outrage that paralleled the more visceral rage of blacks themselves.

Finally, their developing new values caused them to view the Viet Nam war not only as personally threatening and disruptive, but also as a brutal and unjust manifestation of the old values that supported the use of U.S. economic and political power abroad in this century—what President Kennedy harshly called "Pax Americana." In short, they were saying that enough wealth, power, and security was enough. More of the same, ever more of the same, was not just vulgar—it was immoral.

Those affluent students who seek careers in business may feel rather less strongly than many others about some of these points. And they may be likely to proceed differently in their searching. But the differences seem more of degree than of kind, and it would be naive to assume otherwise.

The impact on corporations of those young men who are even relatively "polite and patient" is thus likely to be significant. They will want their organizations to contribute to "righting the wrongs" (note the accusation implicit in the words) of society, as well as permit—indeed, encourage—within corporations the search for more personally meaningful lives that is associated with the new human values. In their moral indignation and their naivete about how slowly change comes, they will want action fast and results NOW.

We must explore how we can help them become more aware of what is unrealistic in their demands, as we learn from them something about their developing new values and thus the extent to which we can integrate new goals into our existing framework and act more quickly to achieve them.

But first it is necessary to dig into the factors that lie behind the demands and counterdemands. What is most visible to us is a surface manifestation of fundamental changes in young people *as persons.* Understanding these basic changes is a prerequisite for intelligent response to them, so it is worth making the effort to understand.

And they are basic changes indeed, involving, among others, a different conception of knowledge. That particular change is relevant to corporations in many ways, and may in part confirm the suspicions of many businessmen that professors have been causing the problems they have to live with. But, as we shall see, it is not as simple as that.

More Frames of Reference

In an intriguing study, William G. Perry, Jr., Director of the Bureau of Study Counsel at Harvard, reports a remarkable shift in the very conception of knowledge since 1900. Perry analyzed the questions given on final examinations at Harvard College in this century.

In 1900, a likely question might have been, "When was the battle of Hastings?" If a student could answer "1066," he was "right." In the late 1960's, a question might have read, "Compare the concepts of authority exemplified by Charles de Gaulle and Mahatma Gandhi." Note that the question does not ask for a comparison of the two men, but for a comparison of the concepts of authority, and these concepts should be ones derived from students' knowledge of the men. Since the ways these concepts are to be compared are not specified, the students must make judgments on the basis of their own values. Their answers could hardly be labeled clearly either "right" or "wrong."

Questions asked of students earlier in this century tended (90% of the time) to require only one frame of reference. Questions more recently tend (80% of the time) to ask students to deal with two or more frames of reference. Consequently, *knowing* means something different for the students of today from what it meant for those of the not very distant past.

To know facts, to remember or memorize them, and be able to produce them on examinations would be regarded by our best students today as a sure sign of a "mickey mouse" course. To Alfred North Whitehead's statement, "Education is the acquisition of the art of the utilization of knowledge," they would probably add, "and thought, and feeling, and values."

Theories, or ways of thinking about phenomena, also seem to have shorter and shorter life spans. Believing them, as one might have in 1910, seems pretty silly; using them until something better comes along seems more sensible. As knowledge (in the "fact" sense of the word) and theories (or "ways of thinking") have become more temporary, is it any wonder that feeling has received increased emphasis, and that the younger generation's own value judgments are assumed to be a necessary part of their approach to problems?

Changes in Development

Perry's work led to a complicated conception of the sequences of students' intellectual and ethical development. The detail of his exciting conception is so rich that, to fit my purposes here, I simplify it at the price of considerable distortion, perhaps. (Those responsible for frequent face-to-face interaction with the young may wish to study Perry's report.) To present the essential aspects briefly, I shall collapse his nine sequences of growth to four levels.

While I use the word "level," it is important at the outset to recognize that I am making no *absolute* value judgment that one is always "better" than another.

Level 1

At the first level a student might say, "Look, knowledge is absolute. It consists of correct answers, one per problem. The teacher's job is to tell me what the relevant questions are, and what the correct answers are. I write them down." The student with this approach might have done very well indeed at most schools 60 years ago. But no longer.

It assumes a right-wrong position, an either-or conception of knowledge. Persons who see things as black or white tend to follow this approach. In my teaching experience, I often see these men as authoritarian, rigid, and moralistic in their thinking.

I recall a recent incident in which a student attacked something I had said in class so strongly that it made me defensive and angry. But after listening and arguing for a while, I finally saw his point, realized I was wrong, and said so. After class, another student came up to me and said, "It is inconceivable that you would admit you're wrong. You've lost the authority a teacher needs."

Level 1 men are not hard to find in any organization, including corporations. While they are increasingly rare in the graduate schools, they are still being graduated by colleges which function largely at the Level 1 conception of knowledge. Many companies find them reliable at lower levels, but when they reach middle management positions, they may act as a barrier preventing men more promising from rising.

Level 2

Most students proceed to a second level that introduces situationalism and relativism to their conception of knowledge. A student at this level might say, "Knowledge consists of the best answer, one per problem. The teacher's job is to pose the relevant problems and offer a number of possible answers. My job is to figure out which answer is the best one, given the situation—which I don't mind too much if the teacher is fair and doesn't make things too obscure." (A change of the word "teacher" to "boss" is likely to remind the reader of some subordinates.)

My experience in the classroom has led me to view Level 2 students across a spectrum. Let me describe its two ends:

Holistic group—these students are often unhappy over the excessive absence of personal relevance in the abstractions that were a part of their prior education, and angry at heavy emphasis on analysis, especially when unrelated to what they are experiencing. They want to sense things, to apprehend them rather than comprehend them.

One student who had top grades in all his courses—thereby demonstrating his analytical skills—refused to analyze an interview he had taped and typed up, which was the assignment. He wrote, "This is too beautiful to analyze." In other words, "Thinking is for what does not have deep feeling for me." In a different context, another student looked at me and said, "The only way you can own a butterfly is to kill it or cage it."

In reaction against abstractions, they seek the territory of important personal experiencing and are reluctant to map that territory with ideas. They affect a deliberate inarticulation, a disdain for precise language. "Like, man, it's groovy" is not a very specific communication.

While their cultivation of personal, unique sensation is satisfying to some extent, it frequently leaves them alienated (as others are affected by drugs). They feel a need to be more connected, however, and so one hears them talking earnestly about community, close groups, and shared experiences, and about intimacy and involvement. But the excessive turning-in to the personal, the inability to commit themselves to others, and the refusal to think about what they feel is important—these often preclude satisfaction.

Analytical group—these students (a larger group) *want* to analyze and comprehend, to be impersonal, objective, distant, and intellectual. They ask, "What is the nature of the game? What are the rules? How do I win?" They like to break things into parts. They enjoy mapping the territory of experience but shy from intense personal experiencing itself. They are uncomfortable with sensing the whole as more than the sum of its parts, and prefer to add up their own conception of parts.

As a result, they often become cynical and see much of life in win-lose terms. They may view others as objects to be manipulated, while others see them as cold and machinelike. I recall one young man in a group, searchingly discussing the existence of God, who suddenly stated, "Let's face it; there is a .5 probability that God exists. Get off it." They frequently act hostilely, though unaware of their feelings. They are the icy-eyed, buttoned-up young men on the make.

Of course, few students are completely at the holistic or the analytic pole. Even the few who are extreme tend to go back and forth from each end, as suggested by the top student who refused to analyze an interview that touched him personally.

Level 3

At the third level of development, a student might say:

Knowledge exists in specific settings. The settings differ, and so do the knowers. Therefore several interpretations are legitimate, depending on the person, his point of view, and his purpose, as well as the setting and the thing being addressed. This leaves me uneasy in a kaleidoscopic world, but I judge my answers, or theories, in terms of how well they fit the data, and predict their behavior, given my purposes in attending to the data.

So the teacher's job is to pose problems and help me see more ways to view them, as well as help me judge better the fit of my thinking, given my purpose, to the data. My values, as well as the teacher's, are to be used here.

(Try reading this again, substituting "boss" or "father" for "teacher," to see if it fits your experience with your subordinates or teen-age children.)

Students at Level 3 try to experience the whole of something, think about it in several ways, and determine which way of thinking, or combination of ways, best fits the thing, given their persons and their purposes. They refuse to be told what the "right" or the "best" way of thinking is, since that leaves them, their purposes, and their values out of it.

I recently observed an example of this approach in a firm. Its senior men, long priding themselves on their professional orientation, had rejected opportunities that promised great financial rewards whenever such opportunities threatened the values they held as "professional men building a professional firm helping corporations." The firm had achieved unusual status and security as a result of this value orientation and business focus.

Then certain younger members began to question both the value orientation and the client focus. Some wanted the firm to get into the financial world directly to increase the incomes of members, while others wanted the firm to serve clients in the public sector, notably the urban part of society, even if the financial rewards were less.

In response, study teams were set up which included some of the young men pressing for change. The financial study team decided that the firm should not "move to Wall Street" for a number of reasons, one being that the "fundamental character of the firm" would be changed. The public sector team concluded that the firm should devote more resources to urban clients and expand its public sector work.

The many young men who were not involved in the studies found it difficult to accept the recommendations, for they could not be sure that their purposes and their values were the ones used to interpret the findings. Since the reports could not include all the thinking of the study teams, the "outsiders" suspected that too few approaches to the subject had been used. They even doubted the findings technically. In short, they would not give up easily their assumption that they, and only they, could decide such issues for themselves. Their willingness to trust others to represent them was low. Such Level 3 people are indeed difficult to "supervise."

Level 4

At Level 4, a person seems to say:

> O.K., I've looked at a great many alternatives, and see the relativism of knowledge and values. Now I've chosen a set of values I intend to live by. I accept these values enough to act on them, and I recognize that my person and my purposes, as well as the settings in which I find myself, have limitations. I also am aware that others will choose to live differently from the way I do, and yet we can accept each other as different.

The basic difference between a Level 3 and a Level 4 man is that the latter is *aware* that his own values, person, purposes, and settings are limited in multiple ways, and he *accepts* the fact that he is relating to others who are different. A Level 4 man "knows" who he is, accepts who others are, and is prepared to live with the differences he finds, in ways he is willing to explore imaginatively.

In the firm I just discussed, there were some young men who found the decision "not to move to Wall Street" possible to understand. Though they did not participate in the study, they were aware of the differing values working on the decision makers and were willing to accept the outcomes as reasonable, if not quite satisfying. So they decided to help achieve many of the goals of the group urging the Wall Street involvement, and were able to create another solution that was sufficiently acceptable to all to be approved.

These Level 4 men, ready to accept others as well as themselves, were imaginative and responsible in dealing with the uncertainty, ambiguity, and imperfection always present in living together in and out of organizations.

If a classroom or a company includes persons at all these levels, the teacher or executive has a complex problem. If he attends to those at Level 1, the others are furious. If he focuses on those at Level 2, the ones at Level 1 are lost and angry ("This guy must be soft or a liberal or something. What's he mean, no clear right or wrong?"); and those at Level 3 are disappointed and bored ("Another incompetent!"). Attending only to those at Level 3 stupefies those at Level 1 and leaves those at Level 2 anxious and resentful. Meanwhile, those at Level 4 may try to help as they can.

Since young men of roughly the same age can be at different levels of development, with each behaving according to where he is and developing from where he is, more than ever before attention is needed to deal with their differences from one another. Unfortunately, corporations, like other large organizations, are accustomed to dealing with what were assumed to be *similarities* among groups of persons who were largely at Levels 1 and 2.

Next we must consider three other changes that bear on our ability to respond skillfully: first, the change in young persons' conception of reality; second (one which hits closer to home), in their conception of authority; and third, in their values.

New Conception of Reality

Western man has passed through several phases of his view of reality. J. Samuel Bois has provided a useful interpretation of those stages:

The Age of Primitive Realism (to 650 B.C.)	The world is what I feel it to be.
The Age of Reason (650 B.C.-350 B.C.)	The world is what I say it is.
The Age of Science (1500-1900)	The world is an immense machine, and I can discover how it works.
The Age of Relativism (1900-1966)	The world consists of the probabilities that I create by my way of looking at them.
The Age of Unity (1966-	My world has a structure that no formulation can encompass; I conceive of the world as my own total experience within it, and I play with my own symbolic constructs in a spirit of [uneasy involvement].

The point here is that the changes previously discussed in the conception of knowledge and in the *development* of students have altered something so profound in man as his very conception of reality and his relation to it.

Most executives seem to be in the Age of Science or Relativism, although one still hears of those back at the Age of Reason. When one of the latter encounters a student who is at home in the Age of Unity, the results are not very happy ones—for either, it must be added.

Perhaps even more painful is the situation in which a teacher who talks at the Age of Relativism but behaves at the Age of Reason encounters a student functioning in the Age of Unity. The student must see the teacher as not only limited but hypocritical. And of course this "perception," sadly, will prepare him well for life in many corporations.

The "uneasy involvement" of the young tends to emphasize that aspect of the world that is made up of individuals, and thus focuses on relationships as a central aspect of reality. The ways persons relate to others loom large in their awareness as they confront the world. Which brings us to what many executives see as the nub of the problem—authority.

Authority Flows Two Ways

Hard as it is for most executives to conceive of attacks from within by young executives, imagine if you will this series of events:

The chief executive officer of a large corporation issues a statement affecting employees, on a policy about which he feels strongly.

There is an outcry of protest from some of his first-line supervisors, and the outcry grows as they gain support from various higher-level executives.

The insurgency becomes so troublesome that division managers from all over the country meet in a hotel to determine what action they should take, only to find a large group of young, promising junior executives sitting in the lobby, where they sing songs and demand that the division managers defy the chief executive.

Later a number of plant managers, young executives, and foremen quit, and even a few senior vice presidents begin to question openly their boss's directive.

Sound incredible? Well, in a general way that is what Pope Paul faced after his encyclical on birth control. And if this could happen to the oldest, most successful organization in the history of the Western world, it clearly could happen to corporations.

Indeed, some companies already report similar events. The shock of such change to top executives is likely to be painful and seen also as a direct challenge to authority.

Man as Subject

Earlier I mentioned that the relative affluence of many of the young has freed them to explore new but not yet fully articulated goals that relate more to what has meaning for man as a human than to efficiency for organizations as economic units. The described changes in orientation to knowledge, reality, and authority include a shift in values, with the individual rather than the group in the center. Since every person is to some extent unique, there is emphasis on what is unique for him. And among the things that are unique for him is the meaning he discovers about himself, his world, and the relationship between the two.

This emphasis on what is unique in the individual flies in the face of practice in most large organizations. It is administratively simpler to focus on what is similar among people in groups and have the false comfort of avoiding the uncertainty, ambiguity, and imperfection of the human condition. As we have developed our administrative practices, they have become more rigid and dehumanizing, for both the managers and the managed.

Many writers, especially in this century, have described eloquently the tendency in organizations for those with power to view man as an object rather than a subject. As object, man is the recipient of action, and the focus is on what impinges on him and on his external behavior. The causes of man's behavior are seen as outside him, and anything occurring inside him is discounted. In short, he becomes an "it."

As subject, man is the doer, the one taking action, the one acting on objects. He is seen as having his own unique way of looking at things, his own desired experiences, and his own mode of changing his environment to fit his desires. Accordingly, his behavior is seen as having reasons rather than causes. The subjective view is essential in understanding individuals.

Yet the objective is still essential in dealing with large numbers of persons. I am not arguing that we should discard the objective view but, rather, that we increase our subjective viewing of persons.

A simple example, useful because it is so obvious, if not crucial, is the variation increasingly evident in the appearance of the young. When I was a graduate business student in the late 1950's, I was told that we were a colony of penguins indistinguishable to the casual eye. This external uniformity was also prevalent then in corporate settings; apparently men who looked alike could more easily be regarded as interchangeable parts without important internal differences.

Much more diversity in attire, length of hair, and facial adornment seems to exist now in corporations, especially at staff levels, and of course vastly more exists in schools preparing future executives. The young do not see external differentiation as threatening, or disloyal, or necessarily suspect.

But they do see it, incidentally, as a way to identify executives for whom they would not want to work. All one has to do is let facial hair grow and, in the job interview, watch for discomfort or an outright complaint. They reason that rejection of what is *on* one's head, in a school setting, is likely to accompany low appreciation for what is *in* it, on the job.

And, like many simple tests, this one works pretty well. If an executive tends to think that a beard identifies the wearer as an artist or hippie, if not an SDS activist, then his capacity to deal with humans as subjects with important internal differences may indeed be low.

To Learn the Future

At the risk of sounding preachy, I suggest that, before reading on, the executive should lean back and ask himself whether, and in what ways, he needs and wants to learn more, to grow as a *person* in his role. I suggest it because the notion that just another set of administrative procedures or a new program in the personnel department—another change one makes from time to time—will do in the present circumstances is really worse than doing nothing, for it promises what it cannot deliver.

Acceptance of the idea that one needs to grow personally may not be easy for men who have "arrived" after a long and arduous trip. To be told that one should set out on still another voyage (an uncharted one) may sound disrespectful of past accomplishments, and threatening to boot. And yet, for some executives, the excitement of personally growing and searching may give new meaning to the rest of their lives.

Let me state plainly the reason for my suggestion. The challenge posed to corporations by the ideas that are taking hold can be met only by individuals—men who have executive position and power and who care enough about themselves as persons, about their companies, and about the world around them to invest heavily in their own growing and their organization's renewal.

The Young Can Teach

So, first, executives should set out to learn, before they attempt to teach or initiate some changes, while resisting others. This requires starting with the disturbing awareness that not only have we something to learn, but that we need to learn it from the young.

Robert Frost said it best in his poem, "What Fifty Said":

> When I was young my teachers were the old.
> I gave up fire for form till I was cold.
> I suffered like a metal being cast.
> I went to school to age to learn the past.
>
> Now I am old my teachers are the young.
> What can't be molded must be cracked and sprung.
> I strain at lessons fit to start a suture.
> I go to school to youth to learn the future.

Those executives who are willing to "strain," to "be cracked and sprung," should have little trouble enrolling in the school of youth. There are many ways to proceed.

The easiest and safest (and so perhaps the least useful if no other ways are used) is to read. Ask someone in your organization who seems irritatingly sympathetic with the young to pull together a set of articles and books that he thinks you should read, even books he knows you won't like. If you find the reading not very uncomfortable, tell him that he should not have played it so safe, and if necessary get yourself another man.

Still another route is to visit a local campus and eat in the student cafeteria (not the president's dining room) or attend a movie-lecture series. Or attend any other campus event and look, listen, and ask questions. (Hold off on responding if you can.) Ask your minister or priest or rabbi to arrange for groups of adults and teen-agers, or college students, to talk with each other. See what they have to tell you before you let them know what you have to give to them. Set up small groups of executives and bring some outspoken campus leaders to talk to you, and with you, and focus on what does make sense in what they say.

This learning can be very rewarding in personal terms. A priest I know, disturbed about the apparent lack of meaning to young people in his church's liturgy, encountered through a young parishioner the rock opera "Tommy," by a group disconcertingly called "The Who." He found in it some clues to what was wrong in his liturgy and discovered a promising direction for himself to explore.

However you go about it, be sure to get in conversation with young people; do not just learn ways of thinking about them. Try to contain the annoyance of learning from your juniors by reminding yourself of Robert Frost. And ask yourself whether your own children might have a lot to tell you if they thought you would really listen because you want to grow too. Finally, remember that it can hurt to grow. Value the discomfort if you can.

The Subjective Organization

Now, take a look at your organization. Try to be tough-minded in gauging the extent to which your company's goals, its means, and its ends are accomplished by overemphasis on the objective. Try to find policies and procedures, rules and regulations that are unnecessarily rigid in design or execution. Experiment with more subjective methods, recognizing that where we are all going is not yet clear, but we must begin to search before we are forced to.

Multiple goals: The kind of searching study I am recommending here must include influence from the top, since the questioning already going on at the bottom creeps up in organizations and results in a malaise, a loss of confidence, that can affect those in the middle unless it is met by the reassuring concern and involvement of the top man, and those close to him.

The time and attention such involvement takes is considerable, and it probably will lead to a question of its impact on profits. Many executives claim that *the* goal of their companies is profit—that is, the goal is singular and quantitative.

But I recently heard the president of a major corporation publicly state that his company's goals were plural, and that the rank order of their importance varied from situation to situation. Sometimes profit was overriding, sometimes not. Sometimes what was right for a person came first, sometimes not. Sometimes growth was most important, sometimes not. And so on. He suggested that corporate leaders who talked *only* profit as a goal seldom actually behaved that way to the degree that they thought they did.

If multiple goals are identified and accepted, and if they are seen as not ranked in one order for all decisions, then it becomes possible to reevaluate virtually every other aspect of corporate life in the light of what I have been trying to say here. Besides organizational structures (especially committees), the actual decision processes currently existing and the policies, rules, and regulations in force can be appraised. And, of course, the range and kind of human beings involved, their informal norms and structures, must be searchingly considered.

It will not take long to find opportunities for change if you mull over the specifics of your situation in terms of the objective-subjective spectrums presented earlier. Having done so, you will be in a position to initiate change rather than react to it. You will be able to see in advance the places where you must stand firm, for now at least; and, having been open yourself to learning, and being one of the sources of exploration and innovation in your organization, you will have earned anew the respect of those who have to live with your *no.*

Better yet, you can help them grow by being more able to explain why your *no* to some things is necessary and useful, if you have your reasons ready, they stand tough questioning, and you are willing to explain and teach.

Let me conclude. Each of us needs to see that:

The overriding conflict between the young and their elders is rooted in the former's excessive emphasis on the subjective and the latter's excessive emphasis on the objective.

Therefore, we are a part of the problem we perceive.

The "solution" to the problem involves our growing and changing as *persons,* so as to integrate more of the views and values of the young.

Our growing can be enhanced by learning from the young.

Such growth can then be expressed in changes in our behavior in our executive roles, as we explore how to renew our organizations skillfully and carefully.

This process will make it possible for us to lead and teach the young more about their own part in the problem we are all having.

Even if you agree with my perception of the problem, you are left with the choice to change. This choice is indeed personal, the effort large, the discomfort great, and the outcome promising if uncertain. Only you can decide—for now, anyway.

PART THREE *Some Specific Societal Problems and Response to Those Problems*

"The deepest ills of the world—nuclear danger, overpopulation, human misery—do not come from affluent capitalism."
George Kateb, *Commentary* **49(1)**, January 1970.

Hail and beware the dead
who will talk life
until you are blue
in the face.
And you will not understand,
what is wrong.

Charles Olson

23. *Selected Problems We Face*

JOHN R. WISH WITH MARY ANN WISH

INTRODUCTION *to part three*

As our nation goes so goes General Motors as well as other businesses large and small. Business depends on a stable society, and one in which faith and trust are uppermost. The violence we read of almost daily shows that in many segments of our society, faith and trust are missing. And the relative stability we have enjoyed is now fluctuating. Thus, the disorder in our nation has resulted in disorder in the marketplace. In this section we will examine parts of three aspects of market disorder; military dominance, overpopulation, and human injustice, all of which are related to technology.

W. E. Merrill in his dissertation written this past year at the University of Oregon made the following statement:

Industrial society as now constituted cannot continue. At best it can commit somewhat selective suicide; at next best, total *homo*cide. *This is now being denied, but not refuted.* Technology seems to be guided by a kind of automatic pilot to oblivion. The task laid out for us by the Rachael Carson's and Harrison Brown's is that of discovering ways of resuming control over our own machinery. Conversations over many years with students, the rhetoric of the New Left, and the anguish of the well-oiled residents of the shores of the Santa Barbara Channel all point to emerging traces of a healthy though tardy fear of technology itself. If that fear continues to grow, it may provide a climate wherein serious search for means of control and rational direction may be supported, but rational control awaits understanding. Rachael Carson put the question which may no longer be left as rhetorical. She sees future historians asking, "How could intelligent beings seek to control a few unwanted species by a method that contaminated the entire environment and brought the threat of disease and death even to their own kind?" The spirit of this question can be extended to the entire range of industrial energy applications, and must be answered. That we are indeed behaving in this fashion is no longer a question. How is it that we do this? Foregoing this question will mean foregoing even the satisfaction of knowing what happened to us.

A growing minority is overtly or covertly supporting disorder, because of their fear of the machine becoming master. This minority is supported by a large number of people, who, because of their affluence, are able to concern themselves with higher order needs concerning the quality of life. So it is out of the very success of our American System that we have the present disorders.

Let's look at military dominance, overpopulation and human misery in some further detail.

Military Dominance

The increasingly vociferous issue of the military industrial complex contributes much to market disorder. The section begins with excerpts from President Eisenhower's 1961 farewell address. It ends with articles discussing the importance of the military in total demand for goods and services. Lest the reader think defense spending is inconsequential, he is reminded that in fiscal year 1969 defense spending was estimated to be almost $80 billion which was 43% of federal spending and was over $340 for each man, woman, and child in the entire country, would you believe $1,258 for each family? No nation spends one half as much on defense as this nation. In 1967, only five countries spent a larger percentage of GNP than we did on "national defense." (See Table 1).

To give two other perspectives on the enormity of defense expenditures:

1. The largest category of consumer expenditures is food. That is to say that we humans spend more on food than any other category (24% of personal consumption is spent on food, beverages and tobacco). Food consumption amounted to $86.1 billion in 1967 of which $69.1 billion was sold by retail food stores. The federal budget outlays for defense in FY 1968 was $80.5 billion. In other words as a society we "purchased" more "defense products" than food. However, we did "consume" more dollars worth of food than "defense."

2. Another fact. Employment is helped by defense spending. In 1967 10.5% of all manufacturing employment was attributable to defense.

Table 1. National Defense Expenditures 1967. The Eleven Nations with the Greatest Percent of GNP and Associated Per Capita Dollar Expenditures[a]

Nation	Percent of GNP Spent on Defense	Rank on Percent of GNP	Dollars in Per Capita Defense Expenditure	Rank of Defense Expenditure on Dollar Per Capita Basis
Israel	13.8	1	121	3
Jordan	12.8	2	53	5
Egypt (U.A.R.)	12.7	3	21	8
Saudi Arabia	11.9	4	71	4
Syria	11.9	4	22	7
Iraq	10.3	5	27	6
United States	9.8	6	368	1
USSR	9.6	7	147	2
China (Mainland)	9.2	8	9	10
South Vietnam (Republic of Vietnam)	8.8	9	11	9
China (Taiwan)	7.9	10	21	8

[a]From 43 countries listed.

Overpopulation

The second aspect with which we attempt to deal is that of overpopulation. Increasingly, we are asking, what price development? As Erhlich suggests, because of "too many people" and because, as Carson mentions, we have accepted industrial progress, we have quality problems with our environment. All the Great Lakes are fast becoming one vast sewer, just as Lake Erie already is. Our major rivers are polluted so that game fish cannot live. Recently one river near Cleveland caught fire because of the oil and flammable content on the water. Our atmosphere is becoming so polluted that people's life expectancy is cut. Trees, centuries old, die because polluted air restricts photosynthesis. In Tokyo, policemen and others who must work the streets wear face masks to protect themselves from the deadly fumes. In the beautiful Willamette Valley, south of Portland, Oregon, visibility has been decreasing constantly for at least the last ten years. Even the Rose City itself, Portland, is having troubles.

Respiratory infections are on the increase. Chemical herbicides are being used in even greater quantities—and many do not decompose. Some writers contend that we are cutting our forests so fast that the balance between plants which use carbon dioxide and motors which exhale carbon monoxide is already broken and there is nothing we can do about it.

That potential markets for pollution control exist is not doubted. But except in a few specific instances, it isn't yet profitable to control pollution.

Human Injustice

In this section we will touch on selected aspects of injustice and misery which can be most easily dealt with by the business sector.

Racism in general.
Problems of consumerism.
Problems of hunger.
Problems of adequate housing.

Malcolm X writes succintly of "racism" and the position of the black man in the market disorder.

What white Americans have never fully understood—but what the Negro can never forget—is that white society is deeply implicated in the ghetto. White institutions maintain it, and white society condones it.

Because of "racism" many of the problems of blacks are shared by other low income families. The poor do pay more. The low income man is subject to greater job insecurity. There is hunger and malnutrition in America and the best estimates indicate that 12% of the families are poorly housed.

Conclusion

The main thrust of this section is that we are in a period of *market disorder.* Some of the solutions to the market disorder lie in the marketing functions of private businesses and other bureaucracies.

To market successfully in the 1970's, one must intellectually understand and personally know of the social and cultural forces at work plus some of the real problems and issues which we must face. We must know that market disorder arises because many who want to be a part of the mainline culture have been excluded by race or by sex. We must know that the market disorder reflects unsatisfied human lives as participants in today's America. Finally we must accept some of the market disorder as part of the total disorder arising from the simple bold belief in the American Dream. If we can get to the moon, we can do anything.

Our plan is to present the problems and the issues as well as the response of business and government organizations to these issues. The response has been limited. Part Four of the book will discuss some changing perceptions, new priorities and make some suggestions for action.

Some Specific Societal Problems:
A. Military Dominance

24. *Farewell Radio and Television Address to the American People. January 17, 1961*

DWIGHT D. EISENHOWER

My fellow Americans:

Three days from now, after half a century in the service of our country, I shall lay down the responsibilities of office as, in traditional and solemn ceremony, the authority of the Presidency is vested in my successor.

This evening I come to you with a message of leave-taking and farewell, and to share a few final thoughts with you, my countrymen.

Like every other citizen, I wish the new President, and all who will labor with him, Godspeed. I pray that the coming years will be blessed with peace and prosperity for all.

We now stand ten years past the midpoint of a century that has witnessed four major wars among great nations. Three of these involved our own country. Despite these holocausts America is today the strongest, the most influential and most productive nation in the world. Understandably proud of this pre-eminence, we yet realize that America's leadership and prestige depend, not merely upon our unmatched material progress, riches and military strength, but on how we use our power in the interests of world peace and human betterment.

Throughout America's adventure in free government, our basic purposes have been to keep the peace; to foster progress in human achievement, and to enhance liberty, dignity and integrity among people and among nations. To strive for less

SOURCE. *Public Papers of the Presidents,* Dwight D. Eisenhower, 1960, published in 1961, "Farewell Radio and Television Address to the American People," January, 1961.

would be unworthy of a free and religious people. Any failure traceable to arrogance, or our lack of comprehension or readiness to sacrifice would inflict upon us grievous hurt both at home and abroad.

A vital element in keeping the peace is our military establishment. Our arms must be mighty, ready for instant action, so that no potential aggressor may be tempted to risk his own destruction.

Our military organization today bears little relation to that known by any of my predecessors in peacetime, or indeed by the fighting men of World War II or Korea.

Until the latest of our world conflicts, the United States had no armaments industry. American makers of plowshares could, with time and as required, make swords as well. But now we can no longer risk emergency improvisation of national defense; we have been compelled to create a permanent armaments industry of vast proportions. Added to this, three and a half million men and women are directly engaged in the defense establishment. We annually spend on military security more than the net income of all United States corporations.

This conjunction of an immense military establishment and a large arms industry is new in the American experience. The total influence—economic, political, even spiritual—is felt in every city, every State house, every office of the Federal government. We recognize the imperative need for this development. Yet we must not fail to comprehend its grave implications. Our toil, resources and livelihood are all involved; so is the very structure of our society.

In the councils of government, we must guard against the acquisition of unwarranted influence, whether sought or unsought, by the military-industrial complex. The potential for the disastrous rise of misplaced power exists and will persist.

We must never let the weight of this combination endanger our liberties or democratic processes. We should take nothing for granted. Only an alert and knowledgeable citizenry can compel the proper meshing of the huge industrial and military machinery of defense with our peaceful methods and goals, so that security and liberty may prosper together.

Akin to, and largely responsible for the sweeping changes in our industrial-military posture, has been the technological revolution during recent decades.

In this revolution, research has become central; it also becomes more formalized, complex, and costly. A steadily increasing share is conducted for, by, or at the direction of, the Federal government.

Today, the solitary inventor, tinkering in his shop, has been overshadowed by task forces of scientists in laboratories and testing fields. In the same fashion, the free university, historically the fountainhead of free ideas and scientific discovery, has experienced a revolution in the conduct of research. Partly because of the huge costs involved, a government contract becomes virtually a substitute for intellectual curiosity. For every old blackboard there are now hundreds of new electronic computers.

The prospect of domination of the nation's scholars by Federal employment, project allocations, and the power of money is ever present—and is gravely to be regarded.

Yet, in holding scientific research and discovery in respect, as we should, we must also be alert to the equal and opposite danger that public policy could itself become the captive of a scientific-technological elite.

It is the task of statesmanship to mold, to balance, and to integrate these and other forces, new and old, within the principles of our democratic system—ever aiming toward the supreme goals of our free society.

Another factor in maintaining balance involves the element of time. As we peer into society's future, we—you and I, and our government—must avoid the impulse to live only for today, plundering, for our own ease and convenience, the precious resources of tomorrow. We cannot mortgage the material assets of our grandchildren without risking the loss also of their political and spiritual heritage. We want democracy to survive for all generations to come, not to become the insolvent phantom of tomorrow.

25. Report from Iron Mountain on the Possibility and Desirability of Peace

LEONARD C. LEWIN

The Nature of War

War is not, as is widely assumed, primarily an instrument of policy utilized by nations to extend or defend their expressed political values or their economic interests. On the contrary, it is itself the principal basis of organization on which all modern societies are constructed. The common proximate cause of war is the apparent interference of one nation with the aspirations of another. But at the root of all ostensible differences of national interest lie the dynamic requirements of the war system itself for periodic armed conflict. Readiness for war characterizes contemporary social systems more broadly than their economic and political structures, which it subsumes.

Economic analyses of the anticipated problems of transition to peace have not recognized the broad pre-eminence of war in the definition of social systems. The same is true, with rare and only partial exceptions, of model disarmament "scenarios." For this reason, the value of this previous work is limited to the mechanical aspects of transition. Certain features of these models may perhaps be applicable to a real situation of conversion to peace; this will depend on their compatibility with a substantive, rather than a procedural, peace plan. Such a plan can be developed only from the premise of full understanding of the nature of the

SOURCE. Reprinted from *Report from Iron Mountain* by Leonard C. Lewin. Copyright © 1967 by Leonard C. Lewin and used by permission of the publisher, The Dial Press.

war system it proposes to abolish, which in turn presupposes detailed comprehension of the functions the war system performs for society. It will require the construction of a detailed and feasible system of substitutes for those functions that are necessary to the stability and survival of human societies.

The Functions of War

The visible, military function of war requires no elucidation; it is not only obvious but also irrelevant to a transition to the condition of peace, in which it will by definition be superfluous. It is also subsidiary in social significance to the implied, nonmilitary functions of war; those critical to transition can be summarized in five principal groupings.

1. *Economic.* War has provided both ancient and modern societies with a dependable system for stabilizing and controlling national economies. No alternate method of control has yet been tested in a complex modern economy that has shown itself remotely comparable in scope or effectiveness.

2. *Political.* The permanent possibility of war is the foundation for stable government; it supplies the basis for general acceptance of political authority. It has enabled societies to maintain necessary class distinctions, and it has ensured the subordination of the citizen to the state, by virtue of the residual war powers inherent in the concept of nationhood. No modern political ruling group has successfully controlled its constituency after failing to sustain the continuing credibility of an external threat of war.

3. *Sociological.* War, through the medium of military institutions, has uniquely served societies, throughout the course of known history, as an indispensable controller of dangerous social dissidence and destructive antisocial tendencies. As the most formidable of threats to life itself, and as the only one susceptible to mitigation by social organization alone, it has played another equally fundamental role: the war system has provided the machinery through which the motivational forces governing human behavior have been translated into binding social allegiance. It has thus ensured the degree of social cohesion necessary to the viability of nations. No other institution, or groups of institutions, in modern societies, has successfully served these functions.

4. *Ecological.* War has been the principal evolutionary device for maintaining a satisfactory ecological balance between gross human population and supplies available for its survival. It is unique to the human species.

5. *Cultural and Scientific.* War-orientation has determined the basic standards of value in the creative arts, and has provided the fundamental motivational source of scientific and technological progress. The concepts that the arts express values independent of their own forms and that the successful pursuit of knowledge has

intrinsic social value have long been accepted in modern societies; the development of the arts and sciences during this period has been corollary to the parallel development of weaponry.

Substitutes for the Functions of War: Criteria

The foregoing functions of war are essential to the survival of the social systems we know today. With two possible exceptions they are also essential to any kind of stable social organization that might survive in a warless world. Discussion of the ways and means of transition to such a world are meaningless unless a) substitute institutions can be devised to fill these functions, or b) it can reasonably be hypothecated that the loss or partial loss of any one function need not destroy the viability of future societies.

Substitutes for the Functions of War: Models

The following substitute institutions, among others, have been proposed for consideration as replacements for the nonmilitary functions of war. That they may not have been originally set forth for that purpose does not preclude or invalidate their possible application here.

1. *Economic.* (a) A comprehensive social-welfare program, directed toward maximum improvement of general conditions of human life. (b) A giant open-end space research program, aimed at unreachable targets. (c) A permanent, ritualized, ultra-elaborate disarmament inspection system, and variants of such a system.

2. *Political.* (a) An omnipresent, virtually omnipotent international police force. (b) An established and recognized extraterrestrial menace. (c) Massive global environmental pollution. (d) Fictitious alternate enemies.

3. *Sociological: Control function.* (a) Programs generally derived from the Peace Corps model. (b) A modern, sophisticated form of slavery. *Motivational function.* (a) Intensified environmental pollution. (b) New religions or other mythologies. (c) Socially oriented blood games. (d) Combination forms.

4. *Ecological.* A comprehensive program of applied eugenics.

5. *Cultural.* No replacement institution offered. *Scientific.* The secondary requirements of the space research, social welfare, and/or eugenics programs.

Substitutes for the Functions of War: Evaluation

The models listed above reflect only the beginning of the quest for substitute institutions for the functions of war, rather than a recapitulation of alternatives.

Nevertheless, some tentative and cursory comments on these proposed functional "solutions" will indicate the scope of the difficulties involved in this area of peace planning.

Economic. The social-welfare model cannot be expected to remain outside the normal economy after the conclusion of its predominantly capital-investment phase; its value in this function can therefore be only temporary. The space-research substitute appears to meet both major criteria, and should be examined in greater detail, especially in respect to its probable effects on other war functions. "Elaborate inspection" schemes, although superficially attractive, are inconsistent with the basic premise of transition to peace. The "unarmed forces" variant, logistically similar, is subject to the same functional criticism as the general social-welfare model.

Political. Like the inspection-scheme surrogates, proposals for plenipotentiary international police are inherently incompatible with the ending of the war system. The "unarmed forces" variant, amended to include unlimited powers of economic sanction, might conceivably be expanded to constitute a credible external menace. Development of an acceptable threat from "outer space," presumably in conjunction with a space-research surrogate for economic control, appears unpromising in terms of credibility. The environmental-pollution model does not seem sufficiently responsive to immediate social control, except through arbitrary acceleration of current pollution trends; this in turn raises questions of political acceptability. New, less regressive, approaches to the creation of fictitious global "enemies" invite further investigation.

Sociological: Control function. Although the various substitutes proposed for this function that are modeled roughly on the Peace Corps appear grossly inadequate in potential scope, they should not be ruled out without further study. Slavery, in a technologically modern and conceptually euphemized form, may prove a more efficient and flexible institution in this area. *Motivational function.* Although none of the proposed substitutes for war as the guarantor of social allegiance can be dismissed out of hand, each presents serious and special difficulties. Intensified environmental threats may raise ecological dangers; mythmaking dissociated from war may no longer be politically feasible; purposeful blood games and rituals can far more readily be devised than implemented. An institution combining this function with the preceding one, based on, but not necessarily imitative of, the precedent of organized ethnic repression, warrants careful consideration.

Ecological. The only apparent problem in the application of an adequate eugenic substitute for war is that of timing; it cannot be effectuated until the transition to peace has been completed, which involves a serious temporary risk of ecological failure.

Cultural. No plausible substitute for this function of war has yet been proposed. It may be, however, that a basic cultural value-determinant is not necessary to the survival of a stable society. *Scientific.* The same might be said for the function of war as the prime mover of the search for knowledge. However, adoption of either a giant space-research program, a comprehensive social-welfare program, or a master program of eugenic control would provide motivation for limited technologies.

General Conclusions

It is apparent, from the foregoing, that no program or combination of programs yet proposed for a transition to peace has remotely approached meeting the comprehensive functional requirements of a world without war. Although one projected system for filling the economic function of war seems promising, similar optimism cannot be expressed in the equally essential political and sociological areas. The other major nonmilitary functions of war—ecological, cultural, scientific—raise very different problems, but it is at least possible that detailed programming of substitutes in these areas is not prerequisite to transition. More important, it is not enough to develop adequate but separate surrogates for the major war functions; they must be fully compatible and in no degree self-canceling.

The principal cause for concern over the continuing effectiveness of the war system, and the more important reason for hedging with peace planning, lies in the backwardness of current war-system programming. Its controls have not kept pace with the technological advances it has made possible. To the best of our knowledge, no serious quantified studies have ever been conducted to determine, for example:

Optimum levels of armament production, for purposes of economic control, at any given series of chronological points and under any given relationship between civilian production and consumption patterns.

Correlation factors between draft recruitment policies and mensurable social dissidence.

Minimum levels of population destruction necessary to maintain war-threat credibility under varying political conditions.

Optimum cyclical frequency of "shooting" wars under varying circumstances of historical relationship.

These and other war-function factors are fully susceptible to analysis by today's computer-based systems but they have not been so treated.

Our final conclusion is that it will be necessary for our government to plan in depth for two general contingencies. The first, and lesser, is the possibility of a viable general peace; the second is the successful continuation of the war system. In our view, careful preparation for the possibility of peace should be extended, not because we take the position that the end of war would necessarily be desirable, if it is in fact possible, but because it may be thrust upon us in some form whether we are ready for it or not. Planning for rationalizing and quantifying the war system, on the other hand, to ensure the effectiveness of its major stabilizing functions, is not only more promising in respect to anticipated results, but is essential; we can no longer take for granted that it will continue to serve our purposes well merely because it always has. The objective of government policy in regard to war and peace, in this period of uncertainty, must be to preserve maximum options.

B. *Overpopulation*

26. *Population + Production = Pollution*

LEAGUE OF WOMEN VOTERS
OF THE UNITED STATES

Pollution is a Problem of People

Water pollution is not so much a water problem as it is a people problem. As people buy more and more products to satisfy their needs and desires, pollution from agriculture and industry mounts. As people continue to move into cities and suburbs, pollution from sewage is increasingly concentrated. As more people seek outdoor recreation, their sheer numbers degrade the quality of the water they crowd to enjoy. It is this increase in population, in urbanization, in production and consumption that makes water pollution a major issue.

Man—The Great Polluter

Pollution is a natural process; no surface or ground water is pure H_2O. Climate, season, temperature of water, kind of rock and soil, plant cover, and animal life affect the solutes and sediment picked up by water in a state of nature. Salt springs in the Arkansas and Red River basin are an example of natural pollution. And so is the process by which lakes fill, age, and disappear naturally as sediment is deposited, water plants multiply, and products of decay increase.

But man is the great polluter, and modern man the greatest polluter of all. People produce personal and household wastes. Industries discharge grease and oil, acids, complex chemicals, salts, and heated water. Run-off from farmland carries sediment, fertilizers, pesticides, and animal wastes into streams. Irrigation water dissolves salts from soil and through reuse becomes too saline for crops. One place or another, these and other pollutants are entering U.S. rivers, lakes, and ground-water limiting the water's usefulness.

Clean Enough to Use Again

Use is not the same for every lake and river in the United States, nor for all parts of a river system, nor even for every section of mainstem or major tributary. Water quality is highly variable, changing from place to place and from day to day, as it responds to amount and kinds of entering wastes and of flow available to dilute them.

In some of the country's river basins the dependable flow is reused, often several times, during low-flow periods. Repeated reuse of water is forecast by all estimates of water needs in 1980 and 2000, for only with reuse will supply meet demand. Waste water is this country's most immediately available water supply; it need not be pumped over divides nor up from deep below the surface. The cheapest, quickest, most flexible way to increase the quantity of usable water is to reduce water pollution.

People's Choice

Use and reuse are key words. Where people want to use rivers only for navigation by tug and barge or for disposal of municipal and industrial waste, polluted water will suffice. Where people want to use rivers for other purposes, such as for the growing number of pleasure boats or for attractive open space in an urban area, they will want cleaner water.

In our super-cities, wastes as well as population and income are being concentrated. Since no organism is able to live in an environment of its own multiplying wastes, the choices before us are *how,* not *whether,* to counteract growing water pollution.

Municipal Wastes

Wastes from towns and cities and wastes from industrial plants exceed all other sources of water pollution. So great has been the increase in wastes municipalities produce that building more and more treatment plants has not been enough to keep streams from growing more polluted. Because municipal sewage treatment does not remove all wastes, waste-discharge after sewage treatment must grow greater as total volume of municipal sewage increases.

Population growth and movement to cities are the main causes, but failure to construct needed treatment works, treatment plant obsolescence or poor management, and increased installation of new devices such as garbage disposals also add to municipal water pollution. There is pressing need for new water treatment processes that will remove more of the contaminants from waste water and do this economically. Complete water renovation by advanced waste treatment is now possible but costly.

Primary is Poorer

Along many waterways, cities are now so close together that their waste water needs more treatment than the cities provide. To know that a city treats its sewage or that a large percentage of jurisdictions in a basin now have treatment plants is not enough. We need to ask, "Is the degree of treatment adequate?"

Unless most towns and all cities move up at least to secondary treatment, pollution of streams will grow worse. It has been suggested that secondary treatment be made the required treatment, with primary treatment allowed only as an exception by permit from a state water pollution control agency.

Secondary treatment is a substantial improvement over primary treatment, but it does not do away with all problems of pollution from domestic sewage and industrial waste. Secondary treatment even aggravates what is known as the "enrichment" problem.

Domestic sewage contains dissolved compounds of nitrogen and phosphorus, which all gardeners recognize as the chief constituents of synthetic fertilizers. Untreated sewage and the liquid discharge from treatment plants (effluent) enrich the receiving waters with plant nutrients and stimulate growth of aquatic plants, particularly algae. Living, an abundance of algae give the water a pea-green, soupy appearance; dying, they cause pollution, disagreeable odors, unpleasant taste. Unfortunately, in secondary treatment of sewage, nitrogen and phosphorus are changed into forms that algae utilize exceptionally well.

Industrial Wastes

To broaden their tax base and increase employment for their people, communities welcome industry. The industries, so eagerly sought, require water for cooling, for washing, for use in manufacturing processes. From their survey of water use in industry, published in 1965, the National Association of Manufacturers and the Chamber of Commerce of the United States report that only 6.7 percent of the water withdrawn for industrial use is consumed (i.e., made unavailable to others in the immediate vicinity or downstream because the water is incorporated in products, evaporated in cooling towers, or lost in other ways).

What happens to the rest? Cooling water is returned to the stream at higher temperatures (thermal pollution) but otherwise unchanged. Much water used for cleaning and other industrial processes also goes back into streams and lakes. Where the water is returned laden with solutes and solids, downstream use is diminished for other than waste-carrying purposes.

Information on industrial waste discharge into U.S. waters has been sparse and difficult to obtain because most companies have chosen to keep it confidential. Where state agencies are allowed by law to collect data on industrial water use and waste discharge, some operate under a legislative proviso that the information will not be revealed. Industries say that to place in the public record the names and quantities of discharged waste materials or descriptions of treatment methods would, in many cases, be tantamount to disclosing a company's secrets to its competitors.

Compounding the Problem

Industrial *organic* waste discharged into U.S. water courses in 1960 was estimated to be twice the municipal waste load. Domestic sewage and industrial wastes (chiefly from food processing, pulp and paper, and non-synthetic textiles) are thought to furnish about equal amounts of organic wastes that break down under today's conventional sewage treatment (degradable pollutants). In addition, chemical companies and fabricators and packagers of chemical compounds discharge synthetic organic wastes that are not removed by natural stream purification processes or by primary or secondary treatment (persistent pollutants).

Industrial processes also release *inorganic* materials—metals, salts, acids—into plant waste water. Inorganic chemicals (whether from industry, agriculture, or homes), like persistent organics, are not removed by primary or secondary treatment.

Water high in dissolved inorganic chemicals corrodes equipment, forms scale, affects color, odor, and taste, and requires additional treatment for industrial and domestic use.

Cutting Back Industrial Waste Discharge

The forecast that industry will require "80 percent or more of the expected increase in total future water requirements and will account for 65 percent or more of all fresh water used in 1980 and 2000" suggests how important industrial waste-handling may be to total U.S. water quality control and to industry itself.

A company's decision on how to handle its waste water is based on economic factors. It costs money to recirculate through cooling towers, construct treatment works, develop new processes that use less water or leave it cleaner. Some industries have found it profitable to recover byproducts from waste water, but more often recovery does not match cost. Installation of treatment systems or process changes with or without waste reclamation seems expensive to a company accustomed to "free" disposal to stream, lake, or ocean.

When social conscience or concern for corporate image make stream pollution distasteful to officers and management or when government regulations limit waste-discharge into public water, companies weigh the net costs of discharging through municipal sewerage systems, altering plant processes, or upgrading company waste-water treatment. The number of plants that discharge industrial waste through municipal sewerage systems is increasing. Smaller plants tend to make use of public facilities; larger ones generally treat their own wastes.

Many companies have given great attention to pollution abatement and invested large sums in preventive measures as, for example, at the new Kimberly-Clark pulp and paper plant on the Sacramento River in California.

In Conclusion

Although unknowns are many and additional research is much needed, deterioration of U.S. waters *can* be slowed down *now*. But clean streams will not be cheap. People must show that they are willing to pay the price, for cost of municipal cleanup will be borne by the taxpayer and cost of industrial improvement ultimately by the consumer.

By taking greater responsibility for supporting and paying for pollution abatement, people can get cleaner water to use and enjoy. Improvement can go forward in the traditional American way, through simultaneous effort by private enterprise, by citizen organizations, by all three levels of government. It can be advanced through widespread growth of popular understanding and popular demand for water quality improvement. Like pollution, pollution control is chiefly a people problem.

27. *The Obligation to Endure*

R A C H E L   C A R S O N

The history of life on earth has been a history of interaction between living things and their surroundings. To a large extent, the physical form and the habits of the earth's vegetation and its animal life have been molded by the environment. Considering the whole span of earthly time, the opposite effect, in which life actually modifies its surroundings, has been relatively slight. Only within the moment of time represented by the present century has one species—man—acquired significant power to alter the nature of his world.

During the past quarter century this power has not only increased to one of disturbing magnitude but it has changed in character. The most alarming of all man's assaults upon the environment is the contamination of air, earth, rivers, and sea with dangerous and even lethal materials. This pollution is for the most part irrecoverable; the chain of evil it initiates not only in the world that must support life but in living tissues is for the most part irreversible. In this now universal contamination of the environment, chemicals are the sinister and little-recognized partners of radiation in changing the very nature of the world—the very nature of its life. Strontium 90, released through nuclear explosions into the air, comes to earth in rain or drifts down as fallout, lodges in soil, enters into the grass or corn or wheat grown there, and in time takes up its abode in the bones of a human being, there to remain until his death. Similarly, chemicals sprayed on croplands or forests

SOURCE. From *Silent Spring.* Copyright © 1962 by Rachel L. Carson. Reprinted by permission of the publisher, Houghton Mifflin Company.

or gardens so long in soil, entering into living organisms, passing from one to another in a chain of poisoning and death. Or they pass mysteriously by underground streams until they emerge and, through the alchemy of air and sunlight, combine into new forms that kill vegetation, sicken cattle, and work unknown harm on those who drink from once-pure wells. As Albert Schweitzer has said, "Man can hardly even recognize the devils of his own creation."

It took hundreds of millions of years to produce the life that now inhabits the earth—eons of time in which that developing and evolving and diversifying life reached a state of adjustment and balance with its surroundings. The environment, rigorously shaping and directing the life it supported, contained elements that were hostile as well as supporting. Certain rocks gave out dangerous radiation; even within the light of the sun, from which all life draws its energy, there were short-wave radiations with power to injure. Given time—time not in years but in millennia—life adjusts, and a balance has been reached. For time is the essential ingredient; but in the modern world there is no time.

The rapidity of change and the speed with which new situations are created follow the impetuous and heedless pace of man rather than the deliberate pace of nature. Radiation is no longer merely the background radiation of rocks, the bombardment of cosmic rays, the ultraviolet of the sun that have existed before there was any life on earth; radiation is now the unnatural creation of man's tampering with the atom. The chemicals to which life is asked to make its adjustment are no longer merely the calcium and silica and copper and all the rest of the minerals washed out of the rocks and carried in rivers to the sea; they are the synthetic creations of man's inventive mind, brewed in his laboratories, and having no counterparts in nature.

To adjust to these chemicals would require time on the scale that is nature's; it would require not merely the years of a man's life but the life of generations. And even this, were it by some miracle possible, would be futile, for the new chemicals come from our laboratories in an endless stream; almost five hundred annually find their way into actual use in the United States alone. The figure is staggering and its implications are not easily grasped—500 new chemicals to which the bodies of men and animals are required somehow to adapt each year, chemicals totally outside the limits of biologic experience.

Among them are many that are used in man's war against nature. Since the mid-1940's over 200 basic chemicals have been created for use in killing insects, weeds, rodents, and other organisms described in the modern vernacular as "pests"; and they are sold under several thousand different brand names.

These sprays, dusts, and aerosols are now applied almost universally to farms, gardens, forests and homes—nonselective chemicals that have the power to kill every insect, the "good" and the "bad," to still the song of birds and the leaping of fish in the streams, to coat the leaves with a deadly film, and to linger on in soil—all this though the intended target may be only a few weeds or insects. Can anyone believe it is possible to lay down such a barrage of poisons on the surface of the earth without making it unfit for all life? They should not be called "insecticides," but "biocides."

The whole process of spraying seems caught up in an endless spiral. Since DDT was released for civilian use, a process of escalation has been going on in which ever more toxic materials must be found. This has happened because insects, in a triumphant vindication of Darwin's principle of the survival of the fittest, have evolved super races immune to the particular insecticide used, hence a deadlier one has always to be developed—and then a deadlier one than that. It has happened also because, for reasons to be described later, destructive insects often undergo a "flare-back," or resurgence, after spraying, in numbers greater than before. Thus the chemical war is never won, and all life is caught in its violent crossfire.

Along with the possibility of the extinction of mankind by nuclear war, the central problem of our age has therefore become the contamination of man's total environment with such substances of incredible potential for harm—substances that accumulate in the tissues of plants and animals and even penetrate the germ cells to shatter or alter the very material of heredity upon which the shape of the future depends.

Some would-be architects of our future look toward a time when it will be possible to alter the human germ plasm by design. But we may easily be doing so now by inadvertence, for many chemicals, like radiation, bring about gene mutations. It is ironic to think that man might determine his own future by something so seemingly trivial as the choice of an insect spray.

All this has been risked—for what? Future historians may well be amazed by our distorted sense of proportion. How could intelligent beings seek to control a few unwanted species by a method that contaminated the entire environment and brought the threat of disease and death even to their own kind? Yet this is precisely what we have done. We have done it, moreover, for reasons that collapse the moment we examine them. We are told that the enormous and expanding use of pesticides is necessary to maintain farm production. Yet is our real problem not one of *overproduction*?

Have we fallen into a mesmerized state that makes us accept as inevitable that which is inferior or detrimental, as though having lost the will or the vision to demand that which is good? Such thinking, in the words of the ecologist Paul Shepard, "idealizes life with only its head out of water, inches above the limits of toleration of the corruption of its own environment . . . Why should we tolerate a diet of weak poisons, a home in insipid surroundings, a circle of acquaintances who are not quite our enemies, the noise of motors with just enough relief to prevent insanity? Who would want to live in a world which is just not quite fatal?"

28. *The Media and Environmental Awareness* JERRY MANDER

It has occurred to me that I am employed in a dying industry.

Advertising is not dying out for any of the usually advocated reasons—immoral or distasteful behavior in the marketplace. Perhaps it should be killed for those reasons but it will not be necessary.

Advertising is a critical element encouraging an economic system committed to growth. Expanding technology is a by-word of political and economic rhetoric, and the country's economic health is judged by the rate at which Gross National Product increases, year by year.

The advertising business—based on a commission system—is particularly tied to the expanding economy. As long as expansion continues, ad revenues increase and so things would seem to be going along just fine for everyone. After all, as David Ogilvy, a well known ad man has pointed out, "Clients are hogs with all four feet in the trough."

However, there is only so much getting bigger possible.

That should have been evident, of course, the moment our astronauts flashed us pictures of the Earth and we noted it was round. The idea of an infinitely expanding Gross National Product on an isolated sphere, a finite system, an island in space, is complete nonsense, to put it as lightly as possible, or, to put it the way I

SOURCE. From *The Environmental Handbook,* ed. by Garrett de Bell. Copyright © 1970 by Garrett de Bell. A Ballantine/Friends of the Earth Book.

personally perceive it, may be, together with population growth, the most dangerous tendency in the world today.

You simply may not have a continually expanding economy within a finite system: Earth. At least not if the economy is based upon anything approaching technological exploitation and production as we now know it. On a round ball, there is only so much of anything. Minerals. Food. Air. Water. Space . . . and things *they* need to stay in balance. An economy which feeds on itself can't keep on eating forever. Or, as Edward Abbey put it, "growth for the sake of growth is the ideology of the cancer cell."

Yet just the other day Mr. Nixon reaffirmed his faith in American industry's abilities to continue its "healthy" growth rate. And the president of U.S. Steel said he doesn't believe in "clean water for its own sake."

The first remark tells us that the patient hasn't yet noticed he's near collapse, and the second tells us that the cancer hasn't noticed it's running out of digestibles.

C. *Human Injustice*

29. *The Autobiography of Malcolm X*

MALCOLM X

My thinking had been opened up wide in Mecca. In the long letters I wrote to friends, I tried to convey to them my new insights into the American black man's struggle and his problems, as well as the depths of my search for truth and justice.

"I've had enough of someone else's propaganda," I had written to these friends. "I'm for truth, no matter who tells it. I'm for justice, no matter who it is for or against. I'm a human being first and foremost, and as such I'm for whoever and whatever benefits humanity *as a whole*."

Largely, the American white man's press refused to convey that I was now attempting to teach Negroes a new direction. With the 1964 "long, hot summer" steadily producing new incidents, I was constantly accused of "stirring up Negroes." Every time I had another radio or television microphone at my mouth, when I was asked about "stirring up Negroes" or "inciting violence," I'd get hot.

"It takes no one to stir up the sociological dynamite that stems from the unemployment, bad housing, and inferior education already in the ghettoes. This explosively criminal condition has existed for so long, it needs no fuse; it fuses itself; it spontaneously combusts from within itself. . . ."

They called me "the angriest Negro in America." I wouldn't deny that charge. I spoke exactly as I felt. "I *believe* in anger. The Bible says there is a *time* for anger." They called me "a teacher, a fomentor of violence." I would say point blank, "That

SOURCE. Reprinted by permission of Grove Press, Inc. Copyright ©1964 by Alex Haley and Malcolm X. Copyright ©1965 by Alex Haley and Betty Shabazz.

is a lie. I'm not for wanton violence, I'm for justice. I feel that if white people were attacked by Negroes—if the forces of law prove unable, or inadequate, or reluctant to protect those whites from those Negroes—then those white people should protect and defend themselves from those Negroes, using arms if necessary. And I feel that when the law fails to protect Negroes from whites' attack, then those Negroes should use arms, if necessary, to defend themselves."

"Malcolm X Advocates Armed Negroes!"

What was wrong with that? I'll tell you what was wrong. I was a black man talking about physical defense against the white man. The white man can lynch and burn and bomb and beat Negroes—that's all right: "Have patience" . . . "The customs are entrenched" . . . "Things are getting better."

Well, I believe it's a crime for anyone who is being brutalized to continue to accept that brutality without doing something to defend himself. If that's how "Christian" philosophy is interpreted, if that's what Gandhian philosophy teaches, well, then, I will call them criminal philosophies.

I tried in every speech I made to clarify my new position regarding white people—"I don't speak against the sincere, well-meaning, good white people. I have learned that there *are* some. I have learned that not all white people are racists. I am speaking against and my right is against the white *racists*. I firmly believe that Negroes have the right to fight against these racists, by any means that are necessary."

But the white reporters kept wanting me linked with that word "violence." I doubt if I had one interview without having to deal with that accusation.

"I *am* for violence if non-violence means we continue postponing a solution to the American black man's problem—just to *avoid* violence. I don't go for non-violence if it also means a delayed solution. To me a delayed solution is a non-solution. Or I'll say it another way. If it must take violence to get the black man his human rights in this country, I'm *for* violence exactly as you know the Irish, the Poles, or Jews would be if they were flagrantly discriminated against. I am just as they would be in that case, and they would be for violence—no matter what the consequences, no matter who was hurt by the violence."

White society *hates* to hear anybody, especially a black man, talk about the crime the white man has perpetrated on the black man. I have always understood that's why I have been so frequently called "a revolutionist." It sounds as if *I* have done some crime! Well, it may be the American black man does need to become involved in a *real* revolution. The word for "revolution" in German is *Umwälzung*. What it means is a complete overturn—a complete change. The overthrow of King Farouk in Egypt and the succession of President Nasser is an example of a true revolution. It means the destroying of an old system, and its replacement with a new system. Another example is the Algerian revolution, led by Ben Bella; they threw out the French who had been there over 100 years. So how does anybody sound talking about the Negro in America waging some "revolution"? Yes, he is condemning a system—but he's not trying to overturn the system, or to destroy it. The Negro's so-called "revolt" is merely an asking to be *accepted* into the existing system! A *true* Negro revolt might entail, for instance, fighting for separate black states within this country—which several groups and individuals have advocated, long before Elijah Muhammad came along.

When the white man came into this country, he certainly wasn't demonstrating any "non-violence." In fact, the very man whose name symbolizes non-violence here today has stated:

"Our nation was born in genocide when it embraced the doctrine that the original American, the Indian, was an inferior race. Even before there were large numbers of Negroes on our shores, the scar of racial hatred had already disfigured colonial society. From the sixteenth century forward, blood flowed in battles over racial supremacy. We are perhaps the only nation which tried as a matter of national policy to wipe out its indigenous population. Moreover, we elevated that tragic experience into a noble crusade. Indeed, even today we have not permitted ourselves to reject or to feel remorse for this shameful episode. Our literature, our films, our drama, our folklore all exalt it. Our children are still taught to respect the violence which reduced a red-skinned people of an earlier culture into a few fragmented groups herded into impoverished reservations."

"Peaceful coexistence!" That's another one the white man has always been quick to cry. Fine! But what have been the deeds of the white man? During his entire advance through history, he has been waving the banner of Christianity . . . and carrying in his other hand the sword and the flintlock.

You can go right back to the very beginning of Christianity. Catholicism, the genesis of Christianity as we know it to be presently constituted, with its hierarchy, was conceived in Africa—by those whom the Christian church calls "The Desert Fathers." The Christian church became infected with racism when it entered white Europe. The Christian church returned to Africa under the banner of the Cross—conquering, killing, exploiting, pillaging, raping, bullying, beating—and teaching white supremacy. This is how the white man thrust himself into the position of leadership of the world—through the use of naked physical power. And he was totally inadequate spiritually. Mankind's history has proved from one era to another that the true criterion of leadership is spiritual. Men are attracted by spirit. By power, men are *forced*. Love is engendered by spirit. By power, anxieties are created.

I am in agreement one hundred per cent with those racists who say that no government laws ever can *force* brotherhood. The only true world solution today is governments guided by true religion—of the spirit. Here in race-torn America, I am convinced that the Islam religion is desperately needed, particularly by the American black man. The black man needs to reflect that he has been America's most fervent Christian—and where has it gotten him? In fact, in the white man's hands, in the white man's interpretation . . . where has Christianity brought this *world?*

A desegregated cup of coffee, a theater, public toilets—the whole range of hypocritical "integration"—these are not atonement.

An American white ambassador in one African country was Africa's most respected American ambassador: I'm glad to say that this was told to me by one ranking African leader. We talked for an entire afternoon. Based on what I had heard of him, I had to believe him when he told me that as long as he was on the African continent, he never thought in terms of race, that he dealt with human beings, never noticing their color. He said he was more aware of language differences than of color differences. He said that only when he returned to America would he become aware of color differences.

I told him, "What you are telling me is that it isn't the American white *man* who is a racist, but it's the American political, economic, and social *atmosphere* that automatically nourishes a racist psychology in the white man." He agreed.

We both agreed that American society makes it next to impossible for humans to meet in America and not be conscious of their color differences. And we both agreed that if racism could be removed, America could offer a society where rich and poor could truly live like human beings.

That discussion with the ambassador gave me a new insight—one which I like: that the white man is *not* inherently evil, but America's racist society influences him to act evilly. The society has produced and nourishes a psychology which brings out the lowest, most base part of human beings.

Politics dominated the American scene while I was traveling abroad this time. In Cairo and again in Accra, the American press wire services reached me with trans-Atlantic calls, asking whom did I favor, Johnson—or Goldwater?

I said I felt that as far as the American black man was concerned they were both just about the same. I felt that it was for the black man only a question of Johnson, the fox, or Goldwater, the wolf.

"Conservatism" in America's politics means "Let's keep the niggers in their place." And "liberalism" means "Let's keep the *knee*-grows in their place—but tell them we'll treat them a little better; let's fool them more, with more promises." With these choices, I felt that the American black man only needed to choose which one to be eaten by, the "liberal" fox or the "conservative" wolf—because both of them would eat him.

I kept having all kinds of troubles trying to develop the kind of Black Nationalist organization I wanted to build for the American Negro. Why Black Nationalism? Well, in the competitive American society, how can there ever by any white-black solidarity before there is first some black solidarity? If you will remember, in my childhood I had been exposed to the Black Nationalist teachings of Marcus

Garvey—which, in fact, I had been told had led to my father's murder. Even when I was a follower of Elijah Muhammad, I had been strongly aware of how the Black Nationalist political, economic and social philosophies had the ability to instill within black men the racial dignity, the incentive, and the confidence that the black race needs today to get up off its knees, and to get on its feet, and get rid of its scars, and to take a stand for itself.

One of the major troubles that I was having in building the organization that I wanted—an all black organization whose ultimate objective was to help create a society in which there could exist honest white-black brotherhood—was that my earlier public image, my old so-called "Black Muslim" image, kept blocking me. I was trying to gradually reshape that image. I was trying to turn a corner, into a new regard by the public, especially Negroes; I was no less angry than I had been, but at the same time the true brotherhood I had seen in the Holy World had influenced me to recognize that anger can blind human vision.

Every free moment I could find, I did a lot of talking to key people whom I knew around Harlem, and I made a lot of speeches, saying: "True Islam taught me that it takes *all* of the religious, political, economic, psychological, and racial ingredients, or characteristics, to make the Human Family and the Human Society complete.

"Since I learned the *truth* in Mecca, my dearest friends have come to include *all* kinds—some Christians, Jews, Buddhists, Hindus, agnostics, and even atheists! I have friends who are called capitalists, Socialists, and Communists! Some of my friends are moderates, conservatives, extremists—some are even Uncle Toms! My friends today are black, brown, red, yellow, and *white!*"

I said to Harlem street audiences that only when mankind would submit to the One God who created all—only then would mankind even approach the "peace" of which so much *talk* could be heard ... but toward which so little *action* was seen.

I said that on the American racial level, we had to approach the black man's struggle against the white man's racism as a human problem, that we had to forget hypocritical politics and propaganda. I said that both races, as human beings, had the obligation, the responsibility, of helping to correct America's human problem. The well-meaning white people, I said, had to combat, actively and directly, the racism in other white people. And the black people had to build within themselves much greater awareness that along with equal rights there had to be the bearing of equal responsibilities.

I knew, better than most Negroes, how many white people truly wanted to see American racial problems solved. I knew that many whites were as frustrated as Negroes. I'll bet I got fifty letters some days from white people. The white people in meeting audiences would throng around me, asking me, after I had addressed them somewhere, "What *can* a sincere white person do?"

When I say that here now, it makes me think about that little co-ed I told you about, the one who flew from her New England college down to New York and came up to me in the Nation of Islam's restaurant in Harlem, and I told her that there was "nothing" she could do. I regret that I told her that. I wish that now I knew her name, or where I could telephone her, or write to her, and tell her what I tell white people now when they present themselves as being sincere, and ask me, one way or another, the same thing that she asked.

The first thing I tell them is that at least where my own particular Black Nationalist organization, the Organization of Afro-American Unity, is concerned, they can't *join* us. I have these very deep feelings that white people who want to join black organizations are really just taking the escapist way to salve their consciences. By visibly hovering near us, they are "proving" that they are "with us." But the hard truth is this *isn't* helping to solve America's racist problem. The Negroes aren't the racists. Where the really sincere white people have got to do their "proving" of themselves is not among the black *victims*, but out on the battle lines of where America's racism really *is*—and that's in their own home communities; America's racism is among their own fellow whites. That's where the sincere whites who really mean to accomplish something have got to work.

Aside from that, I mean nothing against any sincere whites when I say that as members of black organizations, generally whites' very presence subtly renders the black organization automatically less effective. Even the best white members will slow down the Negroes' discovery of what they need to do, and particularly of what they can do—for themselves, working by themselves, among their own kind, in their own communities.

I sure don't want to hurt anybody's feelings, but in fact I'll even go so far as to say that I never really trust the kind of white people who are always so anxious to hang around Negroes, or to hang around in Negro communities. I don't trust the kind of whites who love having Negroes always hanging around them. I don't know—this feeling may be a throwback to the years when I was hustling in Harlem and all of those red-faced, drunk whites in the afterhours clubs were always grabbing hold of some Negroes and talking about "I just want you to know you're just as good as I am—" And then they got back in their taxicabs and black limousines and went back downtown to the places where they lived and worked, where no blacks except servants had better get caught. But, anyway, I know that every time that whites join a black organization, you watch, pretty soon the blacks will be leaning on the whites to support it, and before you know it a black may be up front with a title, but the whites, because of their money, are the real controllers.

I tell sincere white people, "Work in conjunction with us—each of us working among our own kind." Let sincere white individuals find all other white people they can who feel as they do—and let them form their own all-white groups, to work trying to convert other white people who are thinking and acting so racist. Let sincere whites go and teach nonviolence to white people!

Sometimes, I have dared to dream to myself that one day, history may even say that my voice—which disturbed the white man's smugness, and his arrogance, and his complacency—that my voice helped to save America from a grave, possibly even a fatal catastrophe.

The goal has always been the same, with the approaches to it as different as mine and Dr. Martin Luther King's nonviolent marching, that dramatizes the brutality and the evil of the white man against defenseless blacks. And in the racial climate of this country today, it is anybody's guess which of the "extremes" in approach to the black man's problems might *personally* meet a fatal catastrophe first—"nonviolent" Dr. King, or so-called "violent" me.

I know, too, that I could suddenly die at the hands of some white racists. Or I could die at the hands of some Negro hired by the white man. Or it could be some brainwashed Negro acting on his own idea that by eliminating me he would be helping out the white man, because I talk about the white man the way I do.

Anyway, now, each day I live as if I am already dead, and I tell you what I would like for you to do. When I *am* dead—I say it that way because from the things I *know*, I do not expect to live long enough to read this book in its finished form—I want you to just watch and see if I'm not right in what I say: that the white man, in his press, is going to identify me with "hate."

He will make use of me dead, as he has made use of me alive, as a convenient symbol of "hatred"—and that will help him to escape facing the truth that all I have been doing is holding up a mirror to reflect, to show, the history of unspeakable crimes that his race has committed against my race.

You watch. I will be labeled as, at best, an "irresponsible" black man. I have always felt about this accusation that the black "leader" whom white men consider to be "responsible" is invariably the black "leader" who never gets any results. You only get action as a black man if you are regarded by the white man as "irresponsible." In fact, this much I had learned when I was just a little boy. And since I have been some kind of a "leader" of black people here in the racist society of America, I have been more reassured each time the white man resisted me, or attacked me harder—because each time made me more certain that I was on the right track in the American black man's best interests. The racist white man's opposition automatically made me know that I did offer the black man something worthwhile.

Yes, I have cherished my "demagogue" role. I know that societies often have killed the people who have helped to change those societies. And if I can die having brought any light, having exposed any meaningful truth that will help to destroy the racist cancer that is malignant in the body of America—then, all of the credit is due to Allah. Only the mistakes have been mine.

𝟛𝟘. *The Riot Commission Report: Summary*

The summer of 1967 again brought racial disorders to American cities, and with them shock, fear and bewilderment to the nation.

The worst came during a two-week period in July, first in Newark and then in Detroit. Each set off a chain reaction in neighboring communities.

On July 28, 1967, the President of the United States established this Commission and directed us to answer three basic questions:

What happened?
Why did it happen?
What can be done to prevent it from happening again?

To respond to these questions, we have undertaken a broad range of studies and investigations. We have visited the riot cities; we have heard many witnesses; we have sought the counsel of experts across the country.

This is our basic conclusion: Our nation is moving toward two societies, one black, one white—separate and unequal.

Reaction to last summer's disorders has quickened the movement and deepened the division. Discrimination and segregation have long permeated much of American life; they now threaten the future of every American.

SOURCE. Report of the National Advisory Commission on Civil Disorders, 1969.

This deepening racial division is not inevitable. The movement apart can be reversed. Choice is still possible. Our principal task is to define that choice and to press for a national resolution.

To pursue our present course will involve the continuing polarization of the American community and, ultimately, the destruction of basic democratic values.

The alternative is not blind repression or capitulation to lawlessness. It is the realization of common opportunities for all within a single society.

This alternative will require a commitment to national action—compassionate, massive and sustained, backed by the resources of the most powerful and the richest nation on this earth. From every American it will require new attitudes, new understanding, and, above all, new will.

The vital needs of the nation must be met; hard choices must be made, and, if necessary, new taxes enacted.

Violence cannot build a better society. Disruption and disorder nourish repression, not justice. They strike at the freedom of every citizen. The community cannot—it will not—tolerate coercion and mob rule.

Violence and destruction must be ended—in the streets of the ghetto and in the lives of people.

Segregation and poverty have created in the racial ghetto a destructive environment totally unknown to most white Americans.

What white Americans have never fully understood—but what the Negro can never forget—is that white society is deeply implicated in the ghetto. White institutions created it, white institutions maintain it, and white society condones it.

It is time now to turn with all the purpose at our command to the major unfinished business of this nation. It is time to adopt strategies for action that will produce quick and visible progress. It is time to make good the promises of American democracy to all citizens—urban and rural, white and black, Spanish-surname, American Indian, and every minority group.

Our recommendations embrace three basic principles:

To mount programs on a scale equal to the dimension of the problems:

To aim these programs for high impact in the immediate future in order to close the gap between promise and performance;

To undertake new initiatives and experiments that can change the system of failure and frustration that now dominates the ghetto and weakens our society.

Conclusion

One of the first witnesses to be invited to appear before this Commission was Dr. Kenneth B. Clark, a distinguished and perceptive scholar. Referring to the reports of earlier riot commissions, he said:

I read that report . . . of the 1919 riot in Chicago, and it is as if I were reading the report of the investigating committee on the Harlem riot of '35, the report of the investigating committee on the Harlem riot of '43, the report of the McCone Commission on the Watts riot.

I must again in candor say to you members of this Commission—it is a kind of Alice in Wonderland—with the same moving picutre re-shown over and over again, the same analysis, the same recommendations, and the same inaction.

These words come to our minds as we conclude this Report.

We have provided an honest beginning. We have learned much. But we have uncovered no startling truths, no unique insights, no simple solutions. The destruction and the bitterness of racial disorder, the harsh polemics of black revolt and white repression have been seen and heard before in this country.

It is time now to end the destruction and the violence, not only in the streets of the ghetto but in the lives of people.

31. *Shady Sales Practices*

DAVID CAPLOVITZ

Bait Advertising and the Switch Sale

A sizable number of the families had been victimized by "bait" advertising. Responding to advertisements for sewing machines, phonographs, washing machines, and other items offered at unusually low prices, they succumbed to the salesmen's "switch-sale" technique by buying a much more expensive model.

The technique is illustrated by the story of a 26-year-old Negro housewife:

> *I saw a TV ad for a $29 sewing machine,* so I wrote to the company and they sent down a salesman who demonstrated it for me. It shook the whole house, but I wanted to buy it anyway. But he kept saying it would disturb all the neighbors by being so noisy, and *went out to the hall and brought in another model costing $185. . . .*

I actually had to pay $220. He promised if I paid within a certain amount of time I would get $35 back. *But since my husband was out of work, we couldn't pay within the time period,* so I didn't get the refund. . . . *I was taken in by the high-pressure sales talk.*

A middle-aged Puerto Rican husband was victimized by a variant of this racket. Instead of responding to an ad, he received a call from a salesman saying that his

SOURCE. Reprinted with permission of The Macmillan Company from *The Poor Pay More* by David Caplovitz. Copyright © 1967 by The Free Press, a Division of The Macmillan Company.

wife had won a sewing machine:

> He brought the machine to the house. It was worth $25, and we ended up buying another one for $186. A friend of mine bought a similar machine, maybe better than mine, for $90. *They tricked me into buying the machine for $186 on credit. . . .*

Another variant of the "something for nothing" appeal is based on the principle of the "pyramid club." Consumers are promised a refund if they help the salesman find a certain number of customers. One instance, reported by an 18-year-old Negro housewife, involved the added inducement of an outright monetary gift:

> My mother sent the vacuum cleaner salesman here. He said that he would give me $5 just to talk to me. Then he said that if I got him nine more sales I could have the vacuum cleaner free. I wasn't able to find any customers and I can't work the vacuum cleaner with all its attachments. I don't want it and I've stopped making the payments on it.

Here we see an example of the great disparity between the more traditional logic of these consumers and the law of installment buying. Whether or not the consumer wants the merchandise has no bearing on the merchant's right to payment once the contract is signed.

Misrepresentation of Prices

The preceding incidents illustrate various schemes through which low-income families are pressured into buying. Other incidents exhibit another fairly common form of duplicity: the misrepresentation of price particularly in credit transactions. Although the merchant is required by law in New York State to enter both the cash price and the finance charges on the installment contract, some circumvent this law either by not explaining the terms of the contract or by not sending the customer his copy of the contract until some time after the sale is consummated. In several instances we found that the consumer did not learn the full cost of his merchandise until he received the payment coupons some time after the sale. This practice is illustrated by the following typical episodes:

> [41-year-old Puerto Rican husband, welfare family] I was cheated on a TV set I bought. At first the price was supposed to be $220. After I signed the contract I found out that it was really $300. *But then it was too late.*

> [34-year-old Puerto Rican housewife] I was told by the salesman that the credit price for the Hi-Fi set was $299. *When I got the payment book, I found out that I had to pay them $347.*

> [28-year-old Negro housewife] I heard an ad on the radio about a special bargain on washing machines for only $100. After I ordered it and had it installed, I got

a bill for $200. I said I wouldn't pay it and they took it away. *I paid a $50 down-payment, and they never gave it back to me. I'm just glad I did not have to pay the balance....*

Substitution of Goods

Not only are prices misrepresented in the low income market, but so is quality. Some families were sold reconditioned merchandise that had been represented as new, and others received merchandise inferior to that ordered.

The sale of used merchandise as new is of course illegal. Yet some merchants hinted that their competitors engaged in this practice. The following reports indicate that this does indeed happen. A 36-year-old Puerto Rican mother on welfare gave this account:

I bought a TV set from a First Avenue store. *It was a used set which was sold as new.* After seven days it broke down. The store took it back and returned it in two weeks. It broke down again and they took it for thirty days. They brought it back and it broke down one week later. They took it away again and I *asked for a refund because there was a guarantee of ninety days which had not run out. But they wouldn't give me back my $100 or bring me another TV.* I went to the store several times but with no results. . . .

The Anonymity of Credit Transactions

Several families responded to the question about cheating by describing pots-and-pans salesmen who sold them poor-quality merchandise at exorbitant prices. The details of these stories are similar. The salesman shows up either with the goods or with a catalogue. He stresses the unusually low payments, gets the housewife to sign a contract, extracts a small down-payment, and then disappears. Sometime later the family receives a payment book from a finance company and frequently learns only then that the set of pots and pans will cost as much as $60. What is striking about these accounts is the anonymity of the transaction. Several interviewees reported that they tried unsuccessfully to find out the name of the store from which they had bought the merchandise. The high-pressure techniques of these salesmen as well as the theme of anonymity are illustrated in this report by a 30-year-old Puerto Rican husband:

This happened about four or five days after we moved in. My wife was home and a man knocked at the door. He was selling pots and he pressured my wife to look at them. He said that they would cost only $5 a month and that he would leave her a piggy bank so she could save for other things. Then he told her to "sign here," and when all the payments were made she'd get a present. He then asked her if he could just leave the pots for a second while he went downstairs. But since she was signed up he never came back. We got a coupon book and mailed $5 each month to a bank in New Jersey. . . . *I don't know the name of the store but I guess it's somewhere in Fenway, New Jersey. I have no records of it.*

[Another young Puerto Rican husband gave a similar account:] A salesman came around selling aluminum pots and pans. They're not worth a damn. I gave him a dollar down and then the bank sent me a book and I had to send in payments. *Some bank in New Jersey. I tried to find out the store's name, but I couldn't.* The set cost $60—$5 a month for twelve months.

These incidents illustrate the various ways in which merchants take advantage of low-income consumers. They show the high pressure tactics, the substitution of goods, the exorbitant prices and the shoddy merchandise that are commonplace in the low-income market.

32. *Hunger in America*

MARGARET MEAD

In 1939, at the end of the Depression and before the United States was involved in World War II, surveys and investigations revealed that one-third of the people of the United States were "ill clothed, ill housed and ill fed." The onset of World War II complicated the questions of housing and clothing but the national leadership recognized that an undernourished and malnourished population was a weak population, and set about to work to remedy this with the motto "America needs us strong."

A nationwide program was mounted, coordinated and inspired by Dr. M. L. Wilson, Director of the Extension Services of the United States Department of Agriculture, providing for coordination among government agencies concerned with food production, food distribution, food research, and the health of children, expectant mothers, the men in the armed services and industrial workers. Advisory committees and boards of natural and social scientists were organized and financed. Nutritional committees were set up in every state, under the leadership of experienced home economists, competent in the details of choice and preparation of foods, budgeting and planning. The food industries and the vitamin manufacturers were involved in demonstration projects on the use of reinforced foods, greater consumption of milk and balanced diets. The mass media were systematically brought into the program; radio, especially, became a continuing and potent force

SOURCE. Hearings before the Select Committee on Nutrition and Human Needs of the U.S. Senate, Part I, Dec. 17, 18, 19, 1968, 90th Congress.

in promoting better use of foods. The rationing system was so related to regional supplies and regional preferences that it worked in spite of the complexities of size and diversity of the United States. Educational programs reached every level of the population, and nutrition became a value which advertisers incorporated in their appeals, a cause which no one could afford to be against.

At the end of World War II enormous progress had been made. The people with the poorest diets, notably in the Southeast, were eating better than they ever had before; reinforced foods were a commonplace throughout the country; it was almost impossible to find a case of pellagra, once one 'of the characteristic deficiency diseases of the Southeast. Vitamin supplements were widespread. The idea of the seven basic foods developed as a framework for good nutrition had become a guide post in school lunches, group feeding and home planning.

The affluence that followed World War II, with full employment, high wages and an abundance of available food made the picture seem even rosier. By the early 1950's it was possible to say that America's major nutritional problem was over-nutrition. Attention shifted to the problems of overeating, and obscure clinical manifestation of malnutrition.

Uneasy under the accusation that Americans were, in fact, overfed, when such a large part of the world's population was starving, American attention turned resolutely away from the question of malnutrition in the United States. Almost the entire elaborate apparatus of research, education and monitoring of health and home practices disappeared. Where in the 1940's the motive power for better food and better nutritional practices had come from within the Department of Agriculture, so that research and education interacted with programs designed to dispose of surplus commodities or promote the growth and sale of special products, by the 1960's the centers within the U.S.D.A., devoted to the care of the American people, had withered away. The Bureau of Home Economics was abolished. The Farm Security agency, once the center of concern for the subsistence farmer, shrank to a ghost of its former self. The Extension department became increasingly concerned with large scale commercial farming. In other agencies it was the same story. Funds once available for nutrition education in high schools were diverted to physical education. In the universities, nutrition departments turned away from the needs of hungry and undernourished people to bio-chemical research. Departments of home economics fell apart. As Americans so often do, we had made a great effort, had great success, and then we completely lost interest.

Meanwhile, mechanization drove people by the thousands from the unproductive farms into the cities. Those who were left behind and those who migrated fell into deep poverty. The programs once operated in close relationship to the leadership of nutritionists and home economists were now sporadically deployed in response to positive and negative political pressures over the country. School lunches and stamp plans and surplus commodities ceased to be answers to growing hunger and extensive malnutrition. Deficiency diseases and the consequences of malnutrition, a high infant death rate, failure to learn in school, began to appear more and more frequently. But there was no adequate research, no national leadership, hardly any local programs to deal with the growing problems.

It is now estimated that we have almost 10,000,000 Americans who are malnourished, and undernourished, and that many of these are on the edge of slow starvation. Thirty years ago, in the midst of a Great War, we were able to tackle the sorry condition of a third of the nation. Today we seem unable to deal with a twentieth of the nation, in spite of our greatly increased productivity and far greater technical resources.

This has all been lost sight of in the local contests that have gone on in poor counties where the agricultural workers who are no longer needed are being starved out; in the towns and cities where the distributing methods make it intolerably difficult for those in need to use the various federal distribution plans; in the failure of health authorities to recognize nutritional disease—somehow the central issue that people are hungry and sick from malnutrition, that infants and children are being irreversibly damaged, that foods are being synthesized and alloyed in ways dangerous to health has been forgotten.

We need to start over, clear the decks of the accumulated petty attacks and counterattacks within and against the agricultural establishment, which is now too devoted to the production end to be a fitting center for a food and nutrition program that is concerned with people rather than products.

We need to face the simple facts: the American people are less well nourished, as a whole, than they were 10 years ago. Those with the fewest resources and least education, those who live in the worst areas and belong to the most disadvantaged groups, are suffering the most. Their need is urgent. The national need is urgent. Evidence is accumulating of the irreversible damage that is done to the mental ability of children who are malnourished. Our future depends upon the capacities of our people to manage a highly technological and demanding society.

The problem of meeting the food and nutrition needs of the American people is not a production problem. We do not live, as people of many other nations do, on the edge of genuine scarcity. Nor is it a problem of transportation, as in China. Nor is it a problem of profiteering in times of scarcity as in some Asian countries. Our problem is one of distribution alone, how to see that the necessary food, containing, either naturally or by supplementation, the necessary nutrients, reaches all of the American people, whatever their age or sex, their economic status, their race or their location. We need to be sure that the right kind of food, in the right quantities, is available to the people who need it, and that they have the means to buy it, the knowledge of what to choose and how to plan and prepare it. We knew how to do all of these things in 1945; it would take a relatively short time to learn how to do them now.

During these dismal years when our people have grown worse nourished, and hungrier and when research on people's habits and people's needs has all but ground to a halt, there has been one set of advances—in our knowledge and ability to supplement and fortify foods in ways that will produce optimum nutritional effects and optimum acceptability. Experience of food supplementation and fortification has demonstrated that the route to a better nourished population is by way of commercially available nutritious products, cheap enough, plentiful enough, well enough distributed so that they are available to those who need them. Properly distributed foods, reinforced and fortified to meet special situations, locally deficient diets, poor food habits, unbalanced supplies in federal distribution plans, school lunches which bear a disproportionate nutritional load, must be combined with money enough to buy them if this threat of malnutrition is to be removed.

We need a national food and nutrition program now.

33. *The Shape of the Nation's Housing Problems*

The 81st Congress passed the National Housing Act of 1949, calling for "the realization as soon as feasible of the goal of a decent home and a suitable living environment for every American family." In August the 90th Congress in its Housing and Urban Development Act of 1968 reaffirmed this historic national housing goal but found it "has not been fully realized for many of the nation's lower income families."

A study of this Committee estimated the current number of "lower-income families" for whom a "decent home" is still unaffordable (the "noneffective demand" in the U.S. housing market):

About 7.8 million American families—one in every eight—cannot now afford to pay the market price for standard housing that would cost no more than 20 percent of their total incomes. (The average ratio of housing costs to gross income for the total population is 15 percent.)

About half of these 7.8 million families are surviving on less that $3,000 a year—the Federal poverty level.

The study projected the size of this gap 10 years from now, assuming no marked changes in current economic trends, national policies and priorities among Federal

SOURCE. From *Report of the President's Committee on Urban Housing, A Decent Home,* 1968.

programs. The projection showed that the prevalence of poverty can be expected to decline only slightly:

In 1978, about 7.5 million families—1 in every 10—would still be unable to afford standard housing. . . .

Characteristics of House-Poor Families

Taking the 1960 U.S. Census and other available data as sources, TEMPO's study group projected the demographic characteristics of 1978's families lacking sufficient income to afford standard housing:

About 70 percent will be white.

About one in four nonwhite families will need housing assistance, compared to 1 in 12 white families.

About half the nonwhite families will be living in the nation's central cities.

According to 1960 census statistics, nonwhites—regardless of income—must earn one-third more than whites in order to afford standard housing (based on allocation of 20 percent of earnings for mortgage payments or rent).

After projecting the characteristics of age and family size, TEMPO estimated these conclusions:

Among the urban white families too poor to afford decent housing in 1978, about half will be elderly (head of the household 65-years-old or more).

Among nonwhite urban families needing housing assistance, only 27 percent will be elderly.

Among needy urban white families, about 70 percent will be small households of one or two persons.

Among nonwhite families, only 43 percent will consist of one or two persons.

Housing Conditions in the United States

TEMPO's estimates of the characteristics and conditions of the nation's total housing inventory suggest a fuller picture. There are about 66 million housing units and 60 million households.

Although there appear to be more than enough rooftops:

An estimated 6.7 million occupied units are substandard dwellings—4 million lacking indoor plumbing and 2.7 million in dilapidated condition.

6.1 million units (both standard and substandard) are overcrowded with more than one person per room.

Among the six million vacant units, only about two million are in standard condition and available for occupancy—the nation's lowest available vacancy rate since 1958.

These estimates suggest a growing shortage of decent housing, not only for lower-income families but for the entire population. TEMPO's projections bear out this assumption. In order to provide enough standard housing for the entire population by 1978, TEMPO estimates the American economy will need to:

Build 13.4 million units for new, young families forming during the decade ahead.

Replace or rehabilitate 8.7 million units that will deteriorate into substandard conditions.

Replace three million standard units that will be either accidentally destroyed or purposefully demolished for non-residential land reuses.

Build 1.6 million units to allow for enough vacancies for our increasingly mobile population.

Based on these and other available projections of the nation's housing needs, this Committee reached a fundamental conclusion: there are two distinct and definable but inseparably interdependent housing problems:

There is an immediate and critical social need for millions of decent dwellings to shelter the nation's lower-income families.

Overlying this need is one raising an unprecedented and challenging production problem. The nation is heading toward a serious shortage of housing for the total population, unless production is sharply increased.

These two problems—housing needs of the poor and total national housing needs—are parts of the same equation. They must be tackled together. So long as there is a severe shortage of housing among all income levels, the goal of meeting the housing needs of the poor will not only be more difficult but in this Committee's judgment, it is also unlikely that it will be politically, socially and economically attainable.

We recommended that the nation commit itself to a goal of producing at least 26 million new and rehabilitated housing units by 1978, including six to eight million Federally subsidized dwellings for families in need of housing assistance.

The U.S. Housing Market and Public Policies

Americans spend about $50 billion a year to buy, rent, and maintain our dwellings, and about another $50 billion on utilities, furniture, and other housing expenses. Residential land and structures represent about a third of our total national wealth. More than a quarter of new annual capital investment goes into all the elements that constitute the broadly defined housing industry.

Yet more than 12 percent of American families cannot afford decent housing and at least 10 percent of the nation's existing shelters are in substandard condition. This gap may imply some gross inefficiency in the American housing market. To the contrary, the Committee has found that such is not the case.

When consumers create an effective demand, the U.S. homebuilding industry and housing market have proven their capabilities for producing a quality product and delivering it at reasonable prices. The staff's comparative analyses of U.S. and foreign housing shows that the prevailing standards of American housing generally equal or surpass housing standards in other nations. Moreover, U.S. consumer price indexes point up that housing and all other items, excepting sharply rising medical care costs, rose roughly in line from 1950 to 1960, after which time all other consumer prices began climbing at a faster rate than housing costs.

A chart prepared by the staff dissects the housing delivery process into four distinct phases: preparation, production, distribution and service. Each phase requires inputs from 6 to 14 different sources, from architects to zoning officials, and each operates within the constraints set up by 5 to 11 separate and different sources for impediments and restrictions. In total, there are 23 major public and private direct participants in the housing production process (some involved in more than one phase) and 17 major public and private sources for laws, rules and practices that restrict and influence the process practically every step of the way.

The Committee concluded that within these sets of existing characteristics and constraints, housing producers operate with greater efficiency and response to innovations than commonly thought. The builder, however, can directly influence only a relatively small portion of housing costs.

The following tables taken from a consultant's report (McGraw-Hill Information Systems' Technical Report) show the cost components in building and occupying housing, and demonstrate that the real costs for housing are spread among more ingredients than the cost for constructing the dwelling itself.

After analyzing the work of our consultants and staff, the Committee reached these major conclusions regarding the cost of housing:

Even with implementation of effective policies to squeeze out every practically attainable cost reduction, we can realistically expect a reduction in monthly housing costs of only about 10 percent in the foreseeable years ahead.

Although a 10 percent reduction in consumer's housing costs would save billions of dollars in resources annually, it would *not* be enough to bring new standard housing within economic reach of lower-income families.

Private enterprise, alone, cannot solve the nation's problems of housing the poor.

Federal housing assistance remains essential for lower-income families.

Rough Breakdown of Initial Development and Construction Costs

	Conventional single-family unit (percent)	Elevator apartment unit (percent)
Developed land	25	13
Materials	36	38
On-site labor	19	22
Overhead and profit...........	14	15
Miscellaneous.................	6	12
	100	100

Rough Breakdown of Monthly Occupancy Cost of Three Kinds of Housing

	Conventional single-family home (percent)	Mobile home (percent)	Elevator unit (percent)
Debt retirement (mortgage payment).................	53	55	42
Site rent......................................		28	....
Taxes......................	26	4	14
Utilities	16	11	9
Maintenance and repair	5	2	6
Admin. and similar costs			13
Vacancies, bad debts, and profit			16
Total	100	100	100

Response of the Marketing System to Those Problems:

A. Military Dominance and Technology's By-Products

34. *Nixon's Iron Curtain on the Cost of the War*

Nixon's new budget takes secrecy in government two steps beyond LBJ. Nixon has blacked out the cost of the war in Vietnam and he has also blacked out military spending from his budgetary projections for the next four years. "A budget," Nixon said in his message, "must be a blueprint for the future." In his blueprint these two main parts are missing. "In the past," Nixon said about his new four-year projections, "the Federal government has been unwilling to pull all the pieces together and present the results of projecting Government finances into the future." He said this was essential for "an enlightened discussion of public policies even though precise figures are, of course, impossible." Why then omit expenditures which eat up more than half the general revenues of the government?

About ten days before the budget was released the Pentagon information office was still telling reporters that the cost of the war during the next fiscal year would be about $17 billion. When Secretary Laird first gave out this figure last October, he said this would mean a $13 billion saving over the $30 billion the war cost in fiscal '69, its peak. Total military costs in '69 ("defense by function") were $81.2 billion. But total military costs budgeted for fiscal '71, instead of being $13 billion less than that (or $68.2 billion) are $73.5 billion, or only $7.7 billion less. This means that non-Vietnam military spending is *up* by $5.3 billion. This *increase* in non-Vietnam military spending is itself more than twice as large as total outlays

SOURCE. From *I. F. Stone's Bi-Weekly,* Vol. XVIII No. 4, Feb. 23, 1970. Reprinted by permission.

budgeted for natural resources ($2.5 billion) including air and water despite all Nixon's "now or never" rhetoric on pollution.

No Austerity On Strategic Arms

This may understate the realities. Proxmire in a Senate speech Feb. 10 estimated that the Pentagon "has heisted $10 billion of the peace dividend." He takes into account not only Laird's predicted cut in Vietnam war costs but his announcement last Oct. 16 that henceforth the Pentagon would plan its level of forces for one major and one minor wars instead of two major and one minor wars as it has since the Kennedy-McNamara period. Proxmire said the money thus saved is going to strategic hardware, including the second phase of the ABM, conversion of Polaris into the MIRVed Poseidon, on which the overruns are now $3 billion; into MIRVed Minuteman III, where the overruns are also about $3 billion; into the Navy, which is getting $2.6 billion to modernize the fleet, an increase of $1 billion over 1967-69 expenditures; and into a huge AWACS, over-the-horizon warning system. "Some $18 billion has already been spent for SAGE and AWACS," Proxmire said of these two anti-bomber systems, "even though the Russians have no modern intercontinental bomber. These huge funds were expended to meet a non-existent threat." This is hardly austere military budgeting.

This brings me to the related blackout the Nixon administration is imposing on military spending and planning. "We have learned," Nixon said in the economic report, "that 1-year planning leads to almost as much confusion as no planning at all." He said that was why he was opening up the books, and making long-range projects "that will enable the people to discuss their choices more effectively." He published a four year projection which shows, among other things, that Nixon's new civilian initiatives including welfare and pollution will go up from $3 billion in the first year to $18 billion in the fourth. Yet there are no similar projections on the military side.

How can Nixon say that he is making long-range 4-year projections available to "enable the people to discuss their choices more effectively" when the military side of these projections—much the biggest single share—is hidden from them? "We must become increasingly aware," Nixon also said in the Budget Message, "that small decisions today often lead to large cash outlays in the future." Of no part of the budget is this more resoundingly true than the military sector. A speech by Congressman Reuss in Milwaukee Feb. 10 provided a swift glimpse of such "small decisions" and the large cash outlays they entail. "There is a $1.5 billion item for the ABM," Reuss said of the new budget, "expected ultimately to cost anywhere from $10 to $50 billion. There is $87 million for AWACS, a new airborne radar system with an ultimate $15 billion price tag. There is almost a billion dollars for continued deployment of the Navy's new F-14 fighter plane, with an expected total program cost of up to $36 billion. There is $370 million in the budget for a start on the F-15, the Air Force's new superiority jet fighter. Costs of this program are expected to exceed $25 billion." These programs impose a heavy mortgage on future budgets, but these are among the military commitments blacked out.

The budget presentation is shot through with deceit. "For the first time in two full decades," Nixon boasted in the message, "the Federal government will spend more money on human resource programs than on national defense." This was illustrated with a pie chart showing 41 cents of the budget dollar going to human resources and only 36 cents to national defense. But if the government's huge social security and other trust fund receipts are deducted, we can see that the military spends 53 cents of every dollar of the general revenues.

35. *Needed: New Rules for Industrial Managers* WILLIAM C. ENGS

External Effects and Residuals

Production and consumption in a highly industrialized society have side effects, or as the economists call them, "externalities" or "external effects."

> External effects may be said to arise when relevant effects on production or welfare go wholly or partially unpriced. Being outside the price system such external effects are sometimes looked upon as byproducts, wanted or unwanted, of other people's activities that immediately or indirectly affect the welfare of other individuals. (Mishan, 1965)

There are many kinds of external effects. External effects can be beneficial—the liquor store which makes its waste cartons available to the public; or they can be detrimental—the soot and smoke produced when waste cartons are incinerated by a store and the soot and smoke is experienced by neighboring property owners. This article will be concerned with the latter, undesirable external effects.

Unwanted external effects may be classified according to the stage of the production-consumption process in which they occur. A basic breakdown of external effects includes the following categories:

(a) *Primary or extractive* resulting from production of raw materials, for example, oil contamination of the Santa Barbara Channel of California associated with oil drilling operations.

(b) Production or processing resulting from manufacturing, for example, odor associated with Kraft process paper mills.

(c) *Consumption* resulting from a consumer's use of a product, for example, smog resulting from the use of automobiles and gasoline. A consumer's use of *services* can also be considered to be part of this category. For example, a person who uses jet air travel is contributing to a noise effect which must be borne involuntarily by others.

Here I will focus on the second category of external effects—production, i.e., those resulting from manufacturing.

There is a variety of undesirable external effects which could be produced by manufacturing, such as noise, odor, urban blight, smoke, and solid and liquid wastes. All of these are serious and deserve detailed study. This report will be concerned with the *type* of external effect which has *residuals*. According to Ayres and Kneese this type of external effect is different from the others because residual matter is produced and dispersed in the environment, and they point out that "technological means for purifying one or another type of waste discharge *do not destroy the residuals but only alter their form*" (italics mine). Ayres and Kneese critique economic theory by stating:

> . . . we persist in referring to the final consumption of goods as though material objects such as fuels, materials, and finished goods somehow disappeared in the void—a practice which was comparatively harmless so long as air and water were almost literally free goods. Of course, residuals from both the production and consumption processes remain and they usually render disservices (like killing fish, increasing the difficulty of water treatment, reducing public health, soiling and deteriorating buildings, etc.) rather than services.

By now we are all familiar with the terms "air pollution" and "water pollution," but, except for the fact that we know these forms of pollution are undesirable, we know little about what is involved. Traditionally, economists have treated air and water as "free goods," i.e., resources which one could use without payment, but increased population and economic development have made it increasingly apparent that air and water are *finite* resources and as the capacity of those resources to dilute and chemically degrade waste products is approached, the resource becomes valuable, by some measure. This happens because in the long run (1) the residuals persist and (2) the environment is a closed system. In the short run, the environment has definite carrying capacities at any time: as long as the capacity of air or water to dilute or disperse is not exceeded, conditions are not too bad; but when exceeded, we have serious "pollution" which may immediately threaten life.

In the long run, there is an accumulation of residuals in the environment whether or not air or water is used as a diffuser, degrader or pipeline. All matter will eventually reside somewhere. Boulding says it is useful to differentiate between entropic processes which diffuse concentrated material (iron ore is mined, manufactured into steel and iron and eventually diffused in innumerable dumps and fragments of rust over the surface of the earth); and anti-entropic processes which concentrate diffused material (such as the Dow process, which concentrates the metal magnesium from the limitable resource of the sea). The entropic process, which is now prevalent, can not go on forever. Application of space technology, closed system concepts are needed:

> ... it is quite possible to visualize an earth of the future which has a stable closed system technology dependent upon the atmosphere and the sea as the basic resources from which diffused elements are concentrated and to which concentrations are eventually returned. Man will then be independent of geological capital.

The Common Property Concept

The distinction between private and public, or common, property rights has important implications for the understanding of how the external effects problems have grown over the years and why no one is really effectively able to deal with them.

As stated earlier, traditionally, air and water were considered to be "free goods," and everyone had a common right to use them without restriction.

In order to show what is happening to air and water resources, Garrett Hardin (1968) has described what happened to land, in a scenario called "the tragedy of the commons," based on life in old England. He tells about a pasture open to all. Hardin says that each owner of cattle would ask himself what would be the utility to himself of adding one more animal to his herd. After considering the positive component of the utility, his gain in income and the negative component, the overgrazing effect, which would be shared by all herdsmen, he finds that the positive component greatly outweighs the negative component.

> ... the rational herdsman concludes that the only sensible course for him to pursue is to add another animal to his herd. And another; and another. ... But this is the conclusion reached by every rational herdsman sharing a commons. Therein is the tragedy. Each man is locked into a system that compels him to increase his herd without limit—in a world that is limited. Ruin is the destination toward which all men rush, each pursuing his own best interest in a society that believes in the freedom of the commons. Freedom in a commons brings ruin to all.

The commons analogy is valid in the modern world and can be applied to other kinds of "commons," air and water resources as well as to land resources. External effects are quantitatively negligible in a low-population or economically underdeveloped setting, but they become progressively more important as the population rises and the level of output increases (i.e., as the natural reservoirs of dilution and assimilative capacity become exhausted). As long as rational man finds that his share of the cost of the wastes he discharges into the commons is less than the cost of purifying, treating, etc., before releasing them, he will likely elect to follow the lower cost alternative.

In the case of the common pasture, the problem can be solved by fencing and thereby limiting the use of land to one individual or a group who will conserve the resource. There is no way to fence off air and water resources, nor is there any way that these can be controlled or owned in the same sense that a government may control or own a road system. Since these resources move around from one area to another they create special problems not present when considering land. When common property is available for use on a no rule basis, so that it may be freely used by anyone for any purpose at any time, it will be overused and, hence deteriorate, just as the common pasture did which was owned by everybody—and nobody. In Dales' opinion,

> Air and water in this country, and in most other countries, have been treated as an unrestricted common property; so long as they are so treated, air and water pollution will increase and the physical condition of our air and water assets will continue to deteriorate.

Individual Decisions and Aggregate Results

Given the "commons view" of air and water ownership and the production process, external effects have not been a problem for private decision-makers. Therefore the true costs of the enterprise are not borne by industrial organization. The rationale of an organization is that its contribution is small compared to the aggregate effect, and being so insignificant, the organization is making only a small contribution to the total problem. Of course all organizations will use the same rationalization, and, on that basis, all will be able to continue to justify what they are doing.

Since the rationale for organizational decision-making appears to be primarily economic with first priority given to survival of the organization and not to survival of human beings, it would seem that those who say that external costs should be internalized have an interesting suggestion.

Conclusions

We are now beginning to observe negative aspects of economic growth and technological progress, but economists continue to act as though the quantitatively measured indicators, "production" and "consumption," are in themselves adequate indicators of economic success. But, if we accept and use as a starting point the concept of our planet as a closed system, economic principles need be made compatible with this concept.

Industrial organizations continue to act as though they were operating in an open system in which unlimited growth and technological progress is possible, and in which any negative effects which are generated will be taken care of by the public sector.

Since it is unlikely that environmental quality can be maintained in the face of the aggregate of undesirable external effects produced as the exports of organizations, some kind of organizational adaptation is going to be necessary.

That necessary adaptation has not yet occurred.

36. *Industry Starts the Big Cleanup*

JOHN DAVENPORT

The disagreeable smell of hydrogen sulphide comes wafting through the magnificent stands of fir and cedar as a kind of early warning signal. Minutes later the highway leading up the northern shore of the Columbia River from Portland tips over a rise, and one looks down on a fortress-like industrial complex, which is wreathed in billowing clouds of steam and vapors worthy of Dante's *Inferno*. This is the great paper mill of the Crown Zellerbach Corp. at Camas, Washington. For years the mill's smoking stacks and chimneys have spelled jobs, opportunity, and prosperity for a land that a century and a half ago was wilderness—the chosen habitat of the Chinook Indians. Today that historic era of pioneering is taken more or less for granted. The big question is how and when Crown Zellerbach can produce paper without obscuring the view of distant Mount Hood, or disturbing the life of the Columbia River salmon, or affronting the nostrils of tourists, not to mention the citizens of this part of the Columbia basin.

This is a task that Crown Zellerbach is taking seriously, spurred on by multiplying state laws as well as by desire to protect its own corporate reputation as a good neighbor. "We have a big job to do, no question," says Francis Boylon, president and chief executive officer. If you count it up, Crown Zellerbach is doing quite a bit. Two years ago the company completed a $3-million settling basin on

SOURCE. Reprinted from the February 1970 issue of *Fortune* Magazine. This article has appeared in a book entitled *The Environment: A National Mission for the Seventies,* published by Harper and Row.

Lady Island, off the Camas waterfront, which screens some 40 million gallons of water per day of their worst woody effluent. Now it is breaking ground for a new $15-million magnefite pulping system, which will recirculate chemicals coming from its sulphite mill. Thereafter it will probably begin to revamp its kraft paper facilities at Camas to reduce their noxious sulphide odor—an objective already attained at its new mill at Waunak eighty miles down the Columbia, and at its older Port Townsend plant on Puget Sound. In other areas of the country, notably at Bogalusa, Louisiana, Crown Zellerbach still has a considerable cleanup job to do. Yet counting in experimental work now in progress, the company is responding to a new kind of industrial challenge.

In doing so, Crown Zellerbach is representative of a much broader trend. In the Northwest there is growing sentiment that just as the lumber industry, after ghastly trial and error, learned how to use the forests without despoiling them, so the paper industry and others can meet the needs of an affluent society without drowning it in effluents. Throughout the nation, similar sentiments have been emanating from the leaders of the steel industry, the chemical industry, and public utilities. Last year industrial spending to clean up the air and the water, on conservative estimates, forged past the $1-billion mark. Meanwhile the manufacture of antipollution equipment—giant electrostatic precipitators for reducing dust and smoke, "scrubbers" for catching noxious gases, and plain old-fashioned valves and gates for controlling polluted water—has become a burgeoning industry in its own right. Companies like Research-Cottrell, Wheelabrator, Zurn Industries, and others have been engaging the attention of Wall Street analysts. On the same day that noted economists were predicting a "serious recession" for the economy as a whole, shares of the antipollution companies led the stock market upward.

"Ideas Have Their Time in History"

All this is an immensely healthy development, because if the U.S. is to achieve a cleaner environment in the Seventies, industry has a critical role to play. Industry is only one contributor to pollution, but it is also the repository of the research and techniques that can bring pollution under control. "Technology—not regulations or good intentions or rhetoric—can preserve our clean water," says David D. Dominick, commissioner for the Federal Water Pollution Control Administration of the Department of the Interior. "Industrial leadership and political leadership must carry on the battle together."

Yet the battle is a curious and complicated one, and in defining industry's job it pays to maintain a sense of perspective and realism. "Ideas have their time in history," says one leading businessman, "and I don't think we should loose our screws about this thing." Analysis shows that the No. 1 polluter of the atmosphere is not the smoking factory or steaming chemical plant but the ubiquitous automobile, which at long last Detroit is trying to equip with antipollution devices whose costs will be borne by the consumer. When it comes to pollution of lakes and rivers, business is by no means the sole offender. Municipalities have been notably laggard in coping with their own raw sewage, and the effluents of industry that they have contracted to handle. If the shad find life uncomfortable in the Delaware River, it is not just because Sun Oil, Scott Paper, and Du Pont discharge wastes into that waterway, but because the citizens of Philadelphia and other cities have preferred all too often to complain about the pollution of the environment, rather than voting the necessary bond issues.

More important, it is unrealistic to think that business "leadership," however well intentioned, can by itself clean up the environment without clear guidelines from government, whose responsibility is to set the framework in which competitive enterprise operates.

When a businessman invests in new equipment he at least knows that the resulting product will be paid for by the consumer, and he hopes it will yield a profit. But when he commits money to bettering the environment, he shoulders, on the near term at least, a dead cost; unless other companies follow suit he will find himself at a competitive disadvantage. This explains why many businessmen, who normally might be opposed to government regulations, have welcomed the Water Quality Act of 1965 and the Air Quality Act of 1967 as at least a beginning effort at setting national standards. Says Charles B. McCoy, president of Du Pont: "Everybody would be delighted if Du Pont or some other company could report that it has found a way to turn the expense of pollution control into an asset." With the present state of technology, he concludes, that just isn't possible.

The Rising Curve

Once these elementals are understood, industry's performance is seen to be neither as bad as sometimes made out nor as good as it should be. With respect to cleansing waste water, industry's expenditures have risen from about $45 million in 1952 to an annual current rate of about $600 million. Expenditures for protecting the atmosphere are somewhat smaller. But these figures do not reflect the full burden that many corporations are assuming. In many cases antipollution devices simply cannot be clamped on to existing facilities; instead whole plants must be redesigned with new productive equipment replacing old.

In the Eye of the Housewife

Forced to operate close to the great metropolitan centers, and an obvious target for every housewife who glances out her window, the electric-power companies have moved to reduce pollution. Increasingly they have installed electrostatic precipitators, cyclonic collectors, and wet scrubbers to reduce emission of particulates, and in new plants such installations are now considered routine. Old and middle-aged plants cannot be abandoned, given recurrent power shortages and the danger of overloading and blackouts, which enrage the public even more than emission of soot and smoke.

Regulation is the only answer, and it is having its effect.

Increasingly the power companies find that air-pollution control authorities in Washington and at the municipal level are increasing their costs, in a way that will force the raising of rates. State power commissions are committed to holding rates down. Caught in the middle, utilities have shown considerable ingenuity in shaving operating expenses. Southern California Edison and Arizona Public Service, plus smaller companies, formed a consortium to share the cost of pollution-control equipment at a huge generating station in New Mexico. Advances in technology are also in evidence. Kansas Power & Light Co. has shown that emissions of sulphur dioxide can be licked even in an old plant by a process devised by Combustion Engineering. Working closely with Pennsylvania Electric and later with Metropolitan Edison, the Monsanto Co. has developed a catalytic oxidation system that turns SO_2 into useful sulphuric acid. The cat-ox equipment is expensive, but sale of sulphuric acid can help in amortizing costs. As Monsanto salesmen are fond of pointing out to utilities, Monsanto can help to market this all-purpose byproduct.

"Closest to Hell"

A breakthrough in curbing sulphur dioxide would not only help the utilities, but also might rescue the steel industry from mounting public criticism. Oxides of sulphur are emitted in large quantities from steel's coking ovens, and are an old irritant in many a steel town. At its old Clairton works outside of Pittsburgh, U.S. Steel has turned to a cryogenic process that recovers some sixty tons of sulphur daily from material that used to go up the flue. Despite this reduction, the atmosphere around Clairton is far from savory, and last April an Allegheny County commissioner complained that Clairton "is the closest to hell I've ever been."

The steel industry also emits yellowish dust from its open hearths, and pollutes water with acid wastes from pickling steel as well as other operations. On one estimate the industry uses eight billion gallons of water per day for cooling and other purposes. Despite progress, it still has a considerable distance to go to obtain a clean bill of health. Pittsburgh's famous Golden Triangle is a kind of island rising from the polluted Allegheny and Monongahela rivers. Still worse is the condition of the Cuyahoga River, which snakes down into Lake Erie at Cleveland. Because of oil slicks and other contaminants, it is known as the "only body of water in North America that is considered a fire hazard."

Yet great and substantial changes are going on, and the lumbering steel giant is bestirring itself.

Technological change is on the march, notably in the matter of replacement of the open-hearth process by basic oxygen furnaces. As these are installed, precipitators, scrubbers, and water-treating facilities go with them. As of today, about 50 percent of all steel is produced by this process, and the conversion is bound to continue to meet competition at home, as well as from Europe and from Japan.

In this instance technological innovation, which conservationists often blame for pollution, actually help to lessen it. The trouble in steel and metalworking generally is that old plants cannot be torn down overnight. Small and marginal companies lack the resources and the cash flow to keep up with multiplying regulation. A case in point is the financial condition of gray-iron foundries, which are usually small independent shops with comparably small resources. "If you apply the same regulations to them as to steel," ruminates one expert, "three-quarters of them would simply go out of business tomorrow."

That would also have been true in the early days of oil. Initially refineries were spouting kettles of pollution, and had modern standards been applied to John D. Rockefeller's first famous still in Cleveland it too would have ignominiously folded to the discomfort of today's householder who might still be periodically rushing down to the basement to stoke his furnace with smoky coal. The thrust of technology and the rise of the great integrated oil company have changed all that. The oil industry may be held indirectly accountable for the automobile, which is the largest polluter of the atmosphere, but thanks to enormous expenditures— running last year to over $300 million—it has made an impressive start in cleaning up its refining operations.

Ducks on the Pond and Gulls on the Beach

In the San Francisco Bay area, for instance, Standard Oil (New Jersey) has loaded its new refinery at Benicia with the latest controls and for good measure has given it an aesthetic exterior. More remarkable has been the success of Standard of California in renovating its Richmond refinery, which nestles close to the city. The original installations here were made as far back as 1902 with little thought of the expansion needs of the future or the problems of contamination. Yet step by step, and often by small little-noticed improvements, the company has more than met required standards by use of precipitators; by extracting hydrogen sulphide from its refinery gases *before* they are reused for combustion (and selling it to a nearby chemical company); by waging unrelenting war on oil leakages; and by bulldozing out large oxidation basins where bacteria work on organic wastes and render them harmless before the water is swirled back to the sea. As if to reassure that stern conservationist, the National Audubon Society, lagoons beneath the cracking towers are the favored resting place of all manner of wildlife—gulls, avocets, godwits, curlews, and ducks.

Yet live ducks on San Francisco Bay will not quite make up for the dead gulls that strewed the beaches of Santa Barbara last year, as the result of the miscarriage of an offshore drilling operation by Union Oil Co. The great California oil spill has tarnished the industry's reputation and is all the more exasperating to many oil executives because in their opinion it was foreseeable and preventable. They point out that thousands of wells have been sunk off the California and Gulf coasts without mishap. Union Oil, it is felt, stretched the rules of the game by not sinking a well casing deep enough in a notably unstable geologic area; and the fact that it had permission to do so from the federal government doesn't mend matters. Clearly, individual companies will have to tighten up on their own drilling practices if they want to continue to exploit vital reserves. They will also have to cope with tanker spillage and with the threat of disasters such as the one that overtook the *Torrey Canyon* off the British Isles—a threat that grows with every increase in the size of tankers. Having made a start on cleaning up its refineries, oil faces a new challenge in production and transportation.

Big utility, steel, and oil companies such as we have been considering will for the most part continue to treat their own effluents. But food-processing companies, and thousands of small miscellaneous manufacturing firms, are already making large use of municipal water-treating plants. In 1968 about 15 percent of the waste water thrown off by all manufacturing establishments was sluiced into the public sewers of cities and smaller towns, and some 40 percent of the wastes handled by municipalities was industrial in origin.

Who's Paying the Bill?

Far from decrying this private use of public facilities, many engineers believe that it makes sound economic sense if full user charges are exacted. In some areas, notably California, municipal authorities have insisted that smaller factories use their water-treating plants on the grounds that this gives government real control over pollution. What is troubling is that the municipalities, even when duly compensated for handling industry's wastes, have been lagging behind in meeting their growing responsibilities.

Here, calculations made by the Interior Department are revealing. On one set of estimates the Federal Water Pollution Control Administration figures that between 1970 and 1974 industry must invest an additional $3 billion to take care of water effluents treated in its own plants. Since industrial investment for this purpose is now running to about $600 million per year, industry seems to be just about on target. By contrast, municipalities will have to invest some $10 billion in the same period to take care of rising population and industrial needs. But at present such investment is running to only about $1 billion per year or half of the total amount required annually.

This lag illustrates the fact that while almost everybody wants cleaner water as well as a cleaner atmosphere, there is much less acceptance of the fact that costs must be borne in one way or another. Industry can, and no doubt will, pass on its added costs through higher prices. It can also be helped by special treatment when it comes to amortization of equipment. But in the public sector the need for higher spending and higher taxes is inescapable. Yet the federal government has been most remiss. Washington has been very free with over-all antipollution legislation. It has been skinflint when it comes to voting the hard appropriations for the legislation's implementation.

B. *Human Injustice*

37. *The Marketer in the Ghetto*

ROY ALEXANDER

In May, 1968, Leonard Sucsy—then a 29-year-old marketing executive—visited New York's Spanish Harlem for the first time. His purpose: to build a low-income housing project. Sucsy lacked both real estate and social work experience.

He did have an untested hypothesis: "Business can help solve social problems—and return a profit to stockholders—at the same time."

He proved the point and in so doing wrote a new chapter in social-economic history.

Sucsy turned an old parking lot into a new apartment house. He moved in 66 families. The result: the first turnkey public housing project in New York. He completed it in 13 months, vs. the 44-month norm via the New York Housing Authority—at 10% less cost. He turned a 3.5% profit.

Winning ushered in a new era in business-social interaction. Sucsy shook The Ghetto. He also surprised The Establishment. Neither will ever be quite the same again. Nor will Sucsy.

New York-born Leonard Graham Sucsy comes by business naturally. His father (a banker) encouraged him to study economics at Denison University in Ohio. He soon changed direction.

"As an economics major," he relates, "I became aware of marketing as the dynamic heart of business. I wanted to be where the action was."

SOURCE. From *Industrial Marketing*, October, 1969, copyright 1969 by Crain Communications Inc., Chicago, Illinois.

While in college, Sucsy worked summers in marketing departments of Dow Chemical and States Marine Lines. He studied French civilization at the Sorbonne. As a U.S. Naval officer, he held top-secret clearance. He got an MBA from Harvard Business School.

In 1967, Sucsy joined American Standard, New York, as assistant to Victor P. Buell, marketing vice-president. By the following spring Sucsy had started a traditional climb up the ladder. Then everything shifted.

"How would you like a completely different kind of job?" Buell asked him. "We're thinking about a joint venture with Celanese Corp. We want to build housing in the Ghetto—at a profit. Want to head up this project?"

Sucsy asked two questions. Would the parent firms really back up this venture? How deep was this commitment? One convincing answer: Buell already had an option on a housing site. Besides, he promised Sucsy a free hand.

In May, 1968, Sucsy gave Buell his answer: yes.

Buell arranged for the incorporation of a joint-venture firm—called Construction for Progress Inc. As over-all advisor on construction, the joint venture added the know-how of William Lyon Homes, Inc., Newport Beach, Calif., an American Standard subsidiary.

Sucsy was named CFP executive vice-president and general manager. In career-building, Sucsy had chosen the high-risk, high-gain route.

On his new job, Leonard Sucsy inherited an option—period. Everything else was theory. From May to October, 1968, he retained architects and contractors, arranged a loan from Chase Manhattan Bank, hammered dozens of East Harlem community groups into agreement. In October, 1968, construction crews broke ground.

In May this year Construction for Progress sold the building to New York City Housing Authority at a profit. Tenants moved in shortly thereafter.

This bare-bones narrative over-simplifies greatly the precedent-setting achievement. How did it all happen? And why?

In 1965, Columbia University created the Urban Action and Experiment Program. Harold Bell, professor of architecture, was named director. In bettering the urban condition, Bell found much government and community group activity—but little business participation.

Business know-how, he reasoned, was the missing leg of a three-legged stool. Money contributions, alone, wouldn't do: management expertise was missing. How could Bell stimulate active business participation in urban problems?

In 1967, Bell attacked the problem frontally. He called a colloquium. He invited major corporations, and delegates from 30 companies attended. Bell explained:

"For the most part, U.S. business had expressed deep interest in social good. Management realizes the nation faces problems and that we must solve them. Business also realizes obligations to stockholders. At this meeting, we are seeking a practical way to meet these dual obligations."

When the meeting broke into discussion groups, William A. Bartel, communications and merchandising vice-president of Celanese, approached Bell.

"Celanese wants to do something meaningful. Not just tokenism," Bartel told Bell. "How can we get started?"

Had Bartel talked with Victor Buell at American Standard? No.

"Well, you should," said Bell. "American Standard is thinking along the same lines. Actual housing construction is a real possibility, they feel."

Bell set up a meeting. Buell and Bartel agreed to form a joint venture. Bell volunteered to act as consultant. To prime the pump, Bell selected a possible site in El Barrio (Spanish Harlem) at 111th St. and First Ave. He put it under option.

"We need a good man to operate this firm on a full-time basis," Buell told Bartel. "I hate to lose Leonard Sucsy even to this excellent cause. But I'll see if he wants the job."

Soon Sucsy was setting up a Construction for Progress office in the American Standard building.

If social service was the goal, Spanish Harlem was an excellent locus for it. East Harlem packs 120,000 people between 95th and 125th Sts., Fifth Ave. and the East River. This Manhattan community—60% Puerto Rican, 35% Black—is probably the most densely populated area in the United States.

On housing need—if on few other points—community groups agree The East Harlem Real Great Society, a community action group, has labeled 50% of East Harlem housing as "deteriorating" and 14% as "dilapidated." Moveover, only 12 new buildings had been erected in Harlem in the last decade.

And, of course, New York's overall housing need is marked. The city's waiting list for public housing is rising steadily—up 11% last year alone.

Statistically, then, the need was enormous. Subjectively, it comes across even stronger. On Leonard Sucsy's first visit to the housing site, he found a land of contrasts. To the north, he saw 1960s-type high-rise apartments built by the city. Structures on three sides, however, were vintage 1930s—and earlier. Broken windows. Cracked and faded paint. Sagging foundations. By the number of children playing outside Sucsy suspected ten to 12 families lived in some of the smaller brownstones.

His inaugural site in hand, Sucsy came to a fork in the road. Should Construction for Progress build and manage the apartments? Or build to sell?

Sucsy first examined the market. A full 70% of East Harlem families were rated "poverty-level" by the U.S. government. This 70% was the biggest market and the greatest need. And since the New York City Housing Authority operated a building acquisition program, Sucsy clearly looked to NYCHA as his best prospective customer.

He also investigated a Federal program called Turnkey. He ended up coupling these two programs together—with a unique variation of his own.

Technically, the government's Turnkey program is designed to encourage private-sector building. Under the program a local housing authority reviews plans, then gives the developer a firm commitment at a specific price before construction. To finance the project, the local authority gets U.S. Housing & Urban Development's Housing Assistance Authority permission to float bonds. Debt service is covered by an annual contributions contract from HUD's HAA.

[But] traditional Turnkey would not work for CFP. Here's why: Wicks Law, a New York State housing statute, requires that Housing Authority construction contracts exceeding $25,000 be let on a sealed bid basis.

Furthermore, the law states, bids must provide separate specifications for plumbing and gas fitting; for heat, hot water, cooling, and air conditioning; and for wiring and lighting.

"These requirements prevented CFP from entering into a firm contract," Sucsy said. "Wicks Law eliminated the possibility of cost savings through efficient management. As a result, costs—and time span—would have been increased considerably."

CFP's legal counsel suggested a possible solution. Why not build first—then sell to the Housing Authority? Since the city wouldn't own it during construction, state laws wouldn't apply.

Sucsy liked the concept. But his marketing instinct cautioned him not to get stuck with an unsalable product.

He then hit on the solution that made it work: *Handshake Turnkey.* Sucsy made this proposal to Albert A. Walsh, chairman of New York City Housing Authority:

"CFP will erect a building to suit Housing Authority specifications and HUD financing requirements. The Housing Authority agrees to buy the building, if we deliver informally as specified. However, we sign no agreement. We merely seal the bargain with a handshake."

Walsh favored it. He consulted Herman D. Hillman, HUD's assistant regional administrator of housing assistance. Another green light.

While Handshake Turnkey breathed new life into CFP, it amplified the problem of borrowing money. In May, 1968, Sucsy approached Chase Manhattan Bank. Even though American Standard and Celanese are both Chase customers, bank officials were leary. Philip Molter of the bank's real estate department asked terms of the Housing Authority agreement. Sucsy repeated words of NYCHA chairman Walsh:

"We say only that we've seen their plans, and that if the building existed today, we probably—repeat, probably—would buy it at the price they indicate they would ask."

Molter shook his head. Not much there to comfort a banker. "If we granted the loan, we'd be providing a standby commitment to purchase the building—if no one else did," Molter said.

Chase agreed to consider it. American Standard and Celanese, as sizeable bank customers, encouraged Molter. Bartel actually visited the bank to urge approval. This helped.

Even then, months went by. Sucsy decided to forge ahead. "We had to assume ultimate financing—from somewhere—or the entire project was doomed. Since that was our assumption, we moved forward."

Construction crews broke ground October 1, 1968. A full month later, with CFP's limited working capital "dangerously low," the Chase loan came through. CFP borrowed $800,000—80% of its construction cost—at 8% annual interest. A 1-1/2% service charge was added, bringing the cost of the loan to 9.5%.

Sucsy soon found, however, that money didn't begin to solve one of his biggest headaches, that of community relations.

A marketing man expects to negotiate with government and banking officials. Sucsy consciously boned up on real estate and construction. But his most surprising and unexpected chore—Harlem community politics—almost did him in.

At first, he took a common-sense approach: "Let's find out what organization represents the community. We'll work with them."

Zot! He found 16 organizations claiming to represent the community. They agreed on only one point: "community control!" By conservative estimate, Sucsy has held at least 500 conversations about community control since he first went to Harlem.

One group that played a large role was the East Harlem Real Great Society. RGS (founded by foundation grants) preps school dropouts, conducts language courses, and works extensively in urban planning.

The society explains community control: "East Harlem is an underdeveloped country. Most of it is owned and controlled by private and governmental interests outside the community. In the past, East Harlem has served these outside interests at the expense of an essentially powerless community, but it will not continue to do so.

"East Harlem is awakening to its rights and abilities for self-control and self-determination. The people have become aware, as part of a nationwide movement, that they must control their own environment in order to determine their own future."

Located on three termite-infested floors of an aging building, the society's 30 suspicious, xenophobic members concentrate on making sure outsiders "don't screw us over."

Inside, a sign proclaims: "Anyone with drugs on them—or in them—is not allowed in this building."

This reflects the view of Harry Quintana, director of the society's urban planning studio. He blames outsiders for drug addiction in East Harlem. "They perpetuate drug addiction and welfare," he states baldly. "Because of this, we must have control."

Sucsy decided to open lines of communication with other groups. He asked Columbia University for help.

Vernon (Ben) Robinson, a graduate assistant to Bell, put Sucsy together with two community action groups—the Real Great Society, a Puerto Rican organization, and MEND, a Negro group.

They met in a dimly lit bar near Columbia. One delegate toyed with a switchblade knife during the discussion. After subsequent meetings in which he talked with nine different community groups, Sucsy divided opinions into two separate and distinct camps:

Faction 1: "Speed in housing is the most important, even if the city ends as owner."

Faction 2: "Community control is all-important—even at loss of speed or increase in cost."

Through these and other experiences, Sucsy became oriented toward community participation, without relinquishing control.

In Jim Soler, official of Cooperating Christian Churches, and a middle-of-the-road neighborhood politician, Sucsy found a mediator. Soler helped form a consortium of nine neighborhood groups: the Concerned Citizens for East Harlem. Humberto Cintron was appointed head of it.

Aided by Robinson of Columbia, Cintron's coalition sifted more than 500 applications in a storefront rental office. A representative screening committee—one Black, one Puerto Rican, one white—made the final choices.

The committee unanimously recommended one elderly couple—40-year residents in the one-time Italian neighborhood.

Ethnic battles did develop. Negro groups demanded Blacks dominate choices. Puerto Rican groups held out for Puerto Ricans. A priest with an Italian parish plumped for Italians.

Soler accepted the strife stoically:

"If Jesus Christ were walking the streets of Harlem today, he'd meet criticism from all sides."

Soler's committee finally drew up a compromise list of 126 names. The Housing Authority agreed to choose the final 66.

The Concerned Citizens proved the key to East Harlem community cooperation —of sorts—for a brief period.

In constructing the apartment building, Sucsy tried to use local suppliers and professionals as far as possible. One community group wanted to specify both contractor and architect. Sucsy's pointed answer was "no."

However, CFP did schedule community participation throughout. Max Bond, former executive director of Architects Renewal Committee in Harlem, served as consultant. So did Nathan Smith, another community resident. CFP retained a non-Harlem architectural firm, Wechsler and Schimenti.

Sucsy considered a Harlem-based construction firm. He called it off when the builder insisted on a cost-plus contract. "That's giving a man a blank check. We couldn't do that."

He finally settled on Valridge Construction Co., non-Harlem. Philip Rosen, Valridge president, was instrumental in arranging minority representation on the construction crews. A Puerto Rican, Felix LaSalde, was signed as foreman. Approximately 40% of construction workers were either Black or Puerto Rican.

In solving CFP's multi-problems, Sucsy gives major credit to two management aides—Frank McMorrow and Paul Meaghar.

McMorrow, on the CEP executive staff, supervised construction and cost-accounting details. Meaghar, a former NYCHA staff member, served as governmental advisor.

McMorrow's old-shoe approach, for instance, was ideal in talking construction with construction men. And Meaghar, in talking with government officials, was immediately accepted as a member of the in-group.

In addition, William Lyon's general management counsel throughout was a key factor in CFP success. These combined abilities produced a salable product.

By May of 1969, construction was complete on an unpretentious six-story elevator building called "335 East 111 St." The building's divided brick facade blended with the brownstone row-house neighborhood. Except for street number, the building carried no identifying public housing label. Apartments range from one- to four-bedroom units.

Time for the final test: would the Housing Authority buy it?

CFP set the price at $1,200,000. This price, approximately 10% lower than if built by the authority, resulted from savings in three areas:

1. Bank funds were not drawn until bills came in from suppliers. Since construction took only 7-1/2 months, CFP paid only a few months' interest on most of its loan.

2. Due to construction speed, CFP paid property taxes for only one year.

3. CFP's single contractor operated more efficiently than the multi-contractor arrangement required by Wicks Law.

"At the same time, we added features—such as a laundry room, garbage compactor, and 6,000-sq. ft. community space—at extra cost," Sucsy says.

City inspectors examined the building. Soon Sucsy had a Certificate of Occupancy (a document stating the building meets city living standards). He presented the certificate—along with final plans and specifications—to Chairman Walsh. He waited. In a few days, "We'll buy," a Walsh aid reported.

Tenants moved in this June. The first low-income turnkey housing project was in operation.

Actually, the city saved money. The final purchase price averaged $18,000 per unit compared to $25,000 per unit of New York typical public housing, Columbia's Bell pointed out.

Was the city happy? Grace Bliss, assistant to Walsh, states: "We think we got a favorable price and the building was put up much faster than we could have put up a building of the same size on the same kind of site."

The Housing Authority, working under the same conditions, would have taken at least 30 months to complete construction, Miss Bliss estimates. Traditional turnkey—advance contract instead of handshake—would have required 21 to 24 months to complete. Rents average $18 per room.

If the Housing Authority's approval was clear-cut, community reaction in East Harlem balanced it out. Community reaction was—and is—negative.

To counter attacks, Sucsy relies on human relations. Connie Rodriguez, a Puerto Rican staffer at CFP, is frequently dispatched door-to-door. She talks to tenants in English or Spanish, as they prefer. This develops good rapport.

CFP continues tenant liaison even though the building is Housing Authority property. Soon, for example, Sucsy is planning to conduct home economics courses in the building as a tenant benefit. These courses will be rotated to other CFP buildings later.

"We are not walking away from our buildings," Sucsy says. "We've made that clear to everyone."

This brand of community relations counters many negative comments.

What are future plans at CFP? Whither tomorrow? Construction for Progress' expansion route is impressive. CFP's new housing projects—11 in all—will account for 1,000 units by mid-year 1970. Leonard Sucsy projects 2,000 units, or $40 million worth of business, by end of 1970. On future projects, he expects to equal, or exceed, the inaugural building's 3.5% profit.

Two CFP South Bronx projects are already under construction. CFP will be expanding nationally. Sucsy considers all 50 states fair game.

The CFP techniques, Sucsy points out, are adaptable to any U.S. area where low-income housing is needed if—*repeat if—project management understands the local political and community environment.*

In reporting on CFP to stockholders, Celanese Corp. said: "The aim of Construction for Progress is not to take Celanese into commercial building. Rather it is to demonstrate how private enterprise can apply financial and managerial resources to solve slum housing problems while providing stockholders a reasonable return on assets employed."

Sucsy sees fewer problems as more firms enter the field. "What the U.S. really needs is an Identity of Interests between government/business/community vis-a-vis social problems," he states. "We have this identity, for example, in the Conquest of Space. Everyone works together to solve the problem. We don't have this identity on the social front—yet. We must develop it before we make effective progress."

An Identity of Interests will require change in government, business, and community, Sucsy attests.

"In the past, business has merely skimmed the surface of social need—and taken credit for doing much more. Government has been overly oriented toward *control* —not geared to results and achievement. Community leaders are—all too often—interested in personal power and pressing idealogical points at expense of genuine accomplishment. Each group must change."

Where is the catalyst to spur this change? Sucsy recommends the professional marketer.

"Who better?" he asks. "The business-to-business marketer has a proved record of getting things done—on time. He's trained in persuasion and communications— two indispensable elements. He's people-oriented. He's seasoned in unsnarling complex problems (legal and government, for example).

"The marketer relates effectively other fields—legal, construction, accounting, social—because he's a generalist. Relating to others is part of his training. Any business executive who enters the business-social swim must be a quick-study in many areas. But, on balance, the marketer has the best chance to succeed."

38. *Practical Guidelines to Business-Social Interaction*

The marketing executive who directs a social-business project in a disadvantaged urban area must be prepared for an entirely new world. To profit from Construction for Progress' definitive experience, consider these guidelines, compiled by Leonard G. Sucsy, CFP chief operating officer.

Sucsy applies these calipers to full-scope corporate participation—not philanthropy. Although CFP was formed to provide low-income housing, Sucsy believes the techniques apply to other business-social activities as well. His advice:

Don't add social responsibilities to work of existing personnel. An ambitious social project requires its own full-time staff. Construction for Progress, for example, operates autonomously from its parent firms.

In assigning personnel to the business-social area, seek generalists—not specialists. Both the real estate man and the social worker, for instance, would have been wrong for Construction for Progress. (The marketer—with his background in communication and persuasion—is often a good candidate. However, he can't expect to write the order and go home.) Characteristics required: objectivity, people-orientation, boldness, persistence—plus high frustration tolerance.

Sure, you're making major contributions to serious needs. But don't expect to be loved—or even appreciated. Most community groups will be critical. Government

SOURCE. Reprinted from *Industrial Marketing.* Copyright 1969 Advertising Publications, Inc. 740 Rush St., Chicago, Ill. 60611.

252

agencies want to do it differently. You'll be obstructed during and scored afterward. The sooner you learn to live with this, the better.

"Community control" is the watchword for most community groups. In implementing both business and social objectives, you'll never please them entirely. (100% community control: give them the money—they take it from there.) Expect constant flak about community control. Decide how far you can go and still meet your business goals. Then hold the line.

Remember, you'll find reams of information—from government and other sources—on real estate and construction. But you'll find little (if any) on interaction with the community—probably your biggest problem. In community relations, you chart your own course.

Don't try to apply logic in disadvantaged areas. In Harlem, community groups dedicated to housing improvement were the biggest roadblocks to Construction for Progress. Rather than viewing the over-all good, most local groups concentrate on parochial needs and power-building.

Establish your operating procedure goals early in the game. When you present plans to community groups, expect opposition. Listen to objections. Accept practical suggestions. But don't permit changes to thwart business objectives. If you try to please everyone, you'll end up not pleasing anyone.

When you enter this kind of project, you're automatically in politics. If you cannot adjust to politics as a daily way-of-life, you're not the man for this job. Your company, too, must prepare for new experiences—up to and including being picketed. If you can't stand the heat, stay out of the kitchen.

All politicians (and this now includes you) must develop a power base. You're sure to develop enemies. Counterbalance with powerful friends, too. Take a tip from the professional politician: every vote counts.

Utilize community suppliers as much as possible. But hew to the line on performance. CFP, for instance, employed a Black architectural consultant and community advisers in several areas. (On the other hand, a Black builder was not retained due to cost-plus contract requirements—which CFP considered not economic). CFP also uses Puerto Rican personnel as liaison with tenants.

Retain expert outside legal counsel at the outset. Socially oriented areas are rife with government red tape. You'll need professional assistance in unraveling architectural and legal skeins. Next, cross-check outside opinion with *inside* attorneys. Don't rely on one source—no matter how authoritative.

Expect legal problems. Laws are geared to government control, on one hand, or business philanthropy, on the other. Present laws make business *participation* in urban affairs difficult. Be prepared for this. Reforms are much needed in this area. More business involvement—and protests about restrictive legislation—will help bring changes.

You're in the People Business. Staff studies and corporate structures do not apply. You must be on the human firing line—daily. Every step forward requires help from individuals in the community. If you cannot get things done through people—often facing heavy resistance—this isn't your bag.

"Meaningful dialog" may be a cliche in Washington. But it's a workable motto for good community relations. Keep two-way lines of communications open. Keep talking. Keep listening.

Once involved with community relations, forget about regular office hours. Community groups are likely to meet during evening hours. You'll need to attend to sell, explain, justify, defend your project.

Your company's community reputation is your most valuable asset. Guard it. Your enemies have long memories. Every action must be above reproach. Be accessible to all community groups. Don't become identified with any one. Project this identity: fair-minded, open-minded, tough-minded—in meeting both business and social obligations.

Plan a continuing community relationship after your project is complete to obviate charges of *exploitation.* (Construction for Progress, for instance, is conducting home economics courses for tenants in its East Harlem building.)

Fight outdated government rules. Regulations of government bureaus frequently remain in force after the original purpose is gone. When this happens, protest. Government responds to how much people want something and how loudly they want it. In the initial CFP building, Housing Authority rules required space in each apartment for a washing machine—despite central laundry facilities in the basement. This regulation—along with dozens of others—must be scrapped.

Work for better laws. Existing laws were not designed to encourage business participation in social projects. This must change. The more companies which protest, the sooner the change. In New York, as CFP found, Wicks Law is a problem. (The situation in each state will differ, of course. Massachusetts, for example, has a law similar to Wicks Law.) Why is such restrictive legislation still on the books? Craft unions support Wicks Law to insure job security. Other vested interests defend traditional construction techniques. The greater good suffers.

Balance your two sets of objectives: business and social. If you cannot meet business objectives, you cannot finance social objectives. When community pressures push you too far, fold up and leave. This is your last resort, of course.

39. *Five Profiles of Exceptional Business Leaders*

He's Busy Lifting a City's Face

Meeting William H. Wendel is a little like seeing his neighboring Niagara Falls for the first time—rather more than you bargained for.

Wendel, who this week received the Business Week citizenship award for "exceptional leadership," is president of Carborundum Co., a $250-million company that produces everything from grinding wheels (300,000-odd models) to Spode china. He is president of the Society for the Promotion, Unification, and Redevelopment of Niagara, Inc. (SPUR), and chairman of the Local Governments Improvement Commission (LOGIC). He is also a man of fierce personal commitment—and the awesome integrity of an umpire who is not afraid of getting beaned by an occasional bottle. "You can't involve yourself and not ruffle a few tempers," Wendel notes. "Sometimes, that's the only way to get things done."

The city of Niagara Falls, despite its romantic honeymoon aura, has long been a place where things needed doing. With representatives from Union Carbide Corp., Du Pont, and some 30 other companies, Wendel first organized SPUR in 1964 as a catalytic organization aimed at mobilizing local resources, and putting a new face on the tired city. Last week, SPUR's development arm, the Niagara Falls Gateway to America Corp., was planning a $20-million downtown complex consisting of a

SOURCE. Reprinted from the November 1, 1969 issue of *Business Week* by special permission. Copyright © 1969 by McGraw-Hill, Inc.

new headquarters building for Carborundum, a museum to house a display of Carborundum's Spode china, a bank, and several plazas.

SPUR is also spurring a major urban renewal program that will cover most of the city's 80-acre downtown area and include a new $17-million convention center. Two other housing corporations that SPUR helped create are now building or rehabilitating nearly 1,000 housing units. To get at a more fundamental problem of ineffective local government, SPUR organized LOGIC to make a study of the area's 21 city, town, and village governments.

Wendel runs SPUR and LOGIC the way he runs his business—with crisp military precision. It comes naturally. A graduate of the U.S. Naval Academy, Wendel spent seven years in the Navy, joined Carborundum in 1947 as assistant to the president, and moved up to the top spot in 1962. He quickly won a reputation, both at Carborundum and in civic affairs, as a man who relished broader, long-range strategy more than narrow, tight control. "American industry," Wendel says, "is turning more and more to management by objectives, to the qualification of targets." Thanks to Wendel, Niagara Falls may be a city that is finally on target.

Style-Setter in Equal Opportunity

Walter Haas, Jr., president of Levi Strauss & Co., always gets a little miffed when someone singles out his company for its good works in the ghetto. "We are doing much," he admits, "and we can and will do more. But instead of being the good example, we would much rather be only one of an overwhelming majority doing what should and must be done." Yet an example his company remains.

After the Detroit riots and the formation of the National Alliance of Businessmen, President Johnson appointed Haas as one of eight regional chairmen to help head the NAB's nationwide ghetto job program. Last April, a Harvard alumni group named Haas "business statesman of the year." And this week, Levi Strauss & Co. received one of two Business Week citizenship awards in recognition of its efforts in "human resources."

For a company that once labeled its popular blue-denim "Levis" as "Made by White Labor," Levi Strauss has come a long way.

Years before it was legally required, Strauss promoted equal opportunity at both its San Francisco headquarters and its 30 plants scattered mainly through the South. After his appointment as an NAB regional chairman, Haas further pledged to hire at least 5% of his company's new employees from among the hardcore unemployed, and set up special training programs that raised their retention rate to 70%—comparable to that of regular employees. Strauss also hired and upgraded minority group members for supervisory and managerial positions. Today, some 10% of the company's 1,000 supervisory and managerial employees come from minority groups. "These are not top-level positions, at least not yet," Haas stresses.

"But they are positions in supervision and management, and they can be steps up the ladder."

At the same time, Strauss has helped set up eight minority-owned clothing stores, and is providing long-term credit to nine stores, as part of a $20-million credit pool organized by Phillips-Van Heusen Corp. and the Menswear Retailers of America.

One typical black retailer who is getting credit help is Rufus Butler, owner of Mister B's Men's Shop in Portland, Ore. "I wrote 'em," Butler told a reporter, speaking of Strauss, "that I didn't know what extended credit was but that we sure needed it. Next thing, their local Levi Strauss man was here saying if he didn't do business with me, his boss would probably fire him."

A Lift for Black Businessmen

Bert Daigre is a black capitalist who has made it. A graduate of Northwestern University, Daigre owns a fleet of 30 taxicabs in Chicago and operates an auto garage and insurance company. But he is a rare exception. "Less than 1% of U.S. businesses are owned by Negroes, despite the fact that we make up 17% of the population," he says. "It has also been shown that 97% of the money spent in Negro ghettos goes out of the community."

To help restore the ghetto's balance of payments, Western Electric Co., the manufacturing and supply arm of the Bell System and recipient of one of this year's two Business Week citizenship awards for "human resources," has launched an unusual program for giving the minority businessman a lift.

Like many other companies, Western Electric took the plunge right after the Detroit riots. "With facilities in 30 states and a purchasing function that deals with 47,000 suppliers in 50 states," says William G. Chaffee, vice-president of Western Electric, "we felt we were in a unique position to help the minority businessman."

To start things off, Western Electric signed the first of $60,000 worth of contracts with Watts Mfg. Co., a black-managed subsidiary of Aerojet-General Corp. and producer of various types of canvas products. Since then, Western Electric has lined up 70 other minority suppliers in a dozen cities, often providing management and technical assistance, training, and sometimes start-up capital. To help such suppliers broaden their base, the company also sponsored—along with several local groups—three suppliers' fairs just for black businessmen. Two were staged in Chicago, one in New York. The latest, held in Chicago's International Amphitheatre in September, drew 510 black suppliers and purchasing agents from 148 companies representing more than $100-million worth of annual purchasing power in the Chicago area.

Cecil Carmickle, who operates a building and remodeling company in Chicago, is typical of the suppliers who flocked in. "There is a lot of small contracting work to be done," he notes. The problem is making that first big important contact. "If you don't know anyone," he asks, "how do you get in?" All told, the three fairs resulted in more than $1-million worth of contracts.

A Mine that Works with the Landscape

There comes a time when every red-blooded American male is tempted, in H. L. Mencken's words, "to spit on his hands, hoist the black flag, and begin slitting throats." Many conservationists feel that way today. "In years past when we had a problem with industry," says Roger Hansen, executive director of the Colorado Open Space Foundation, "we tried to settle it over a conference table; then if that failed we brought pressure, and if that failed we went to court. Now many groups start out assuming that business won't cooperate, and they are increasingly going straight to court."

One company that is cooperating—and to an almost unrivaled degree—is American Metal Climax, Inc., a $600-million natural resources developer and the recipient of one of two Business Week citizenship awards in the "physical environment" area.

Working closely with the Colorado Open Space Foundation, a large private conservation group, AMAX has launched a unique "Experiment in Ecology" at its new $200-million Henderson molybdenum mine high in the Colorado Rockies 50 miles west of Denver.

To avoid the usual drab appearance of mining installations, the buildings are being designed with colored siding to match the surroundings. Access roads have been rerouted to preserve as many trees as possible. Some 6,000 acres of woodland have been thrown open for hunting, hiking, and camping.

AMAX's biggest concession to the environment, however, is its system for handling "tailing"—finely ground ore waste that leaves the mill in the form of 60% water and 40% solid material. For convenience, tailing is normally stored in ponds near the mine. At Henderson, that would have put it within a short eagle's glide of a major highway. So AMAX engineers are tunneling 9.3 miles through Red Mountain, building a 13-mile railroad at a cost of $25-million, and putting their mill and tailing pond far from the public's—and conservationists'—view.

Dr. Beatrice Willard, an ecologist and one of the foundation's more militant members, is impressed with results thus far. But she feels there are still several matters to be ironed out. "I want to do considerably more research on wind patterns around the tailing pond," she says. "If wind lifts the tailing into the air and drops it on plants, we can have all kinds of problems." Whatever her research shows, one certainty has come out of "Experiment in Ecology"—AMAX already knows which way the wind is blowing.

Master Builder of a Model City

"The problem of the city," says James Rouse, his eyes twinkling with excitement, "is not just congestion, pollution, deterioration—nor crime, disease, and rats; nor housing, nor unemployment. It is all of these, of course, but underlying all these conditions are the questions: How did it happen? How did the city get this way? What causes our cities to rot away physically and socially?"

As president of Rouse Co. and a highly successful mortgage banker and master builder, Rouse is now trying to answer his own questions. On 14,000 acres of Maryland countryside midway between Baltimore and Washington, Rouse Co.— recipient of one of two Business Week citizenship awards for "physical environment"—is buidling a self-contained model city called Columbia, on the thesis that the problems of today's city are not so much social or economic, as environmental. As part of its model environment, Columbia will offer handy shopping, a full range of cultural and recreational activities, and such unusual urban amenities as 3,000 acres of forest, five lakes, and 26 miles of riding trails.

By creating an environment that "serves, rather than dictates," Rouse hopes to reestablish vital urban inter-relationships that most other cities smother or destroy.

"Think how a good neighborhood environment might affect education," he rhapsodizes, "and how education, in turn, could affect the development of skills, and how job-training resources in a good neighborhood could influence new employment opportunities. Think how health education and preventive medicine might work its way out into the people from neighborhood health and activity centers, how this might reduce critical illness, loss of time at work, and thus increase individual incomes, sense of well being, human effectiveness. And think how all of this together might affect educability, employability, growth of the person, the family."

Some three years after Rouse Co. turned its first earth in Columbia, the city is now well on its way. Twenty-six industries and 83 businesses have acquired space in Columbia, developers have bought land for 4,600 dwelling units, and the city's population itself is above 5,000—on its way to a projected 100,000 by 1980.

40. *One Year Later—Conclusions*

The Nation has not reversed the movement apart. Blacks and whites remain deeply divided in their perceptions and experiences of American society. The deepening of concern about conditions in the slums and ghettos on the part of some white persons and institutions has been counterbalanced—perhaps over-balanced—by a deepening of aversion and resistance on the part of others. The mood of the blacks, wherever it stands precisely in the spectrum between militancy and submission, is not moving in the direction of patience. The black neighborhoods in the cities remain slums, marked by poverty and decay; they remain ghettos, marked by racial concentration and confinement. The nation has not yet made available—to the cities or the blacks themselves—the resources to improve these neighborhoods enough to make a significant change in their residents' lives. Nor has it offered those who might want it the alternative of escape.

Neither has the nation made a choice among the alternative futures described by the Commission, which is the same as choosing what the Commission called "present policies." The present policies alternative, the Commission said, "may well involve changes in many social and economic programs—but not enough to produce fundamental alterations in the key factors of Negro concentration, racial segregation, and the lack of sufficient enrichment to arrest the decay of deprived neighborhoods."

SOURCE. Reprinted with permission, "One Year Later," copyright 1969 The National Urban Coalition.

It is worth looking again at the Commission's description of where this choice would lead:

"We believe that the present policies choice would lead to a larger number of violent incidents of the kind that have stimulated recent major disorders.

"First, it does nothing to raise the hopes, absorb the energies, or constructively challenge the talents of the rapidly growing number of young Negro men in central cities. The proportion of unemployed or underemployed among them will remain very high. These young men have contributed disproportionately to crime and violence in cities in the past, and there is danger, obviously, that they will continue to do so.

"Second, under these conditions, a rising proportion of Negroes in disadvantaged city areas might come to look upon the deprivation and segregation they suffer as proper justification for violent protest or for extending support to now isolated extremists who advocate civil disruption by guerrilla tactics.

"More incidents would not necessarily mean more or worse riots. For the near future, there is substantial likelihood that even an increased number of incidents could be controlled before becoming major disorders, if society undertakes to improve police and National Guard forces so that they can respond to potential disorders with more prompt and disciplined use of force.

"In fact, the likelihood of incidents mushrooming into major disorders would be only slightly higher in the near future under the present policies choice than under the other two possible choices. For no new policies or programs could possibly alter basic ghetto conditions immediately. And the announcement of new programs under the other choices would immediately generate new expectations. Expectations inevitably increase faster than performance. In the short run, they might even increase the level of frustration.

"In the long run, however, the present policies choice risks a seriously greater probability of major disorders, worse, possibly, than those already experienced.

"If the Negro population as a whole developed even stronger feelings of being wrongly 'penned in' and discriminated against, many of its members might come to support not only riots, but the rebellion now being preached by only a handful. Large-scale violence, followed by white retaliation, could follow. This spiral could quite conceivably lead to a kind of urban *apartheid* with semimartial law in many major cities, enforced residence of Negroes in segregated areas, and a drastic reduction in personal freedom for all Americans, particularly Negroes."

The Commission's description of the immediate consequences of the present policies choice sounds strikingly like a description of the year since its report was issued: some change but not enough; more incidents but less full-scale disorder because of improved police and military response; a decline in expectations and therefore in short-run frustrations. If the Commission is equally correct about the long run, the nation in its neglect may be sowing the seeds of unprecedented future disorder and division. For a year later, we are a year closer to being two societies, black and white, increasingly separate and scarcely less unequal.

41. *Cooperatives in the Ghetto: A Brief History of the Cooperative Movement*

WILLIAM E. COX, JR., AND

SUE R. SEIDMAN

The consumer cooperative movement was started in 1844 by twenty-eight poverty stricken workers in Rochdale, England, in protest against excessive prices and adulteration of goods. They, therefore, decided to pool their funds and supply themselves.

For the operation of their association, the Rochdale workers evolved what have come to be known as the Rochdale Principles and Practices, which are now recognized as "the standards" wherever consumers' cooperatives are formed. The Rochdale Principles are:

1. A consumer's cooperative society shall be democratically controlled.

2. There shall be open membership. No persons shall be denied membership unless it be known that they wish to join for the purpose of doing harm to the organization.

3. Money invested in a cooperative society if it receive interest shall receive a fixed percentage which shall not be more than the prevailing current rate.

4. If a cooperative society makes a profit that profit shall be returned to the consumers who patronize the society on the basis of their amount of purchases.

The Rochdale Practices are:

1. A cooperative society shall be composed of members who voluntarily join.

SOURCE. *American Marketing Association Meetings,* "Cooperatives in the Ghetto," William E. Cox, Jr., and Sue R. Seidman, August 1969.

2. Business shall be for cash.

3. Goods and services shall be sold at prevailing prices.

4. A portion of profits shall be used for educational purposes in the field of cooperation.

5. At each inventory, reserves shall be set aside to cover depreciation and unforeseen difficulties arising in the operation of the business.

6. Labor shall be fairly treated.

7. Cooperative societies shall cooperate with one another.

Prior to 1900, the cooperative movement in the United States had some brief spurts of success but it is generally conceded that the movement was a failure. Just after the turn of the century, there was a revival of interest in consumer's cooperatives. This period was marked by the formation of many cooperatives among immigrant groups as well as farm and labor organizations. Movement toward nationwide coordination of cooperative activities began with the organization of the Cooperative League of America in 1916.

Cooperatives started to become popular for the first time in the United States after World War I and the decades of the twenties and the thirties were times of prosperity for the cooperative movement. During World War II, cooperatives continued to grow in importance and apparently reached their peak in the late 1940's and early 1950's, with Census data showing their greatest penetration in 1954. Even then, cooperatives accounted for only 0.2% of total retail store sales of consumer goods. Since that time, cooperatives have lost ground and appear to be in about the same relative position in retailing as they were at the close of World War II.

While consumer cooperatives have never been significant factors in American retailing, they are much more important in Western Europe. Carson has estimated that cooperatives handle an average of 6.2% of the retail trade in Western Europe, with Switzerland, Sweden, and Great Britain reporting 9.0% or more.

Two Successful Cooperatives

Two of the most successful retail cooperatives in the United States today are Greenbelt Consumer Services, Inc. of Beltsville, Maryland, and The Hyde Park Cooperative Society of Hyde Park, Chicago. The history, membership and financial data, services offered, and the cooperative commitment of the members of these two cooperatives are examined in this section of the paper.

Greenbelt Consumer Services, Inc.

The town of Greenbelt, Maryland, was built during the early 1930's under the auspices of the Government Farm Security Program to (1) give employment to the unemployed who were on relief, (2) to demonstrate the soundness of planning and operating towns in accordance with certain "garden city" principles, and (3) to provide low-rent housing in good physical and social environment for low income families. It was to be built with a large wooded area separating it physically from Washington, D.C., and surrounding suburban areas; hence the name Greenbelt. This physical isolation created the need for a variety of services including a retail grocery market.

The story of the Greenbelt cooperative, now the leading non-farm consumers' cooperative in the United States, is one of continuous growth, expansion, and success. By 1943, Greenbelt's sales passed the million dollar mark and its membership had risen to 1283. At the end of 1954 the cooperative had over 5,500 members, seventy-five per cent of whom were government employees. Gross volume for the year was over $5,450,000 from which $55,400 was returned on patronage in addition to five per cent interest on share capital.

Although it operates only in the Washington area, in 1960 Greenbelt opened its tenth shopping center. In 1964 Greenbelt's sales amounted to $22 million and by 1968 they had risen to $40 million.

As of July 1, 1968, Greenbelt Consumer Services had approximately 19,000 member families, each of whom had paid a membership fee of $10.00 per share. Greenbelt now has the greatest appeal for well-educated upper-middle-income people, with sixty to seventy per cent of its members employed by the government.

Greenbelt operates a wide variety of stores, including supermarkets; its furniture store, Scan, which is the largest importer of Scandinavian furniture in North America; petroleum service stations, and pharmacies. Other member benefits include life insurance, auto leasing, and insurance; travel programs; and a co-op newsletter, "The Co-op Consumer." In addition, the cooperative employs several full-time home economists who are available to members for demonstrations or consultations.

As Greenbelt's membership has grown, a single annual membership meeting has become impractical as a method of democratic control. Therefore a "congress" system based on district organization and representative government has been devised and has worked quite well. At present the congress of Greenbelt is made up of 114 delegates elected from the membership. Its primary purpose is to provide a closer link between the members and the board of directors as well as to maintain and promote effective membership control. Another important function of the congress is to provide a training program for future member leadership. The numerous committees of the congress that provide a broad array of services to the Greenbelt membership also provide leadership training.

Hyde Park Cooperative Society, Inc.

The Hyde Park Co-op is in the heart of Chicago's racially mixed south side. Some years ago as the population of Hyde Park began to change and some general deterioration of the neighborhood seemed to be setting in, a general exodus of business establishments began. Instead of moving, the members of the Hyde Park Cooperative Society provide a core of people determined to redevelop Hyde Park instead of abandoning it. Thus around this neighborhood-owned business there began to grow a new community spirit. A redevelopment plan conceived by the University of Chicago and executed by the City of Chicago included a new shopping center to replace several blocks of run-down commercial buildings. The supermarket in that center, the largest in Chicago, was assigned to the Hyde Park Cooperative.

The Hyde Park Co-op was originally organized by a group of families centered around the University of Chicago who needed a convenient place to shop. Today it is owned by some 10,000 member families that have paid $9.00 to join. Its membership is racially integrated as is the community in which it operates. Members are in the upper-middle income brackets and are university-oriented. Mr. Gilbert Spenser, General Manager of the Hyde Park Cooperative Society, estimates that over sixty per cent of Hyde Park's members are connected with the University of Chicago in some capacity and over eighty per cent are college graduates. The cooperative is the only complete, convenient, and modern supermarket for some five square miles.

Only two commercial operations are directly part of the cooperative: The grocery and the FORM furniture store. The grocery is the largest single supermarket in the Chicago area and not only is it an efficient merchandising business, it also supports many worthwhile community enterprises and welfare agencies on Chicago's south side.

FORM, the cooperative's Scandinavian furniture store, opened in September 1967. It provides quality imported furniture at reasonable prices. The operation was patterned after a similar successful operation run by Greenbelt Co-op which provides Hyde Park with much valuable consulting service. The Co-op has helped its members develop a number of other cooperative activities, though none are directly connected with the society. These services include the Credit Union, Fuel Co-op, Chicago Memorial Association and the Sitters' Swap. Additional membership services of the cooperative are the employment of a full-time economist on the staff of the grocery and the twice-monthly publication of the Society's newsletter, *Evergreen*.

Hyde Park's financial operations have been both sound and profitable. In 1963 sales totaled $4,868,591 with dividends on cash stock of four per cent and patronage refund of three per cent. By 1966 sales totaled $6,117,449, and dividends and patronage refunds have continued at the same level.

The Greenbelt and Hyde Park cooperatives have a number of factors in common: (1) emphasize food marketing, (2) relatively little competition from large scale, efficient retailers, (3) highly educated membership, (4) capable leadership dedicated to cooperative principles, (5) experienced, professional management, and (6) large, modern, fully competitive stores. Members have been drawn primarily from long-term residents of the area, and while incomes were relatively low at the time the cooperatives were formed, members were not at the poverty level or below. Moreover, members for the last twenty years have been at the middle income level. Among the government and university employees that dominate the membership of both cooperatives are many leaders and potential leaders who have been willing to spend considerable amounts of time and energy to insure the success of the cooperatives.

Greenbelt and Hyde Park have survived and prospered as consumer cooperatives primarily because of the special character of the membership of the two associations. Without a sizeable number of members who are deeply involved in the cooperative movement and philosophically committed to cooperative principles, it would be difficult for Greenbelt and Hyde Park to maintain their success over an extended period. These associations have been subsidized by the voluntary contributions of their leadership cores and it is this subsidy that permitted Greenbelt and Hyde Park to remain competitive with the corporate chains, particularly in their early years.

Current Marketing Experiments with Cooperative Elements

Five examples of retail marketing operations that incorporate some cooperative elements and are operating in ghetto areas have been selected for examination. Four of the five: Harlem River Consumer's Cooperative, the Hunterspoint Neighborhood Co-op, the Jet Food Corporation, and the Hough Family Service Cooperative have been established in the last four years. The fifth example, about which very little has been written, The Morningside Heights Consumers' Cooperative, has been operating successfully for well over a decade.

The Harlem River Consumer Cooperative, Inc.

Many residents of black ghettos believe that their retail stores are poorly stocked and charge exorbitant prices; the Harlem River Consumer Cooperative was organized to help change this situation. Several business firms aided the Harlem co-op in opening its doors in June 1968 by advancing funds to buy refrigeration equipment and improve store facilities, helping the co-op to hire and train employees, and serving as consultants.

The cooperative is located on the ground floor of the Esplanade Garden Apartments and serves as the principal market for the residents of the 1,870 apartments, as well as the surrounding neighborhood. Although the store is relatively small

(10,000 square feet), its bright interior and range of nationally branded merchandise compares favorably with any suburban market. Most of the cooperative's merchandise is purchased through Mid-Eastern, Inc., a regional wholesale agency that serves some thirty-five local cooperative associations. About sixty percent of the volume is in national brands; the remainder is sold under the Co-op label.

The community itself has provided most of the sixteen members of the Board of Directors and the 4300 members, who have purchased $264,000 in shares at $5.00 each.

The Jet Food Corporation

The Jet Food Corporation was organized in October 1966 as a franchise program to develop modern supermarkets in the inner city. The cooperative element of the program is that stock is sold to residents of the areas where stores are constructed. In November 1967, the Jet Food Corporation opened the first Super Jet Store in Baltimore as a prototype unit. Stock subscriptions at $5.00 per share were sold to area residents and $180,000 of the store's $500,000 initial costs were raised in this manner. Jet Food plans to expand their operations into ten other cities and opened their first supermarket in Cleveland in June 1969.

Jet Food emphasizes the need to adapt the product assortment of its stores to the buying habits of ghetto residents. Thus national brands, rather than a co-op brand, are featured and little prepackaging is used. Forty percent of the Baltimore store's volume is in meats, compared to the 25 percent national average for all supermarket chains. Two additional examples of the recognition of low income buying habits are the absence of large size packages and containers and little use of multiple pricing techniques.

Hunterspoint Neighborhood Co-op

Since its opening in 1965, the Hunterspoint Neighborhood Co-op has been in trouble. Among the reasons cited for the difficulties of this San Francisco ghetto cooperative are: (1) poor location with insufficient parking facilities, (2) lack of consumer interest, (3) inexperienced management, and (4) an insufficient and inappropriate inventory high in gourmet items (such as imported wines) and low in national brands. In 1965, the Co-op was robbed of $12,000, and with only $2,000 insurance, suffered a severe financial setback.

Safeway Stores learned of the Co-op's problems and for the past year has been providing management consulting services for $1.00. Safeway personnel have supervised interior and exterior alterations to the Co-op store, restocking the shelves with a more appropriate inventory, and moving in new equipment.

Morningside Heights Consumers' Co-op

Many cooperatives both within and outside low income areas fail from an inability to compete successfully, but New York's Morningside Heights Consumers' Co-op, not far from Harlem, has been a going concern for nearly a decade. Last year it returned a 4.8 percent cash rebate to members and twelve percent dividend on their $25.00 a share stock.

The Morningside Heights membership is racially mixed, as is its neighborhood. Approximately fifty per cent are Negroes and Puerto Ricans, the other half are whites. Though the members are predominantly low income, many of the Co-op's white members with upper-middle incomes are connected with nearby Columbia University and are deeply committed to the principles of cooperation and to the Co-op itself.

Morningside Heights furnishes an excellent example of effective cooperative action in a predominantly low income area. Over a decade ago, the Morningside Heights area had a substantially unfulfilled need for more efficient grocery services. This need was recognized by both the low income families in the area and some members of the university, also living in the area, who were willing to furnish a leadership core. This leadership core carefully studied and analysed the lack of adequate marketing services and decided that a pooling of resources of interested individuals in the area would provide the most effective method for meeting their marketing needs.

Hough Family Service Cooperative, Inc. (HFSC)

HFSC was started in April of 1968 in Cleveland, Ohio by Mr. William Stewart, project director of the Urban Demonstration Program of the Cooperative League of the United States. It is funded jointly by the Office of Economic Opportunity and the Cooperative League of the United States. Since 1968 it has enrolled 473 members at a $5.00 per share membership fee and a $2.00 non-refundable joining fee. Any member obtains full membership rights with the purchase of his first share. Among these rights are: using any services of the Co-op, voting in all elections and helping to make policy decisions. Among the services HFSC plans to offer are: (1) discounts of food purchased in bulk (primary current service), (2) discounts on appliances, (3) tires and batteries, (4) home maintenance and appliance repair service, and (5) consumer education and information to help members get better values for their money.

HFSC eventually hopes to pool the purchasing power of thousands of members to allow purchases of a variety of goods and services at close to or below wholesale cost while retaining all of the services normally available to consumers. At present HFSC has one small store that depends heavily on outside funding for its continued existence.

Among the five cooperatives in ghetto areas reviewed in the preceding section, the oldest and most successful (Morningside Heights Consumers' Co-op) is very similar to the Greenbelt and Hyde Park cooperatives. The only significant differ-ence is that a higher percentage of Morningside's membership is non-white. Morningside Heights has the same advantages of having many members affiliated with a university and is therefore able to draw leadership resources from an educated membership with a strong commitment to cooperative principles. In each of the other four cooperatives in ghetto areas, there is no sizeable group of members with a high educational level, government or university affiliation, and a strong dedication to cooperative principles. Although these organizations appear to meet some criteria as cooperatives, the absence of the traditional membership base that has been associated with successful cooperatives raises serious questions about the ability of cooperatives to succeed in the ghetto.

42. *Marketers Fiddle While Consumers Burn* E. B. WEISS

It was in 1962 that President John F. Kennedy proclaimed the consumer's four-pronged Magna Charta:

1. The right to safety.
2. The right to be informed.
3. The right to choose.
4. The right to be heard.

These four "rights" symbolized—and heralded—consumerism. They became the basis for auto and tire safety legislation, the truth-in-packaging bill, and truth-in-credit regulations. And they will spawn six to ten additional consumer bills over the next several years.

In 1962, industry tended to shrug off consumerism as a political gambit that would soon fizzle out. During the six ensuing years, each industry affected by proposed legislation has tended, on balance, to oppose uncompromisingly each new legislative proposal on behalf of consumerism. The food industry fought truth-in-packaging bills for five years. Truth-in-credit legislation was opposed by the credit industry for seven years. The meat packers' initial posture was one of confrontation; reluctant collaboration came only toward the end of the debate.

SOURCE. "Marketers Fiddle While Consumers Burn," E.B. Weiss, *Harvard Business Review,* July-August 1968, © 1968 by the President and Fellows of Harvard College; all rights reserved.

Clearly, industry has been unwilling to accept the philosophy that what is good for the public is good for business. That is why few corporate managements have directed the organizational changes necessitated by consumerism, why even fewer managements have charted an imaginative course to guide present consumer legislation to beneficial socioeconomic ends, and why few managements have ordered a study of impending consumer legislation so as to have an appropriate marketing program ready in advance.

In short, after six years of tuning up, Washington is literally racing toward additional consumerism legislation, regulation, and organization. State governments are doing the same thing, and so are many city governments. But industry's attitude tends to remain a mixture of confrontation, lamentation, and pious posturing. The marketing fraternity, especially, is almost united in its opposition. Marketing conventions resound with wails of anguish, of frustration, of bewilderment. Thunderous applause is reserved for the speaker who ties Communism and consumerism into an unholy alliance.

This is the road to a quasi-utility status for marketing. I do not predict that corporate marketing departments will be supervised in the minute way that railroads or power companies are. But I do foresee a future in which, rightly or wrongly, marketing will be regulated by law far more than it has ever been before. Most marketing leaders have only themselves to blame if they do not like this prospect.

The "Smugly" Americans

I will concede that at the very top management level, consumerism is tending to be accepted as part of the new dimensions of corporate social responsibility. But, at the marketing level, fanatical and tearful defense of the status quo remains typical.

A very high-ranking advertising executive unquestionably spoke for the majority of marketing officials when he complained that the government was using consumerism "as a divisive issue." He admitted "confusion" over the "dissension" existing between government and business. Striking the pious pose typical of too many marketing men, he said, "The business people I know feel they are trying their best to make a meaningful contribution to the welfare of the country, and they are hurt when the government portrays them as hawks and consumers as doves requiring protection." He warned that this situation will lead to "severe damage" to the economic and social structure of the country. With supreme irony—remember that this was a meeting presumably called to develop collaboration between government and marketing—he added that there was "need for more humility on the government's part" and called on the government to "remedy the damage" done to business!

Fortunately, voices from another direction are also being heard. For example:

Beyond question, the emerging ethics are challenging business orthodoxy, said A.N. McFarlane, the chairman of the board of Corn Products Company, recently.

What concerns me is how the business community may respond to these ethical changes. It would be a grave error to view them only as a threat, as something to resist. As I see it, they are an expression of public thinking which we attack or disregard only at great peril. . . .

Putting it another way, we have to decide whether, in the marketplace for ideas, we will allow ourselves to become alienated from the mainstream of public thought. . . .

We can respond to the new emphasis on the quality of life—as opposed to the quantity of things—not only by modifying our product mix, but by more sensitive handling of business actions and communications—advertising included. . . .

It is probable that the top managements of many companies will direct their marketing departments to adopt policies and practices more responsive to the public's desires. If this happens, it will help. But in view of marketing's abysmal record to date, I am dubious that it can save itself in time from substantial extensions of government regulation.

Who Needs 1,000 Eyes?

The Chinese say the buyer needs a thousand eyes—the seller but one. Marketing wants to keep it that way. However, consumerism now says the *seller* needs a thousand eyes—the buyer but one.

The buyer will never be protected to that degree, but he will need fewer than 1,000 eyes in the future. Years ago, when the employer became legally responsible for reasonable diligence in providing safe working conditions for his employees, and when workmen's compensation laws emerged, both the incidence and the severity of on-the-job injuries were sharply reduced. Is it unreasonable to conclude that new legal concepts of the seller's responsibilities and liabilities could accomplish similar results for the general public?

Consumer exploitation has been replacing labor exploitation as the real problem of our times. *We would not permit the things to be done to people as workers that we allow to be done to them as shoppers!* A more intelligent society, especially its younger generation, insists this must change.

But the market is self-policing, argues the marketing man, because the shopper is sovereign. This is true in a legalistic sense, perhaps—and it may check with the precepts of classical economics. But to the U.S. public of today it sounds more and more like pure poppycock.

No marketing man hissed (but hundreds applauded) when the former president of a large publishing enterprise declared:

> Freedom of shopping decision is a fundamental prerogative—even the freedom to be wrong, to make a wrong choice. No one has to buy anything, at any price, at any time. . . . Some degree of responsibility must rest on and with the consumer. He cannot be regarded as a pitiable imbecile. He cannot be wholly protected in every move and every purchase he makes, every day of his life.

Now, there is an interesting combination of truth and misjudgment in this argument. Who could disagree that "no one has to buy anything, at any price, at any time"? Who could disagree that "some degree of responsibility must rest on and with the consumer"? Who could disagree that it is foolish to regard the consumer as a "pitiable imbecile"? Who wants the consumer to be "wholly protected in every move and every purchase he makes, every day of his life"? Yet we err in going on (as so many businessmen seem to do) to insist not only that the consumer has a *right* to be wrong, but that marketing must make sure he exercises that right! I rather doubt that a sophisticated, affluent society—especially the properly critical younger generation—will offer much of a mass market for products that cater to the public's right to be *wrong*.

Bewildered Buyers

The fact is that technology is expanding at such an unprecedented rate and spawning such a torrent of new products that it is difficult for the trade, not to mention consumers, to keep fully informed about them. Should shoppers be expected to be able to differentiate between a latex foam mattress and a urethane foam mattress? How many consumers can be expected to understand the difference between a transistorized and a solid-state radio or TV?

Technology has brought unparalleled abundance and opportunity to the consumer. It has also exposed him to new complexities and hazards. It has made his choices more difficult. He cannot be chemist, mechanic, electrician, nutritionist, *and* a walking computer (very necessary when shopping for fractionated-ounce food packages)! Faced with almost infinite product differentiation (plus contrived product virtues that are purely semantic), considerable price differentiation, the added complexities of trading stamps, the subtleties of cents-off deals, and other complications, the shopper is expected to choose wisely under circumstances that baffle professional buyers. His job is not made easier by the fact that prices tend *not* to be uniform in different stores even of the same food chain, and may vary daily. Moreover, if he is like most of us, he has to decide in a hurry.

Let us suppose he stops to buy a can opener. He finds there are hand, wall, and table models, manually operated or electrically powered. Some are combined with knife sharpeners. They are finished with various materials. They come in a range of colors. Some differences are functional and practical others are merely for appearance or for promotion. Moreover, he must usually choose the can opener without the aid of a salesclerk. (If a clerk is present, he is apt to be as confused and unknowing as the customer!)

Flunking the Shopping Test!

Several years ago, California's Consumer Counsel decided to conduct a test to see how a shopper might fare in a typical unarmed encounter with a supermarket. According to a then current survey by Du Pont, the average shopper on an average visit bought 13.7 items in an average time of 27 minutes. Accordingly, a list of 14 items was drawn up. These were all packaged products—common staple foods and household necessities. Then a typical supermarket in the Sacramento area was selected. In the case of the 14 items, the store offered a total of *246 possible choices.*

Five housewives were selected to participate in the test. Though picked at random, they were not average shoppers; each had had some college training as well as considerable family-marketing experience. Their instructions were simple: to make their selections solely on the basis of quantity and cost—i.e., get the most possible for their money.

Each of the five women was given $10 and sent into the supermarket to buy the 14 items. They were clocked from the time they entered the store till they reached the checkout counter.

Only one of the women finished in less time than the average found in the Du Pont survey; she completed her shopping in 25 minutes. The other four women took, respectively, 35, 40, 55, and 60 minutes.

How did they fare? All five succeeded in picking the lowest-priced package of one item, cheddar cheese. But that was their only triumph. In the case of 2 of the 14 products, all five were baffled by the maze of prices and package sizes. For instance, there were 14 different packages of white rice; not one was in a one-pound package! The same was true of the 6 packages of salt, which ran a confusing range from 4/10 ounce to 5 pounds. Toilet tissue was packed in rolls of 650, 800, and 1,000 sheets—some single-ply, some double-ply. Of the 10 cans of tuna, none was one pound or one half pound; 7 were fractional ounces.

In summary, possessing better-than-average educations, and spending more than the average amount of time, the five housewives as a group succeeded 36 times and failed 34 times to pick the most economical items.

Caveat Venditor

I am not arguing that prices should not fluctuate, that various package sizes should not be offered, or that different models, brands, and colors should not be displayed. My point is simply that the shopper is dazed—and understandably so. U.S.

marketers should be taking far more responsibility than they have thus far to help the customer make decisions. Just how much protection does he or she need? That is a question about which reasonable and sincere men differ; but the need for offering *much more* than at present is, in my opinion, beyond dispute.

A free economy depends on rational consumer choice. If consumers cannot choose wisely, if they regularly reach their decisions in a state of wonder and perplexity, if they make their choices on the basis of meaningless and irrelevant claims, a free economy suffers.

Just as a rational voting procedure is necessary to a free political system, so a rational shopping system is necessary to a free market. The marketplace displays more irrationality than rationality. The better educated, more sophisticated shopper of today is beginning to rebel. Politicians are paying heed; marketers are not.

Needed: VPs of Consumerism

How must corporations be restructured, in philosophy and in organization, to conform with and profit from the consumerism trend? The logical starting points would seem to be:

1. The formulation of an up-to-date "consumerism code" that summarizes top management's philosophy and provides a practical framework of policy for line executives.
2. A staff and line reorganization.
3. A program to facilitate implementation of the code.

Arjay Miller, Ford Motor Company's vice chairman, puts it this way:

> The corporation must go beyond its traditional role of business enterprise and seek to anticipate, rather than simply react to, social needs or problems. This may require the establishment of a long-range planning function to make sure a firm will be able to respond to what society wants it to do. It may involve not only changed 'product,' but also changed internal organization.

Miller's new post at Ford was described by Henry Ford II as "recognition of the need for a senior officer to concentrate on the company's external affairs—to maintain better relations with government and with the public." For similar reasons, I propose that companies establish the position of *vice president—consumerism*. The executive holding this position would function at the staff level. He would be concerned with the corporation's external affairs and with the internal functions that have implications for consumerism. It would be his responsibility to:

> Develop an organizational structure and procedures that would ensure more consideration of ethical issues in decision making.

Work out strategic and tactical plans for keeping the company abreast of its responsibilities to consumerism.

Spell out the duties and responsibilities to the buying public of each department and function in the company, along with precise objectives and methods of measuring performance in accomplishing these objectives.

The vice president—consumerism would review marketing programs regularly. Policies must be periodically reexamined and, if necessary, their objectives redefined in order for the company to keep in step with the volatile demands of a more sophisticated and therefore more critical and demanding marketplace. He would also collaborate with:

1. Congress (as well as state legislatures and local civic authorities) in drafting new consumer legislation and regulations—and in drafting changes in existing consumer legislation and regulations.
2. The regulatory and enforcement departments and officials of government.
3. The various public consumer organizations—national, state, and local

Further Steps

The next organizational step might be the establishment of a task force which would report to the vice president—consumerism and represent him at meetings of line executives. This task force would also report on profit opportunities in existing and future consumer legislation.

The vice president—consumerism might organize a panel consisting of representatives of the public and of the trade. The purpose of the panel would be to provide management with a continuing playback on consumerism programs. It would also provide a listening post that would help management to anticipate potential consumerism trends.

The legal department would, of course, be closely aligned with the department headed by the vice president—consumerism. A practical resolution of this departmental kinship will obviously require a high degree of corporate statesmanship. (The strictly legal approach to the requirements of a "consumeristic" society is sterile and self-defeating.) In addition, the legal department should be restructured to include specialists in consumerism legislation and even specialists in certain aspects of consumer legislation that particularly affect the corporation.

Moreover, communications between the legal department and other departments on matters that affect consumerism must be reexamined. The tendency is for the legal department's conclusions to prevail—and that, too often, can be poor policy in our present-day society.

It would also appear advantageous to arrange for closer collaboration between the new department and the legal and marketing departments during the discussion stage of certain marketing programs so as to lessen the likelihood of a negative conclusion being reached later by the legal department.

The vice president—consumerism would, of course, maintain the closest liaison with the marketing department.

Trade Association Action

Trade associations, too, should make changes in their philosophy, organization, programs, and personnel budgets to meet the needs of consumerism. On balance, our trade associations, over the last several decades, have been immobilized by fears, made impotent by legal counsel, and operated with utterly inadequate budgets. Most of them have been slow to reorganize and to reorient themselves so as to provide government and industry members with the leadership and guidance called for by consumerism. And where they have recognized the gathering forces of consumerism, their typical posture has been annoyance, aggravation, frustration, resentment—and a fierce determination to defend the status quo to the last detail.

Recently a few trade associations have taken a different approach. If their example were followed by others, and if this trend were to gather momentum, U.S. industry would benefit greatly.

Conclusion

As I review the events and experience of recent years, several conclusions stand out:

First, technological progress will continue to require that marketing provide more guidance to the consumer.

Second, additional consumerism legislation is inevitable—and for years to come.

Third, marketing can avoid becoming a new type of quasi-utility only if it collaborates with government. However, its response to date has involved more confrontation than collaboration. The question seems to be *how* much utility-type regulation marketing will let itself in for, not *whether* it will become more controlled.

Fourth, the new generation of corporate executives (e.g., the new members of the Committee for Economic Development, who have shown an extraordinary grasp of the expanding opportunities and responsibilities of corporate citizenship) will insist on new and higher levels of marketing integrity. Under their enlightened direction, marketing will find profit, as well as other satisfactions, in greater public service.

43. *Situation Report — Black and White*

The economic gap between white and black is still tremendous, but it is narrowing. Negro median family income rose from 54% as much as white income in 1965 to 60% in 1968. The difference is less dramatic if the South, where half the blacks still live, is excluded. In the North Central and Western states, black family income runs 75% to 80% as high as white income.

The number of Negro families existing below the poverty level ($3,553 for a nonfarm family of four) dropped from 48% in 1959 to 29% in 1968. Poverty depends partly on whether there is a man around the house. During the 1959-68 period, the number of nonwhite "poverty" families headed by men declined from 1,452,000 to 697,000, but those headed by women rose from 683,000 to 734,000. The number of black families with incomes of $8,000 or more tripled in the 1950s and nearly tripled again in the 1960s.

But blacks' wages tend to run much lower than whites'. The Negro who completes four years of high school earns less than the white who finishes only eight years of elementary school. The black with four years of college has a median income of $7,754—or less than the $8,154 earned by the white who has only four years of high school. "Underemployment"—work in seasonal or part-time jobs—is

SOURCE. Reprinted by permission from *Time*, The Weekly Newsmagazine; Copyright Time Inc. 1970.

more common than for whites. Result: a black family often has to have two or more workers to earn as much as a white family with one member at work.

	Black	White
Median Family Income	$5,359	$8,936
Below Poverty Level	29%	8%
Below $5,000 a year	46.9%	19.9%
$8,000 and above	29.5%	57.6%
$25,000 and above	.4%	2.8%
Per Capita Income	$1,348	$2,616
Unemployment Overall (Feb. '70)	7.0%*	3.8%
Unemployment Among Married Men	2.5%*	1.4%
Unemployment Among Teen-Agers (Feb. '70)	25.3%*	11.7%
Receiving Welfare	16%*	3%
Number of Professional Workers (doctors, lawyers, teachers, etc.)	692,000*	10,031,000
Increase in Professional Jobs in 1960s	109%*	41%
Managerial Workers	254,000*	7,721,000
Increase in Managerial Jobs in 1960s	43%*	12%
Self-Employed (nonfarm)	293,000*	4,964,000
Own Home	38%*	64%
Own Car	40.3%	51.8%
Own Black-and-White TV	81.9%	77.5%
Own Color TV	12.4%	33.5%
Average Insurance Coverage	$2,750*	$6,600

*Includes all "nonwhites"—Americans of Indian, Chinese, Japanese and other origins, as well as blacks, who make up about 92% of the total.

PART FOUR
Future
Directions

A. *Problems and Fears*

INTRODUCTION *to part four*

We are the first society in history to have had the technical capability and wealth to bring the good life, no matter how we define it. But we have not yet agreed on any change in priorities away from the heavy, heavy burden of military expenditures. Seligman suggests that today's rebellion of youth is different from other generations, because today's youth are rejecting war and are arguing for a very different life style. Ross writes about William Shirer, who believes the United States is likely to become a fascist nation. Boulding speaks of our international interdependence on "Spaceship Earth." Lazer suggests ways the marketing system can help bring about the good life. Heilbroner lists some new priorities and Gamble and Mosman tell the reader that our perception of reality affects our actions.

Galbraith, Hoover and Maddox, Knauer, and Sullivan all have prescriptions of what to do about specific problems. And it is likely that the changing attitudes of citizens will have a major influence on marketing processes in the near future.

One person's solution is presented in the *Time* article about Ralph Nader, "The U.S.'s Toughest Customer." We are in the new era and some individuals are taking actions that seem right for them. Both Shaffer and Illich mention some of the questions we need to ask. At the University of Oregon we have been making some attempts at restructuring the educational experience so that we try some new and different ideas to help ensure that man's creations serve rather than destroy him. Part Four, "Future Directions," has nothing about solutions to the problems of human justice.

There are no simple solutions. Possibly only individuals acting and reacting within or beyond the bureaucracies can offer any real and viable solution.

44. *A Special Kind of Rebellion*

DANIEL SELIGMAN

The phrase itself is beginning to grate, but it seems more evident every week that the "generation gap" is a rather serious matter. It would be nice to believe that it isn't—that what we are witnessing is only the latest act in history's continuous-run tragicomedy about the rebellion of restless, rootless youth against the world of its elders. A fair number of Americans are in fact clinging to some such agreeable notion about the generation gap. The notion is agreeable because it implies that this young generation too will eventually come to terms with its elders and their institutions; that the arguments now swirling around the campuses will pass; and that at some point, looking back through a nostalgic haze, we will perceive they young rebels of the 1960's as legitimate successors to the flappers of the 1920's, the campus radicals of the 1930's, and the "beats" of the 1950's, all of whom influenced our society in one way or another but were ultimately absorbed into it.

But there is undeniably something special in the educational level of today's youth. Educated youth have to be taken seriously in any society; even when they condemn it bitterly, they are presumed to be its future leaders. Almost eight million members of the young generation today are or have been in college (versus about two million for that 1938 group). No other society in history has ever had to deal with *mass* educated youth.

These particular masses, furthermore, are condemning society in the most sweeping and extravagant terms. Some of their views have a quite revolutionary potential,

SOURCE. Reprinted from the January 1969 issue of *Fortune* Magazine by special permission; © 1968 Time, Inc.

involving challenges to constituted legal authority and to democratic procedures in general. Some formulations challenge the "moral authority" of the business system. Some are more concerned with established ideas about personal conduct and with other familiar bourgeois notions about style and taste, work and play, what's reasonable and what isn't, and what, in general, people should do with their lives. These revolutionary attitudes are not, of course, held by all or even most of the young; even on the campuses they are held only by a minority.

The minority is fairly sizable, however, and it appears to be growing. Its members include the well-publicized activists, who are—or, more precisely, play at being—"revolutionaries" in the traditional sense of the word; but they also include a much larger group that, without having done much about it, has accepted, almost casually it seems, many new-left formulations about the utter depravity of American society.

Some Votes for Che Guevara

This summary of youthful attitudes is based partly on a considerable amount of on-campus reporting by contributors to this special issue of FORTUNE, who together visited about forty colleges and universities. The summary also reflects extensive plowing through recent scholarly literature on youth; the "youth subculture" has become a large new field of inquiry for social scientists, some of whom are solemnly rendering the rites and customs of young Americans in accents reminiscent of Ruth Benedict on the Kwakiutl Indians. In addition, FORTUNE commissioned, and Daniel Yankelovich, Inc., a major attitude-research firm, executed, a depth survey of the beliefs of college-educated men and women who are eighteen through twenty-four.

The most important finding of all has to do with a sharp division on the campuses between those who are "practical-minded" and are in college because it looks like the natural route to the high-paying high-rank jobs, and those who, in effect, take good jobs and affluence for granted and are in college for a variety of less tangible reasons. This division seems to be extremely significant: students on one side of the line have attitudes about a wide range of issues that are strikingly different from those on the other side. Something like three-fifths of college students are on the "practical" side of the line. In general, their feelings about what they want from life and their beliefs about some public issues are remarkably similar to those of young men and women who have never attended college; whatever it may have done for their career prospects, higher education has certainly not revolutionized their basic values.

It is hard to find a label for the two-fifths who are in the minority, since they are defined, not by any particular beliefs or practices, but mainly by their *lack of concern* about making money. On the assumption that, as our society grows more affluent, some such unconcern will become widespread, we will refer to this minority as the "forerunner" group. Not surprisingly, the forerunners are more likely than the practical students to have privileged backgrounds. They are most likely to be majoring in the humanities. They are not only disdainful of "careerist," values, but are somewhat more likely than most students to be vague about their own career expectations; in general, however, they seem interested in finding work that is intellectually challenging and somehow relevant to their social concerns. The college environment seems to have fortified them in these attitudes. It has also led them to embrace positions that are dissident and extreme on many different public issues.

Half of the forerunners (versus only 25 percent of the practical group) said that none of the three major presidential candidates in last year's election held views close to their own. All three actually ran behind Che Guevara in a list of "personalities admired" by the forerunners.

About two-thirds of the group believe it approriate to engage in civil disobedience to further causes they support. Almost 10 percent say they would support civil disobedience *no matter what issues were involved.* (Presumably, a good many in this group don't really mean what they say; it is hard to envision many of them supporting disobedience by, for example, the Ku Klux Klan. Still, the response suggests a strong predisposition to nihilist attitudes.)

Two-thirds of the forerunners support draft resistance—i.e., efforts to disrupt and refusal to cooperate with the Selective Service System.

Well over half, when shown a list of reasons that have been advanced to justify going to war, registered doubts about all of the following: protection of "national interests," preserving "our honor," "protecting allies," and "keeping commitments"; only 14 percent said it was clearly worth going to war to keep commitments.

About half of the group indicated that they have less faith than their parents in democratic processes.

About half believe that the U.S. is a sick society.

45. The Self-Fulfilling Prophecy Related to Social Change and Marketing Systems

S. H. GAMBLE AND J. M. MOSSMAN

"If men define situations as real, they are real in their consequences."
W. J. THOMAS

In the early 1900's a German mathematician owned a horse called "Clever Hans." This animal was reported to perform mathematical computations, spell words, and even solve problems in musical harmony by tapping his feet. A panel of scientists ruled that fraud was not involved. These scientists could not detect cues given to the horse which might cause him to start and stop tapping his feet. In fact, the scientists pointed out that even members of an unfamiliar audience, who presented questions to the horse, usually received correct answers.

Not until Oscar Pfungst's famous experiments of 1911 was the truth about Clever Hans recognized. Pfungst discovered that Hans could not answer the questions correctly unless the questioner knew the answer and could be seen by the horse. Pfungst determined that it was the unwitting signals of the questioner, resulting from his own expectations of the horse's behavior, which gave Hans subtle cues. Thus, the horse's perception of the questioner's expectations, in the form of facial expressions or other physical movements, was responsible for Hans' amazing feats.

The Story of Clever Hans illustrates how expectations may possibly influence final outcomes. *This process of expected outcomes, resulting in the actual occurrence of these outcomes, is called "The Self-Fulfilling Prophecy Process."*

In general, the story of Clever Hans illustrates that there may be, from time to time, unimportant isolated occurrences of an unusual phenomenon called the Self-Fulfilling Prophecy. However, this is a gross understatement. In reality there are countless numbers of such processes operating constantly and some of these processes influence outcomes which are very important to individuals, organizations and/ or our society.

290

The idea of the Self-Fulfilling Prophecy (hereafter referred to as SFP) originated with the sociologist Robert Merton.[1] Merton conceptualized the SFP phenomenon as being ". . . in the beginning, a false definition of a situation evoking a new behavior which makes the originally false concept come true." In other words, *a prophecy (expectation) is self fulfilling if the original expectation of a future situation becomes a reality, and if the prophecy (expectation) is responsible for its own realization.*

The objective of this article is to establish that the self-fulfilling prophecy does exist, and to describe how it is important to our society in areas affecting marketing.

I. Self-Fulfilling Prophecies Have Been Identified by Researchers from Many Disciplines

Cases of the self-fulfilling prophecy have been discovered in many areas of the social sciences, particularly in psychology and sociology. But application of the SFP is not limited solely to the social sciences. Indeed, SFP effects have been found in areas as diverse as political science, medicine and economics. A selection of some of the most notable cases which are evidence of SFP are cited below.

Psychology: Robert Rosenthal and others have demonstrated in controlled experiments that SFP does exist in the laboratory and in the environment. Rosenthal selected ten undergraduate and graduate psychology students who were all proficient in conducting research. Twenty students were assigned to each researcher. Each of the subjects (the students) was shown photographs of people's faces, one at a time, by the researcher. The subject was then instructed to rate the degree of success or failure reflected in the facial expression of the person in the photo. Each face could be rated from −10 (extreme failure) to +10 (extreme success). Actually all the faces in the photos were quite natural; thus, the average total ratings should have produced a numerical score of zero.

All ten researchers were given identical instructions to read to their subjects as well as identical instructions on how to conduct the experiment. They were warned not to deviate from these instructions.

Finally, the researchers were informed that the purpose of the experiment was to see how well they could duplicate results which had already been well established. Half of the researchers were told that the "well established" finding was that people rated the faces in the photos as successful (+5). The other half were told that people rated the faces as unsuccessful (−5). Rosenthal reports:

> The results were clear-cut. Every researcher who was led to expect that the photographed people were successful obtained a higher average rating of success

[1] Robert K. Merton, *Social Theory and Social Structures,* Glencoe, Illinois: The Free Press, 1957, p. 423.

from his group than did any experimenter who expected low success ratings.

We repeated this experiment twice with different groups with the same results. Research in other laboratories has shown much the same result. Although not every experiment showed a significant effect, the probability that results of these experiments occurred by chance is less than one in a thousand billion.

Sociology. Robert Merton cites an even more general and critical example of SFP's effect in our society. Merton suggests that many Americans believe that Negroes are inferior; thus, they see to it that funds for education are not wasted on these "incompetents." They proceed to proclaim that their assumptions about the Negro's inferiority are validated by the fact that Negroes have proportionately "only" one-fifth as many college students as the whites do. Merton remarks, "One can scarcely be amazed by this transparent bit of legerdemain."

Economics. Expectations are closely related to the behavior of our economy and related economic variables. The following are two examples of relationships between expectation and economic variables.

Research has shown that the more publication of income statistics will push the average income upward, primarily because many of those whose incomes are below average will make greater efforts to attain an income level consistent with their expectation of themselves.

The announcement of an expected upturn or downturn in economic activity will result in that occurrence becoming more likely. This is true to the extent that the information source is credible. President Nixon's special effort in 1969 to gather industrial leaders for a special session in which he attempted to convince them that they should expect a cooling of the economy is one example of a belief in this principle. The relationship between William M. Martin's press commentaries and fluctuations in the stock market for over two decades also tends to confirm this principle.

In summary, the studies and examples included here suggest that people actually do abide by their own expectations and communicate these expectations to others in a multitude of conscious and unconscious ways. Hot dog stands and Clever Hans, politicians and placebos, black Americans and Band Wagons all provide evidence of how the self-fulfilling prophecy manifests itself in a broad range of environments and activities in our society. The preceding examples illustrate the importance of SFP as an influence on some critical issues facing our nation.

However, our main concern in this article is to show how the SFP relates to the marketing system. There is wide-open opportunity for using the SFP to solve many important social and organizational problems related to marketing. Two reasons are apparent: Many major problems of society and organizations are closely related to marketing, and the relationships between SFP and these problems are not clearly recognized.

II. SFP May Have a Critical Influence on a Broad Range of Problems in Our Society Which Are Related to Marketing

More now than ever before, marketing processes and knowledge are being applied to a broad range of societal and organizational problems by a large group of business executives, public administrators, and academicians. As a result of writings, such as Philip Kotler and Sidney Levy's "Broadening the Concept of Marketing" (see p. 39),[2] the boundaries of the application of marketing expertise are widening.

SFP is related in some way to most problems of marketing systems, whether they are in particular organizations or in the general society. Because of the importance of these problems and the lack of understanding of the particular relationships between SFP and problem solving, the opportunity for improvement through additional investigation is considerable.

Each of the examples below is a major issue in our society or in organizations. Each is also an important problem for marketers and a problem closely related to SFP.

Problem I. Our Society Underutilizes Present and Potential Black Entrepreneurs

As mentioned earlier, Robert Merton states that many Americans believe that Negroes are inferior. More specifically, the general attitude exists that Negroes cannot be good businessmen. As usual, supporters of the inherent inferiority idea have found statistics to support their position. They point out:

That only 45,000 of the 5,000,000 businesses in this country are owned and operated by Negroes.[3]

That in an almost entirely black area like Harlem, not more than 20% of the businesses are owned by Negroes, and[4]

That in the important commercial activity of food retailing, not more than 3% of the Negro food bill is spent in black grocery stores.[5]

Unfortunately, these statistics describe the "what" not the "why" of the Negro's poor performance. The actual cause is closely tied to the Self-Fulfilling Prophecy. A careful examination of the following statements by John H. Johnson and Abraham

[2]Philip Kotler and Sidney Levy, "Broadening the Concept of Marketing," *The Journal of Marketing,* January 1969, Vol. 33, No. 1, pp. 10-15.

[3]Eugene Foley, "The Negro Businessman: In Search of a Tradition," in *The American Negro,* Talcott Parsons and Kenneth B. Clark, Eds., Boston: Beacon Press, 1965, p. 559.

[4]"The Urban Crises," *Fortune,* January 1968, p. 180.

[5]"Mobilizing Dorman Resources: Negro Entrepreneurs," *The MBA,* May 1967.

S. Venable indicate that both men, generally, recognize the role of individual and reference group expectations in guiding occupational choice and performance.

John H. Johnson,[6] president of the $12-million-a-year Johnson Publishing Company says:

> The trouble is that the Negro has no heritage in business. When he was a boy, he did not hear business discussed at the dinner table. To the extent that he has been exposed to success, it has been among ministers, lawyers, and other professional people. He does not identify with the Business Man.

Abraham S. Venable had the following comment on the Negro attitude toward business:

> More often than not, many Negro businessmen are a symbol of frustration and hopelessness rather than an example of success and leadership. As a result, "business" per se is not a polite word in the Negro community, and Negro parents as a rule tend to discourage their children from pursuing business careers either as employees or as entrepreneurs.

The major point from both men is that Negro males have reference groups which do not instill in them an expectation or aspiration to be business entrepreneurs. And Johnson and Venable suggest that this negative expectation prevents these men from becoming successful businessmen. If this is the case, or even partially true, then the Self-Fulfilling Prophecy is a strong influence on the entrepreneurial success of blacks.

To the extent that negative expectations result in no performance or a poor performance by blacks, a shift to more positive expectations, would, to some extent, result in a more favorable entrepreneurial performance. At present our society is underutilizing a great many persons in minority groups because of some of the conditions mentioned. Marketers and marketing systems can contribute to a solution to this problem by applying, in an organized fashion, a program for shifting expectations to a more realistic level. Wroe Alderson[7] in the "Mission of Marketing" (see p. 49) mentions that one of the major jobs of marketing is to bring new people into the market economy. The Self-Fulfilling Prophecy process is an additional tool to help marketers resolve the problem of underutilization of human resources.

---

[6]"How John Johnson Made It," *Fortune,* January 1968, p. 180.

[7]Wroe Alderson, "The Mission of Marketing," in Wroe Alderson and Michael H. Halbert, *Men, Motives, and Markets,* Englewood Cliffs, New Jersey: Prentice-Hall, 1968.

Problem II.   The High Price of Retail Goods
in the Inner City

Fred Sturdivant,[8] David Caplovitz,[9] and John Wish[10] have all provided evidence that the prices of goods in retail outlets in the inner city are higher than in surrounding areas. The diseconomies of small, neighborhood, retail outlets is partially responsible for this situation. However, many reasons exist for higher prices in the inner city and many of them are related to SFP effects. For example:

> Inner city dwellers do not expect what their suburban counterparts consider to be quality goods, at competitive prices, free from misleading selling practices.

> Few large self-service outlets build and operate units in the inner city because they do not believe that large operations in this area can be profitable.

> Companies which build outlets in the inner city tend to place low quality managers in the outlets because they do not expect the outlet to do well. Because top management candidates—who have the first opportunity to choose their work location—choose outlets which they believe will perform best during their administration, inner city outlets are usually not among the first locations to be chosen.

> The transportation systems operate under the belief that the inner city is a low-volume marginal operation, and therefore it uses older, smaller equipment in this geographical area.

These and other factors combine to increase the price of goods in the inner city. Unfortunately, some of the evidence which causes these expectations is accurate. The potential sales volume of supermarkets in the inner city is lower than in suburbia for these reasons: low family incomes, more shoplifting, less mobility in shopping, dependence on credit, reluctance to patronize a new untested seller, and less awareness or interest in price differences.

In spite of the fact that some causes of high prices in the urban-core area are based on apparent economic facts, expectations play a crucial role in the continuing cycle of high price-low income-low opportunity-despair which exists in the inner city.

The cycle might be shifted and these expectations might be realized to a greater degree if consumers began to *expect* lower prices; if food sellers began to *value* more highly the performance of store managers in the inner city; if young managers began to *expect* that their performance in an inner city store was an effective means

[8]Fred Sturdivant, "Better Deal for Ghetto Shoppers," *Harvard Business Review.*

[9]David Caplovitz, *The Poor Pay More.*

[10]John Wish, Unpublished Study of Retail Prices of Foods in Portland, Oregon.

to help their careers; if food sellers *expected* that more sales were possible with a concentrated promotional effort to change consumers' buying habits, and distribution systems *expected* that greater profitability was possible in the inner city with the addition of larger and better equipment. In other words, a new and more optimistic Self-Fulfilling Prophecy might help alleviate the problems of the existing subculture because new expectations could result in the realization of a new cycle similar to the expectations of the sellers, distributors, and consumers who are the major participants in the system.

Further investigation and trial are necessary to know what specific changes might occur, but it seems plausible that SFP could contribute to a more desirable sequence of events.

Problem III. Unconcern for a Quality of Life

Why have organizations not brought more people into the work force? Why have organizations been allowed to pollute the environment? And of equal importance, why haven't polluters not been forced to pay for the damage they have done to earth's living systems? The answer is mostly expectations.

Historically, Americans have perceived the private sector as a group of organizations who were primarily concerned with profit. Remnants of the puritan ethic and *laissez faire* have had a strong influence on the public's attitude toward organizational behavior. Faith in free enterprise and the price mechanism has diminished criticism of the means used to attain profitable ends. In short, our society has not expected organizations to be concerned with their social responsibilities and their overall influence on the resources they consume: therefore organizations have behaved in ways consistent with these expectations.

The Sherman Act of 1890 and other acts since have limited the means whereby organizations can attain profit, but not until the late 1950's and the early 60's did our society begin to change its attitude about the responsibilities of the business organization. In the early sixties, public spokesmen began to express increased concern about the social responsibilities of organizations. Since 1960, more and more persons have become concerned with the means to the ends, as well as the ends themselves.

The above discussion are examples where SFP is influencing important processes in our society. And very important, the expectations are being marketed. This is probably a major reason why the more common SFP process which tends to discourage a change of the status quo and the present establishment is being redirected by the expectations of a signficant minority group.

The question for the future for all SFP's and all social issues is which mixes of communication will be most effective in communicating the kinds of expectations we have been discussing and how can society best direct SFP's in meeting society's long-range needs.

46. *The Part-Time Buyer and the Marketing Profession*

VIRGINIA KNAUER

The marketing profession has shown that it can create a desire for the new as well as the old. The responsible use of this talent is necessary if we are to retain our system of free enterprise.

The consumer is, as you know, a vital part of this system.

One of the AMA's major objectives, as you also know, is to uphold sound honest practices and to keep marketing on a high ethical plane. There can be no quarrel with the statement that sound honest marketing practices, and ethical marketing are the consumer's best protection.

The welfare of the American consumer is my business—and yours.

It is on his behalf that I wish to enlist your thoughts today.

When I received your invitation, I wondered what I should say to you that would secure your support for a new imaginative approach toward the consumer. How I could persuade you that the problems that underlie the press for consumer rights must be solved, not shelved.

Should I, I wondered, repeat what all thoughtful economists, businessmen and educators have stressed; that our population is not the only thing that has exploded in recent years?

So have our technical skills.

SOURCE. *American Marketing Association Meetings*, "The Part-Time Buyer and the Marketing Profession," speech by Virginia Knauer, August 1969.

That explosion has brought with it a vast increase in the sophistication of our equipment, products and materials in our markets and in our marketing techniques.

This brave new world of machines that can do almost anything, of products so numerous one cannot count them, of markets so vast that one cannot envisage them, has, in turn, generated a new responsibility on the part of business to give the consumer the information and the protection he must have if he is to buy safely, wisely and well.

Today's consumer cannot cope with the complexity of today's market, as we used to, and as we wished we could. Although we know a great deal more than we did before about a great many more products, we do not know more than the country's best chemists, mechanics, electricians and nutritionists who are responsible for those innovations.

Our creativity, our innovation, our rapid technological advance tend to make our information obsolete, almost before we digest it, let alone act on it.

We are amateur, part-time buyers. And as such, we cannot possibly compete with the professional full-time seller even on one product, to say nothing of the enormous number we have today.

Products that must be bought repeatedly come in a bewildering profusion of sizes, shapes, and prices, often with incomplete and misleading claims concerning their contents, capacity, capability and care.

The buyer must ask himself:

Is "improved" really improved when it doesn't do as good a job as the original unimproved version?

Is it fair to our children to buy products that are harmful?

What does "hours of protection" mean? Will the spray that is said to be good for "hours" be effective until it is washed off? Or does it contain an ingredient that makes it evaporate? In one hour, in two hours, in three, when?

Will the suit shrink, the dress run, the zipper break on that one day when it is most important that it does not?

How, in Heaven's name, does one know that a durable billed as "jumbo" is really smaller than a similar one not so billed, until one compares them?

These are questions the consumer has to answer every time he goes to market.

It takes time to answer them.

Economists know that today time is money.

So does the busy consumer, and he resents having to spend his time checking the marketer's claims.

Nobody wants a computer on his shopping cart. Nobody wants mumbo jumbo, in place of good hard fact.

We all know that a satisfied customer is a repeat customer.

But the customer is not satisfied.

And he will not be until he obtains the labels or packaging he needs to enable him to make basic unit price comparisons between the products he buys, without spending all day at it.

Marketers are well aware that the market is no longer controlled by the simple fact that good products sell, bad ones don't.

It is no longer true that the market is self-policing because the buyer is king.

King buyer is in danger of being checkmated by the complexity of the market.

47. *On Institutional Obsolescence and Innovation — Background for Professional Dialogue on Public Policy*

JAMES DUNCAN SHAFFER

The Emerging Political Economy

The Bureaucracies.—If I were called upon to name the emerging political economy after its most obvious characteristic, the name would be bureaucracy. In our concern for the growing discrepancy between potential and achieved quality of life, we must examine the behavior of bureaucratic organizations. A bureaucracy has among its characteristics the following: It has a life of its own—the incentives perceived by its management may be quite independent of the intentions of its "owners," be they stockholders, legislators, citizens, or members; it spends much of its energy in protective tactics designed for a survival independent of performance; in a changing society, the bounds of control of a bureaucracy frequently become inappropriate to the problems with which it is intended to deal; it is frequently structured to a narrow interest and responsibility, but with capacity for extensive external effects; and it creates positions of extensive power and control, often undisciplined.

Yet, organized technical competence is indispensable to the modern political economy; technology, specialization, and essential protection of society's interests dictate it. We must rethink our ideas of instituting bureaucracies to make them more responsive to the needs of society.

SOURCE. Abridged from the original article which appeared in the *American Journal of Agricultural Economics,* May 1969. Reprinted by permission.

The Corporation.—Berle reminds us that the founding fathers specifically denied the federal government the power to create corporations, because of concern for the potential concentration of power inherent in the corporation. Their concern was prophetic. By 1967, the 100 largest corporations held 48 percent of the assets in manufacturing in the U.S. And Berle argues that "if a rather larger group is taken, the statistics would probably show that about two-thirds of the economically productive assets in the United States, excluding agriculture, are owned by a group of not more than five hundred corporations." The control of these giant corporations is in the hands of the managing bureaucracy, with 100 or so trust departments of banks managing very large stock holdings for individuals and pension trust funds with power to check the performance of the management. Surely this represents the greatest concentration of economic power in history. What institutional innovations are needed to insure that this power will be exercised in the public interest?

The bureaucracies of the large corporations follow a number of practices (protective institutions) which significantly modify the outcome of the market. They avoid uncertainty and improve vertical coordination through vertical integration and contracts, thus substituting administrative coordination and negotiation for spot market coordination. They have the capacity, within limits set by monopolistic competition, to manage prices. They avoid the uncertainty of the capital market, at least to some extent, by assuring a large part of financing from retained earnings. This gives them significant advantage over small firms. The uncertainties of the labor market are reduced by negotiations with labor unions (thus individual workers avoid marginal evaluation of their effort). Product markets are modified by negotiated contracts with buyers, especially with the government, and by managing consumer demand through advertising, promotion, and product design.

According to Galbraith, a number of the needs of the corporate bureaucracy are also provided by the state. The state trains technicians and spends large sums on technical research valuable to the expansion of the corporation and the economy. And the state reduces risk to the corporate bureaucracy by providing programs for price stabilization and growth; planning is more successful with a small but regular rate of inflation.

We are only beginning to understand the implications of the institutions associated with product differentiation and promotion. They are clearly very significant protective institutions for the firm. Advertising, offering very great economies of scale, is an incentive to larger size and an effective barrier to entry by small firms. And advertising creates a new property in the form of the *image* of the product. Advertising represents about 10 percent of the value added by consumer goods manufacturers.

Advertising has another dimension in the emerging political economy, since it is designed to change preferences and has substantial effects on the content of the mass media. The concept of the "good life" and acceptable behavior for many Americans is defined in their many hours of exposure to television sponsored by the large advertisers.

On the Role of Applied Social Scientists

Public policy is concerned with changes in the formal rules that regulate the activities of members of the society. These rules specify rights and obligations. By and large, the social science disciplines have taken the position that these rules cannot be judged. They are the province of ethics and moral philosophy. But surely the rules of the political economy must be judged, and I believe that applied social scientists have a major role to play in the process.

Alternative rules lead to different consequences. It is the province of applied social science to understand the complex social systems and predict the consequences of alternative sets of rules.

The variables considered relevant in any policy issue will clearly affect any predictions made. To a large extent, the variables considered relevant are determined by the discipline of the social scientists. And, the very high levels of specialization by the different social science disciplines bring a narrow perspective to their analysis, greatly reducing the effectiveness of social science in policy formulation. A part of the present problem in U.S. public policy is the failure to consider the essential variables involved in our critical policy issues. For example, the sociologist's basic question concerning the factors that hold the society together must be considered along with the questions about *economic* growth. Too many of our socio-economic policies have effects quite unintended by the policy makers.

Prediction of consequences depends upon description of the system, which can be approached as an activity of pure science. In this connection, I have been wondering if the habits of thought imposed by our equilibrium models may not restrict an understanding of the complex evolving system. Buckley contrasts equilibrium, homeostatic, and complex adaptive models, describing the latter in part as ". . . open 'internally' as well as externally in that the interchanges among their components may result in significant changes in the nature of the components themselves with important consequences for the system as a whole . . . True feedback loops make possible not only self-regulation, but self-direction or, at least, adaptation to a changing environment, such that the system may change or elaborate its structure as a condition of survival or viability." Buckley argues that the socio-cultural system more closely fits the complex adaptive model. I do not believe the dynamic system can be described by equilibrium models or theories of advantage. We need also accept the fact that the system is too complex to ever completely specify, and we will have to live with a fairly high level of uncertainty as to outcome of the dynamic system.

I believe a substantial effort should be spent in diagnosis of society's ills and prescription of institutional innovations to deal with the problems. Prescription involves art as well as science. We need to develop the skill to create the concepts of new institutions that will serve the purposes of society. For social scientists of this persuasion, this means being a social critic. *The universities should nurture the social critic and support extensive dialogue on issues of public policy, as should the academic professional associations. It is an essential input to the development of the emerging society.* And university professors need much more aggressively to perform this essential social function.

Our technology has liberated us from the base tyranny of the environment, but we have not adjusted to the new freedom with its implicit premise that a meaningful life for all the members of our society is limited only by our will and creativity in structuring our institutions.

B. *Some Possibilities*

48. *Can U.S. Go Fascist?*

NANCY L. ROSS

WASHINGTON—"We may be the first country to go fascist democratically."

Author William L. Shirer, who chronicled the rise of Naziism and the takeover of the Vichy government, finds disturbing parallels between prewar Germany and France and the United States of 30 years later.

Shirer, whose "Rise and Fall of the Third Reich" was a best seller nearly a decade ago, was in town to promote his latest book, "The Collapse of the Third Republic," published last November.

Interviewed at his hotel, the former CBS foreign correspondent whose early World War II broadcasts from Berlin, like those of Edward R. Murrow from London, made his voice familiar to millions of Americans remarked, "I used to believe only totalitarian states brainwashed people."

Now 65, Shirer sees history repeating itself in what he considers Vice President Agnew's threat of government action against the press, in government propaganda about Vietnam, in small-town accents on patriotism and in the swing of labor, police and the "petite bourgeoisie" to George Wallace.

"We saw it in France during the 1934 riots. The press and the people went over to the right, which showed it could almost overthrow a republic. It was the small people who went to Naziism, who supported fascism.

"In this country, support of reactionary policies is unduly widespread among the very people who would suffer the most under them. Fascism does nothing for them."

SOURCE. Reprinted with permission from *The Washington Post.*

Shirer now lives in Lenox, Mass., best known as the home of the Berkshire Music Center and Alice's Restaurant. During last November's Vietnam moratorium, he joined Arlo Guthrie and other young demonstrators on the town square. Few adults showed up.

"The American people are afraid of so many things now," concluded Shirer. "Afraid to demonstrate, pressed to conform. Like the French who couldn't see their own interests during the '30s for all their petty treaties, Americans today are afraid to face reality in foreign policy."

49. *The Economics of the Coming Spaceship Earth* KENNETH BOULDING

We are now in the middle of a long process of transition in the nature of the image which man has of himself and his environment. Primitive men, and to a large extent also men of the early civilizations, imagined themselves to be living on a virtually illimitable plane. There was almost always somewhere beyond the known limits of human habitation, and over a very large part of the time that man has been on earth, there has been something like a frontier. That is, there was always some place else to go when things got too difficult, either by reason of the deterioration of the natural environment or a deterioration of the social structure in places where people happened to live. The image of the frontier is probably one of the oldest images of mankind, and it is not surprising that we find it hard to get rid of.

Gradually, however, man has been accustoming himself to the notion of the spherical earth and a closed sphere of human activity. A few unusual spirits among the ancient Greeks perceived that the earth was a sphere. It was only with the circumnavigations and the geographical explorations of the fifteenth and sixteenth centuries, however, that the fact that the earth was a sphere became at all widely known and accepted. Even in the nineteenth century, the commonest map was Mercator's projection, which visualizes the earth as an illimitable cylinder, essentially a plane wrapped around the globe, and it was not until the Second World War and the development of the air age that the global nature of the planet really

SOURCE. From *Beyond Economics*, copyright 1969 by The University of Michigan Press, Ann Arbor, Mich. Reprinted by permission.

entered the popular imagination. Even now we are very far from having made the moral, political, and psychological adjustments which are implied in this transition from the illimitable plane to the closed sphere.

Economists in particular, for the most part, have failed to come to grips with the ultimate consequences of the transition from the open to the closed earth. One hesitates to use the terms "open" and "closed" in this connection, as they have been used with so many different shades of meaning. Nevertheless, it is hard to find equivalents. The open system, indeed, has some similarities to the open system of von Bertalanffy, in that it implies that some kind of a structure is maintained in the midst of a throughput from inputs to outputs. In a closed system, the outputs of all parts of the system are linked to the inputs of other parts. There are no inputs from outside and no outputs to the outside; indeed, there is no outside at all. Closed systems, in fact, are very rare in human experience, in fact almost by definition unknowable, for if there are genuinely closed systems around us, we have no way of getting information into them or out of them; and hence if they are really closed, we would be quite unaware of their existence. We can only find out about a closed system if we participate in it. Some isolated primitive societies may have approximated to this, but even these had to take inputs from the environment and give outputs to it. All living organisms, including man himself, are open systems. They have to receive inputs in the shape of air, food, water, and give off outputs in the form of effluvia and excrement. Deprivation of input of air, even for a few minutes, is fatal. Deprivation of the ability to obtain any input or to dispose of any output is fatal in a relatively short time. All human societies have likewise been open systems. They receive inputs from the earth, the atmosphere, and the waters, and they give outputs into these reservoirs; they also produce inputs internally in the shape of babies and outputs in the shape of corpses. Given a capacity to draw upon inputs and to get rid of outputs, an open system of this kind can persist indefinitely.

There are some systems—such as the biological phenotype, for instance the human body—which cannot maintain themselves indefinitely by inputs and outputs because of the phenomenon of aging. This process is very little understood. It occurs, evidently, because there are some outputs which cannot be replaced by any known input. There is not the same necessity for aging in organizations and in societies, although an analogous phenomenon may take place. The structure and composition of an organization or society, however, can be maintained by inputs of fresh personnel from birth and education as the existing personnel ages and eventually dies. Here we have an interesting example of a system which seems to maintain itself by the self-generation of inputs, and in this sense is moving towards closure. The input of people (that is, babies) is also an output of people (that is, parents).

Systems may be open or closed in respect to a number of classes of inputs and outputs. Three important classes are matter, energy, and information. The present world economy is open in regard to all three. We can think of the world economy or "econosphere" as a subset of the "world set," which is the set of all objects of possible discourse in the world. We then think of the state of the econopshere at any one moment as being the total capital stock, that is, the set of all objects, people, organizations, and so on, which are interesting from the point of view of the system of exchange. This total stock of capital is clearly an open system in the sense that it has inputs and outputs, inputs being production which adds to the capital stock, outputs being consumption which subtracts from it. From a material point of view, we see objects passing from the noneconomic into the economic set in the process of production, and we similarly see products passing out of the economic set as their value becomes zero. Thus we see the econosphere as a material process involving the discovery and mining of fossil fuels, ores, etc., and at the other end a process by which the effluents of the system are passed out into noneconomic reservoirs—for instance, the atmosphere and the oceans—which are not appropriated and do not enter into the exchange system.

From the point of view of the energy system, the econosphere involves inputs of available energy in the form, say, of water power, fossil fuels, or sunlight, which are necessary in order to create the material throughput and to move matter from the noneconomic set into the economic set or even out of it again; and energy itself is given off by the system in a less available form, mostly in the form of heat. These inputs of available energy must come either from the sun (the energy supplied by other stars being assumed to be negligible) or it may come from the earth itself, either through its internal heat or through its energy of rotation or other motions, which generate, for instance, the energy of the tides. Agriculture, a few solar machines, and water power use the current available energy income. In advanced societies this is supplemented very extensively by the use of fossil fuels, which represent as it were a capital stock of stored-up sunshine. Because of this capital stock of energy, we have been able to maintain an energy input into the system, particularly over the last two centuries, much larger than we would have been able to do with existing techniques if we had had to rely on the current input of available energy from the sun or the earth itself. This supplementary input, however, is by its very nature exhaustible.

The inputs and outputs of information are more subtle and harder to trace, but also represent an open system, related to, but not wholly dependent on, the transformations of matter and energy. By far the larger amount of information and knowledge is self-generated by the human society, though a certain amount of information comes into the sociosphere in the form of light from the universe outside. The information that comes from the universe has certainly affected man's image of himself and of his environment, as we can easily visualize if we suppose that we lived on a planet with a total cloud-cover that kept out all information from the exterior universe. It is only in very recent times, of course, that the information coming in from the universe has been captured and coded into the form of a complex image of what the universe is like outside the earth; but even in primitive times, man's perception of the heavenly bodies has always profoundly affected his image of earth and of himself. It is the information generated within the planet, however, and particularly that generated by man himself, which forms by far the larger part of the information system. We can think of the stock of knowledge, or as Teilhard de Chardin called it, the "nöosphere," and consider this as an open system, losing knowledge through aging and death and gaining it through birth and education and the ordinary experience of life.

From the human point of view, knowledge or information is by far the most important of the three systems. Matter only acquires significance and only enters the sociosphere or the econosphere insofar as it becomes an object of human knowledge. We can think of capital, indeed, as frozen knowledge or knowledge imposed on the material world in the form of improbable arrangements. A machine, for instance, originated in the mind of man, and both its construction and its use involve information processes imposed on the material world by man himself. The cumulation of knowledge, that is, the excess of its production over its consumption, is the key to human development of all kinds, especially to economic development. We can see this preeminence of knowledge very clearly in the experiences of countries where the material capital has been destroyed by a war, as in Japan and Germany. The knowledge of the people was not destroyed, and it did not take long, therefore, certainly not more than ten years, for most of the material capital to be reestablished again. In a country such as Indonesia, however, where the knowledge did not exist, the material capital did not come into being either. By "knowledge" here I mean, of course, the whole cognitive structure, which includes valuations and motivations as well as images of the factual world.

The concept of entropy, used in a somewhat loose sense, can be applied to all three of these open systems. In the case of material systems, we can distinguish between entropic processes, which take concentrated materials and diffuse them through the oceans or over the earth's surface or into the atmosphere, and anti-entropic processes, which take diffuse materials and concentrate them. Material entropy can be taken as a measure of the uniformity of the distribution of elements and, more uncertainly, compounds and other structures on the earth's surface. There is, fortunately, no law of increasing material entropy, as there is in the corresponding case of energy, as it is quite possible to concentrate diffused materials if energy inputs are allowed. Thus the processes for fixation of nitrogen from the air, processes for the extraction of magnesium or other elements from the sea, and processes for the desalinization of sea water are anti-entropic in the material sense, though the reduction of material entropy has to be paid for by inputs of energy and also inputs of information, or at least a stock of information in the system. In regard to matter, therefore, a closed system is conceivable, that is, a system in which there is neither increase nor decrease in material entropy. In such a system all outputs from consumption would constantly be recycled to become inputs for production, as for instance, nitrogen in the nitrogen cycle of the natural ecosystem.

In regard to the energy system there is, unfortunately, no escape from the grim Second Law of Thermodynamics; and if there were no energy inputs into the earth, any evolutionary or developmental process would be impossible. The large energy inputs which we have obtained from fossil fuels are strictly temporary. Even the most optimistic predictions would expect the easily available supply of fossil fuels to be exhausted in a mere matter of centuries at present rates of use. If the rest of the world were to rise to American standards of power consumption, and still more if world population continues to increase, the exhaustion of fossil fuels would be even more rapid. The development of nuclear energy has improved this picture, but has not fundamentally altered it, at least in present technologies, for fissionable material is still relatively scarce. If we should achieve the economic use of energy through fusion, of course, a much larger source of energy materials would be available, which would expand the time horizons of supplementary energy input into an open social system by perhaps tens to hundreds of thousands of years. Failing this, however, the time is not very far distant, historically speaking, when man will once more have to retreat to his current energy input from the sun, even though this could be used much more effectively than in the past with increased knowledge. Up to now, certainly, we have not got very far with the technology of using current solar energy, but the possibility of substantial improvements in the future is certainly high. It may be, indeed, that the biological revolution which is just beginning will produce a solution to this problem, as we develop artificial organisms which are capable of much more efficient transformation of solar energy into easily available forms than any that we now have. As Richard Meier has suggested, we may run our machines in the future with methane-producing algae.

The question of whether there is anything corresponding to entropy in the information system is a puzzling one, though of great interest. There are certainly many examples of social systems and cultures which have lost knowledge, especially in transition from one generation to the next, and in which the culture has therefore degenerated. One only has to look at the folk culture of the Appalachian migrants to American cities to see a culture which started out as a fairly rich European folk culture in Elizabethan times and which seems to have lost both skills, adaptability, folk tales, songs, and almost everything that goes up to make richness and complexity in a culture, in the course of about ten generations. The Americans Indians on reservations provide another example of such degradation of the information and knowledge system. On the other hand, over a great part of human history, the growth of knowledge in the earth as a whole seems to have been almost continuous, even though there have been times of relatively slow growth and times of rapid growth. As it is knowledge of certain kinds that produces the growth of knowledge in general, we have here a very subtle and complicated system, and it is hard to put one's finger on the particular elements in a culture which make knowledge grow more or less rapidly, or even which make it decline. One of the great puzzles in this connection, for instance, is why the take-off into science, which represents an "acceleration," or an increase in the rate of growth of knowledge in European society in the sixteenth century, did not take place in China, which at that time (about 1600) was unquestionably ahead of Europe, and one would think even more ready for the breakthrough. This is perhaps the most crucial question in the theory of social development, yet we must confess that it is very little understood. Perhaps the most significant factor in this connection is the existence of "slack" in the culture, which permits a divergence from established patterns and activity which is not merely devoted to reproducing the existing society but is devoted to changing it. China was perhaps too well-organized and had too little slack in its society to produce the kind of acceleration which we find in the somewhat poorer and less well-organized but more diverse societies of Europe.

The closed earth of the future requires economic principles which are somewhat different from those of the open earth of the past. For the sake of picturesqueness, I am tempted to call the open economy the "cowboy economy," the cowboy being symbolic of the illimitable plains and also associated with reckless, exploitative, romantic, and violent behavior, which is characteristic of open societies. The closed economy of the future might similarly be called the "spaceman" economy, in which the earth has become a single spaceship, without unlimited reservoirs of anything, either for extraction or for pollution, and in which, therefore, man must find his place in a cyclical ecological system which is capable of continuous reproduction of material form even though it cannot escape having inputs of energy. The difference between the two types of economy becomes most apparent in the attitude towards consumption. In the cowboy economy, consumption is regarded as a good thing and production likewise; and the success of the economy is measured by the amount of the throughput from the "factors of production," a part of which, at any rate, is extracted from the reservoirs of raw materials and noneconomic objects, and another part of which is output into the reservoirs of pollution. If there are infinite reservoirs from which material can be obtained and into which effluvia can be deposited, then the throughput is at least a plausible measure of the success of the economy. The gross national product is a rough measure of this total throughput. It should be possible, however, to distinguish that part of the GNP which is derived from exhaustible and that which is derived from reproducible resources, as well as that part of consumption which represents effluvia and that which represents input into the productive system again. Nobody, as far as I know, has ever attempted to break down the GNP in this way, although it would be an interesting and extremely important exercise, which is unfortunately beyond the scope of this paper.

By contrast, in the spaceman economy, throughput is by no means a desideratum, and is indeed to be regarded as something to be minimized rather than maximized. The essential measure of the success of the economy is not production and consumption at all, but the nature, extent, quality, and complexity of the total capital stock, including in this the state of the human bodies and minds included in the system. In the spaceman economy, what we are primarily concerned with is stock maintenance, and any technological change which results in the maintenance of a given total stock with a lessened throughput (that is, less production and consumption) is clearly a gain. This idea that both production and consumption are bad things rather than good things is very strange to economists, who have been obsessed with the income-flow concepts to the exclusion, almost, of capital-stock concepts.

There are actually some very tricky and unsolved problems involved in the questions as to whether human welfare or well-being is to be regarded as a stock or a flow. Something of both these elements seems actually to be involved in it, and as far as I know there have been practically no studies directed towards identifying these two dimensions of human satisfaction. Is it, for instance, eating that is a good thing, or is it being well fed? Does economic welfare involve having nice clothes, fine houses, good equipment, and so on, or is it to be measured by the depreciation and the wearing out of these things? I am inclined myself to regard the stock concept as most fundamental, that is, to think of being well fed as more important than eating, and to think even of so-called services as essentially involving the restoration of a depleting psychic capital. Thus I have argued that we go to a concert in order to restore a psychic condition which might be called "just having gone to a concert," which, once established, tends to depreciate. When it depreciates beyond a certain point, we go to another concert in order to restore it. If it depreciates rapidly, we go to a lot of concerts; if it depreciates slowly, we go to few. On this view, similarly, we eat primarily to restore bodily homeostasis, that is, to maintain a condition of being well fed, and so on. On this view, there is nothing desirable in consumption at all. The less consumption we can maintain a given state with, the better off we are. If we had clothes that did not wear out, houses that did not depreciate, and even if we could maintain our bodily condition without eating, we would clearly be much better off.

It is this last consideration, perhaps, which makes one pause. Would we, for instance, really want an operation that would enable us to restore all our bodily tissues by intravenous feeding while we slept? Is there not, that is to say, a certain virtue in throughput itself, in activity itself, in production and consumption itself, in raising food and in eating it? It would certainly be rash to exclude this possibility. Further interesting problems are raised by the demand for variety. We certainly do not want a constant state to be maintained; we want fluctuations in the state. Otherwise there would be no demand for variety in food, for variety in scene, as in travel, for variety in social contact, and so on. The demand for variety can, of course, be costly, and sometimes it seems to be too costly to be tolerated or at least legitimated, as in the case of marital partners, where the maintenance of a homeostatic state in the family is usually regarded as much more desirable than the variety and excessive throughput of the libertine. There are problems here which the economics profession has neglected with astonishing singlemindedness. My own attempts to call attention to some of them, for instance, in two articles, as far as I can judge, produced no response whatever; and economists continue to think and act as if production, consumption, throughput, and the GNP were the sufficient and adequate measure of economic success.

It may be said, of course, why worry about all this when the spaceman economy is still a good way off (at least beyond the lifetimes of any now living), so let us eat, drink, spend, extract and pollute, and be as merry as we can, and let posterity worry about the spaceship earth. It is always a little hard to find a convincing answer to the man who says, "What has posterity ever done for me?" and the conservationist has always had to fall back on rather vague ethical principles postulating identity of the individual with some human community or society which extends not only back into the past but forward into the future. Unless the individual identifies with some community of this kind, conservation is obviously "irrational." Why should we not maximize the welfare of this generation at the cost of posterity? *"Après nous, le déluge"* has been the motto of not insignificant numbers of human societies. The only answer to this, as far as I can see, is to point out that the welfare of the individual depends on the extent to which he can identify himself with others, and that the most satisfactory individual identity is that which identifies not only with a community in space but also with a community extending over time from the past into the future. If this kind of identity is recognized as desirable, then posterity has a voice, even if it does not have a vote; and in a sense, if its voice can influence votes, it has votes too. This whole problem is linked up with the much larger one of the determinants of the morale, legitimacy, and "nerve" of a society, and there is a great deal of historical evidence to suggest that a society which loses its identity with posterity and which loses its positive image of the future loses also its capacity to deal with present problems, and soon falls apart.

Even if we concede that posterity is relevant to our present problems, we still face the question of time-discounting and the closely related question of uncertainty-discounting. It is a well-known phenomenon that individuals discount the future, even in their own lives. The very existence of a positive rate of interest may be taken as at least strong supporting evidence of this hypothesis. If we discount our own future, it is certainly not unreasonable to discount posterity's future even more, even if we do give posterity a vote. If we discount this at 5 per cent per annum, posterity's vote or dollar halves every fourteen years as we look into the future, and after even a mere hundred years it is pretty small—only about 1½ cents on the dollar. If we add another 5 per cent for uncertainty, even the vote of our grandchildren reduces almost to insignificance. We can argue, of course, that the ethical thing to do is not to discount the future at all, that time-discounting is mainly the result of myopia and perspective, and hence is an illusion which the moral man should not tolerate. It is a very popular illusion, however, and one that must certainly be taken into consideration in the formulation of policies. It explains, perhaps, why conservationist policies almost have to be sold under some other excuse which seems more urgent, and why, indeed, necessities which are visualized as urgent, such as defense, always seem to hold priority over those which involve the future.

All these considerations add some credence to the point of view which says that we should not worry about the spaceman economy at all, and that we should just go on increasing the GNP and indeed the gross world product, or GWP, in the expectation that the problems of the future can be left to the future, that when scarcities arise, whether this is of raw materials or of pollutable reservoirs, the needs of the then present will determine the solutions of the then present, and there is no use giving ourselves ulcers by worrying about problems that we really do not have to solve. There is even high ethical authority for this point of view in the New Testament, which advocates that we should take no thought for tomorrow and let the dead bury their dead. There has always been something rather refreshing in the view that we should live like the birds, and perhaps posterity is for the birds in more senses than one; so perhaps we should all call it a day and go out and pollute something cheerfully. As an old taker of thought for the morrow, however, I cannot quite accept this solution; and I would argue, furthermore, that tomorrow is not only very close, but in many respects it is already here. The shadow of the future spaceship, indeed, is already falling over our spendthrift merriment. Oddly enough, it seems to be in pollution rather than in exhaustion that the problem is first becoming salient. Los Angeles has run out of air, Lake Erie has become a cesspool, the oceans are getting full of lead and DDT, and the atmosphere may become man's major problem in another generation, at the rate at which we are filling it up with gunk. It is, of course, true that at least on a microscale, things have been worse at times in the past. The cities of today, with all their foul air and polluted waterways, are probably not as bad as the filthy cities of the pretechnical age. Nevertheless, that fouling of the nest which has been typical of man's activity in the past on a local scale now seems to be extending to the whole world society; and one certainly cannot view with equanimity the present rate of pollution of any of the natural reservoirs, whether the atmosphere, the lakes, or even the oceans.

I would argue strongly also that our obsession with production and consumption to the exclusion of the "state" aspects of human welfare distorts the process of technological change in a most undesirable way. We are all familiar, of course, with the wastes involved in planned obsolescence, in competitive advertising, and in poor quality of consumer goods. These problems may not be so important as the "view with alarm" school indicates, and indeed the evidence at many points is conflicting. New materials especially seem to edge towards the side of improved durability, such as, for instance, neolite soles for footwear, nylon socks, wash and wear shirts, and so on. The case of household equipment and automobiles is a little less clear. Housing and building construction generally almost certainly has declined in durability since the Middle Ages, but this decline also reflects a change in tastes towards flexibility and fashion and a need for novelty, so that it is not easy to assess. What is clear is that no serious attempt has been made to assess the impact over the whole of economic life of changes in durability, that is, in the ratio of capital in the widest possible sense to income. I suspect that we have under-estimated, even in our spendthrift society, the gains from increased durability, and that this might very well be one of the places where the price system needs correction through government-sponsored research and development. The problems which the spaceship earth is going to present, therefore, are not all in the future by any means, and a strong case can be made for paying much more attention to them in the present than we now do.

It may be complained that the considerations I have been putting forth relate only to the very long run, and they do not much concern our immediate problems. There may be some justice in this criticism, and my main excuse is that other writers have dealt adequately with the more immediate problems of deterioration in the quality of the environment. It is true, for instance, that many of the immediate problems of pollution of the atmosphere or of bodies of water arise because of the failure of the price system, and many of them could be solved by corrective tax-ation. If people had to pay the losses due to the nuisances which they create, a good deal more resources would go into the prevention of nuisances. These argu-ments involving external economies and diseconomies are familiar to economists, and there is no need to recapitulate them. The law of torts is quite inadequate to provide for the correction of the price system which is required, simply because where damages are widespread and their incidence on any particular person is small, the ordinary remedies of the civil law are quite inadequate and inappropriate. There needs, therefore, to be special legislation to cover these cases, and though such legislation seems hard to get in practice, mainly because of the widespread and small personal incidence of the injuries, the technical problems involved are not insuperable. If we were to adopt in principle a law for tax penalties for social damages, with an apparatus for making assessments under it, a very large proportion of current pollution and deterioration of the environment would be prevented. There are tricky problems of equity involved, particularly where old established nuisances create a kind of "right by purchase" to perpetuate themselves, but these are problems again which a few rather arbitrary decisions can bring to some kind of solution.

The problems which I have been raising in this paper are of larger scale and perhaps much harder to solve than the more practical and immediate problems of the above paragraph. Our success in dealing with the larger problems, however, is not unrelated to the development of skill in the solution of the more immediate and perhaps less difficult problems. One can hope, therefore, that as a succession of mounting crises, especially in pollution, arouse public opinion and mobilize support for the solution of the immediate problems, a learning process will be set in motion which will eventually lead to an appreciation of and perhaps solutions for the larger ones. My neglect of the immediate problems, therefore, is in no way intended to deny their importance, for unless we at least make a beginning on a process for solving the immediate problems we will not have much chance of solving the larger ones. On the other hand, it may also be true that a long-run vision, as it were, of the deep crisis which faces mankind may predispose people to taking more interest in the immediate problems and to devote more effort for their solution. This may sound like a rather modest optimism, but perhaps a modest optimism is better than no optimism at all.

50. *Marketing's Changing Social Relationships* WILLIAM LAZER

The purpose, of this article is to present some viewpoints and ideas on topics concerning marketing's changing social relationships. The author hopes to stimulate discussion and encourage work by others concerned with the marketing discipline, rather than to present a definitive set of statements. He first presents a brief discussion of marketing and our life style, and marketing's role beyond the realm of profit. This is followed by the development of some ideas and viewpoints on marketing and consumption under conditions of abundance, with a particular focus on changing consumption norms. The last section is concerned with changing marketing boundaries and emerging social perspectives.

Marketing and Life Style

Since the American economy is a materialistic, acquisitive, thing-minded, abundant market economy, marketing becomes one of the cores for understanding and influencing life styles; and marketers assume the role of taste counselors. Since American tastes are being emulated in other parts of the world such as Europe, Japan, and Latin America, the impact of our values and norms reverberate throughout a broad international community.

SOURCE. Reprinted from *Journal of Marketing,* published by the American Marketing Association, Vol. 33, January 1969.

Yet a basic difference exists between the orientation of the American life style, which is interwoven with marketing, and the life style of many other countries, particularly of the emerging and lesser-developed countries, although the differences are blurring. American norms include a general belief in equality of opportunity to strive for a better standard of living; the achievement of status and success through individual initiative, sacrifice, and personal skills; the provision and maintenance of a relatively open society with upward economic and social movement; the availability of education which is a route for social achievement, occupational advancement, and higher income. Yet, there are contradictory and conflicting concepts operating within this value system. One contradiction is seen in the conflict between concepts of equality for all on the one hand and the visible rank and status orderings in society. Another conflict much discussed today concerns the conflicts between the coexisting values of our affluent society and the pockets of poverty in the United States.

In their scheme of norms the majority of Americans, even younger Americans, exude optimism in the materialistic productivity of our society. They feel confident that the economic future will be much better than the present, that our standard of living and consumption will expand and increase, that pleasures will be multiplied, and that there is little need to curb desires.

Questions have been raised about priorities of expenditures, and authority has been challenged. Various marketing processes and institutions have been attacked. But, by and large, there exists a general expectation of increasing growth, the availability of more and more, and a brighter and better future. As a result of this perspective, economic opportunities and growth are perceived not so much in terms of curbing consumer desires as is the case in many other societies, particularly in underdeveloped economies, but in increasing desires; in attempting to stimulate people to try to realize themselves to the fullest extent of their resources and capabilities by acquiring complementary goods and symbols. Similarly, the emerging nations now have rising economic expectations and aspiration levels, and their life style perspectives are changing. They expect to share in the economic abundance achieved by highly industrialized economies.

Beyond the Realm of Profit

One of the next marketing frontiers may well be related to markets that extend beyond mere profit considerations to intrinsic values—to markets based on social concern, markets of the mind, and markets concerned with the development of people to the fullest extent of their capabilities. This may be considered a macro frontier of marketing, one geared to interpersonal and social development, to social concern.

From this perspective one of marketing's roles may be to encourage increasing expenditures by consumers of dollars and time to develop themselves socially, intellectually, and morally. Another may be the direction of marketing to help solve some of the fundamental problems that nations face today. To help solve such problems, in addition to its current sense of purpose in the firm, marketing must develop its sense of community, its societal commitments and obligations, and accept the challenges inherent in any institution of social control.

But one may ask whether social welfare is consonant with the bilateral transfer characteristics of an exchange or market economy, or can it be realized only through the unilateral transfer of a grants economy? This is a pregnant social question now confronting marketing.

Business executives operating in a market economy can achieve the degree of adaptation necessary to accept their social responsibilities and still meet the demands of both markets and the business enterprise. At the very least, the exchange economy will support the necessary supplementary grants economy. Currently we are witnessing several examples of this. The National Alliance for Businessmen composed of 50 top business executives is seeking jobs in 50 of our largest cities for 500,000 hard-core unemployed; the Urban Coalition, composed of religious, labor, government, and business leaders, as well as several individual companies, is actively seeking ways of attacking the problem of unemployment among the disadvantaged; and the insurance companies are investing and spending millions for new housing developments in slum areas. It even seems likely that business executives, operating in a market environment, stimulated by the profit motive, may well succeed in meeting certain challenges of social responsibility where social planners and governmental agencies have not.

Governmental agencies alone cannot meet the social tasks. A spirit of mutual endeavor must be developed encompassing a marketing thrust.

The development of the societal dimensions of marketing by industry and/or other institutions is necessary to mold a society in which every person has the opportunity to grow to the fullest extent of his capabilities, in which older people can play out their roles in a dignified manner, in which human potentials are recognized and nurtured, and in which the dignity of the individual is accepted. While prone to point out the undesirable impact of marketing in our life style (as they should), social critics have neglected to indicate the progress and the contributions that have been made.

In achieving its sense of broad community interest and participation, marketing performs its social role in two ways. First, marketing faces social challenges in the same sense as the government and other institutions. But unlike the government, marketing finds its major social justification through offering product-service mixes and commercially unified applications of the results of technology to the marketplace for a profit. Second, it participates in welfare and cultural efforts extending beyond mere profit considerations, and these include various community services and charitable and welfare activities.

A fundamental value question to be answered is not one of the absolute morality or lack of problems in our economic system and marketing activities, as many critics suggest. Rather, it is one concerning the *relative* desirability of our life style with its norms, its emphasis on materialism, its hedonistic thrust, its imperfections, injustices, and poverty, as contrasted with other life styles that have different emphases. Great materialistic stress and accomplishment is not inherently sinful and bad. Moral values are not vitiated (as many critics might lead one to believe) by substantial material acquisitions. Increasing leisure time does not automatically lead to the decay and decline of a civilization. History seems to confirm this; for great artistic and cultural advancements were at least accompanied by, if not directly stimulated by, periods of flourishing trade and commerce.

Marketing and Consumption Under Abundance

American consumers are confronted with a dilemma. On the one hand, they live in a very abundant, automated economy that provides a surplus of products, an increasing amount of leisure, and an opportunity for a relative life of ease. On the other hand, they have a rich tradition of hard physical work, sweat, perseverance in the face of adversity, earning a living through hard labor, being thrifty, and "saving for a rainy day."

American consumers still adhere to many puritanical concepts of consumption, which are relevant in an economy of scarcity but not in our economy of abundance. Our society faces a task of making consumers accept comfortably the fact that a life style of relative leisure and luxury that eliminates much hard physical labor and drudgery, and permits us to alter unpleasant environments, is actually one of the major accomplishments of our age, rather than the indication of a sick, failing, or decaying society.

In essence, our consumption philosophy must change. It must be brought into line with our age of plenty, with an age of automation and mass production, with a highly industrialized mass-consumption society. To do so, the abundant life style must be accepted as a moral one, as an ethical one, as a life which can be inherently good.

In our society, is it not desirable to urge consumers to acquire additional material objects? Cannot the extension of consumer wants and needs be a great force for improvement and for increasing societal awareness and social contributions? Is it not part of marketing's social responsibility to help stimulate the desire to improve the quality of life—particularly the economic quality—and so serve the public interest?

Yet some very significant questions may be posed. Can or should American consumers feel comfortable, physically and psychologically, with a life of relative luxury while they are fully cognizant of the existence of poverty in the midst of plenty, of practice of discrimination in a democratic society, the feeling of hope-lessness and despair among many in our expanding and increasingly productive economy, and the prevalence of ignorance in a relatively enlightened age? Or, on a broader base, can or should Americans feel comfortable with their luxuries, regular model and style changes, gadgetry, packaging variations, and waste while people in other nations of the world confront starvation? These are among the questions related to priorities in the allocation of our resources, particularly between the public and private sectors and between the national and international boundaries that have been discussed by social and economic commentators such as Galbraith and Toynbee.

These are not easy questions to answer. The answers depend on the perspective adopted (whether macro or micro), on the personal philosophy adhered to (religious and otherwise), and on the social concern of individuals, groups, and nations. No perfect economic system has or will ever exist, and the market system is no exception. Economic and social problems and conflicts will remain, but we should strive to eliminate the undesirable features of our market system. And it is clear that when abundance prevails individuals and nations can afford to, and do, exercise increasing social concern.

Toynbee, in assessing our norms and value systems (particularly advertising), wrote that if it is true that personal consumption stimulated by advertising is essential for growth and full employment in our economy (which we in marketing believe), then it demonstrates automatically to his mind that an economy of abundance is a spiritually unhealthy way of life and that the sooner it is reformed, the better. Thus, he concluded that our way of life, based on personal consumption stimulated by advertising, needs immediate reform. But let us ponder for a moment these rather strong indictments of our norms and the impact of marketing on our value systems and life style.

When economic abundance prevails, the limitations and constraints on both our economic system and various parts of our life style shift. The most critical point in the functioning of society shifts from physical production to consumption. Accord-ingly, the culture must be reoriented: a producers' culture must be converted into a consumers' culture. Society must adjust to a new set of drives and values in which consumption, and hence marketing activities, becomes paramount. Buckminster Fuller has referred to the necessity of creating regenerative consumers in our affluent society. The need for consumers willing and able to expand their purchases both quantitatively and qualitatively is now apparent in the United States. It is becoming increasingly so in Russia, and it will be so in the future among the underdeveloped and emerging nations. Herein lies a challenge for marketing—the challenge of changing norms and values to bring them into line with the require-ments of an abundant economy.

Although some social critics and observers might lead us to believe that we should be ashamed of our life style, and although our affluent society is widely criticized, it is circumspect to observe that other nations of the world are struggling to achieve the stage of affluence that has been delivered by our economic system. When they achieve it, they will be forced to wrestle with similar problems of abundance, materialism, consumption, and marketing that we now face.

Consumption Activities and Norms

Consumption should not be considered an automatic or a happenstance activity. To achieve our stated economic goals of stability, growth, and full employment, marketing must be viewed as a force that will shape economic destiny by expanding and stabilizing consumption.

To date the major determinant of consumption has been income. But as economic abundance increases, the consumption constraints change. By the year 2000 it has been noted that the customer will experience as his first constraint not money, but time. As time takes on greater utility, affluence will permit the purchase of more time-saving products and services.

In other ages, the wealthy achieved more free time through the purchase of personal services and the use of servants. In our society, a multitude of products with built-in services extend free time to consumers on a broad base.

The concept of consumption usually conjures a false image. Consumption generally seems to be related to chronic scarcity. It is associated with hunger, with the bare necessities of life, and with the struggle to obtain adequate food, shelter, and clothing. It is associated with the perception of economics as the "dismal science," with the study of the allocation of scarce resources.

But what happens to norms and values when people have suitably gratified their "needs"? What happens after the acquisition of the third automobile, the second color television set, and three or four larger and more luxurious houses? Maslow (see p. 117) has noted that consumers then become motivated in a manner different from that explained by his hierarchy of motives. They become devoted to tasks outside themselves.

Maslow also makes a distinction between the realm of being, the "B-realm," and the realm of deficiencies, the "D-realm,"—between the external and the practical. For example, in the practical realm of marketing with its daily pressures, executives tend to be responders. They react to stimuli, rewards, punishments, emergencies, and the demands of others. However, given an economy of abundance with a "saturation of materialism," they can turn attentions to the intrinsic values and implied norms—seeking to expose themselves to great cultural activities, to natural beauty, to the developments of those "B" values.

Our society has reached the stage of affluence without having developed an acceptable justification for our economic system, and for the eventual life of abundance and relative leisure that it will supply. Herein lies a challenge for marketing: to justify and stimulate our age of consumption. We must learn to realize ourselves in an affluent life and to enjoy it without pangs of guilt. What is required is a set of norms and a concept of morality and ethics that corresponds to our age.

Advertising is the institution uniquely identified with abundance, particularly in America. But the institution that is actually brought into being by abundance without previous emphasis or existence in the same form is marketing. It is marketing expressed not only through advertising. It is also expressed in the emphasis on consumption in our society, new approaches to product development, the role of credit, the use of marketing research and marketing planning, the implementation of the marketing concept, the management of innovation, the utilization of effective merchandising techniques, and the cultivation of mass markets. Such institutions and techniques as self-service, supermarkets, discount houses, advertising, credit plans, and marketing research are spreading marketing and the American life style through other parts of the world.

Changing Marketing Boundaries

We may well ask, what are the boundaries of marketing in modern society? This is an important question that cannot be answered simply. But surely these boundaries have changed and now extend beyond the profit motive. Marketing ethics, values, responsibilities, and marketing-government relationships are involved. These marketing dimensions will unquestionably receive increasing scrutiny by practitioners and academicians in a variety of areas, and the result will be some very challenging and basic questions that must be answered.

We might ask, for example, can or should marketing, as a function of business, possess a social role distinct from the personal social roles of individuals who are charged with marketing responsibilities? Does the business as a legal entity possess a conscience and a personality whose sum is greater than the respective attributes of its individual managers and owners? Should each member of management be held personally accountable for social acts committed or omitted in the name of the business? Answers to such questions change with times and situations, but the trend is surely to a broadening recognition of greater social responsibilities—the development of marketing's social role.

Few marketing practitioners or academicians disagree totally with the concept that marketing has important social dimensions and can be viewed as a social instrument in a highly industrialized society. Disagreement exists, however, about the relative importance of marketing's social dimensions as compared to its managerial or technical dimensions.

The more traditional view has been that marketing management fulfills the greater part of its responsibility by providing products and services to satisfy consumer needs profitably and efficiently. Those adopting this view believe that as a natural consequence of its efficiency, customers are satisfied, firms prosper, and the well-being of society follows automatically. They fear that the acceptance of any other responsibilities by marketing managers, particularly social responsibilities, tends to threaten the very foundation of our economic system. Most questions about who will establish the guidelines, who will determine what these social responsibilities should be, and who will enforce departures from any standards established, are raised.

However, an emerging view is one that does not take issue with the ends of customer satisfaction, the profit focus, the market economy, and economic growth. Rather, its premise seems to be that the tasks of marketing and its concomitant responsibilities are much wider than purely economic concerns. It views the market process as one of the controlling elements of the world's social and economic growth. Because marketing is a social instrument through which a standard of living is transmitted to society, as a discipline it is a social one with commensurate social responsibilities that cannot merely be the exclusive concern of companies and consumers.

Perhaps nowhere is the inner self of the populace more openly demonstrated than in the marketplace; for the marketplace is an arena where actions are the proof of words and transactions represent values, both physical and moral.

Marketing's responsibility is only partially fulfilled through economic processes. There is a greater responsibility to consumers and to the human dignity that is vital to the marketplace—the concern for marketing beyond the profit motive.

Academicians and executives will be forced to rethink and reevaluate such situations in the immediate future just by the sheer weight of government concern and decisions if by nothing else. In the last year, there have been governmental decisions about safety standards, devices for controlling air pollution, implied product warranties, packaging rules and regulations, the relationship of national brands to private labels, pricing practices, credit practices, and mergers. There have been discussions about limiting the amount that can be spent on advertising for a product, about controlling trading stamps, about investigating various promotional devices and marketing activities. Such actions pose serious questions about marketing's social role. If we do not answer them, others will; and perhaps in a manner not too pleasing, or even realistic.

51. *Priorities for the Seventies*

ROBERT L. HEILBRONER

To talk about national priorities is to talk about precedence, the order in which things are ranked. It is not difficult to establish what that order is in America today. Military needs rank above civilian needs. Private interests rank above public interests. The claims of the affluent take precedence over those of the poor. This is all so familiar that it no longer even has the power to rouse us to indignation.

But I do not want to expatiate on the present order of things. For I presume that to talk of priorities is to determine what they *should* be. What should come first? What ought to be on top of the agenda?

To ask such questions is to invite pious answers. I shall try to avoid the pieties by grouping my priorities into three categories. The first has to do with our immediate survival—not as a nation-state, but as a *decent* nation-state. The second has to do with our ultimate salvation. The third with our moving from survival to salvation.

The initial set of priorities is simple to specify. It consists of three courses of action necessary to restore American society to life. The first of these is the demilitarization of the national budget. That budget now calls for the expenditure of $80-billion a year for military purposes. Its rationale is that it will permit us to fight simultaneously two "major" (though, of course, non-nuclear) wars and one "minor" or "brushfire" war. This requires the maintenance of eighteen army

SOURCE. Condensed from the *Saturday Review,* January 3, 1970, copyright 1969 Saturday Review, Inc.

divisions, as against eleven in 1961; of 11,000 deliverable nuclear warheads, compared with 1,100 in 1961; of a naval force far larger than that of any other nation in the world.

Politically, economically—even militarily—this budget is a disaster for America. It has sucked into the service of fear and death the energies and resources desperately needed for hope and life. Until and unless that budget is significantly cut, there will be little chance of restoring vitality to American society.

Here let us make a first approximation as to how much the military budget can be cut by determining how large are the life-giving aims to which we must now give priority. I see two of these as being essential for the attainment of decency in American society. One is the long overdue relief of poverty. In 1967, 10 per cent of all white families, 35 per cent of all black families, and 58 per cent of all black families over age sixty-five, lived in poverty—a condition that we define by the expenditure for food of $4.90 per person per week. *Per week.* To raise these families to levels of minimum adequacy will require annual transfer payments of approximately $10- to $15-billion. This is half the annual cost of the Vietnam war. I would make this conversion of death into life a first guide to the demilitarization of the budget.

A second guide is provided by the remaining essential priority for American decency. This is the need to rebuild the cities before they collapse on us. This means not only replacing the hideous tenements and junkyards and prison-like schools of the slums, but providing the services needed to make urban living tolerable—regular garbage collection, dependable police protection, and adequate recreational facilities.

These objectives are minimal requirements for America. Fortunately, they are easy to accomplish—at least in a technical sense. There will be no problem in cutting the military budget by the necessary $30- to $40-billion once that task is entrusted to men who are not prisoners of the military-industrial superiority complex. There are no great problems in the alleviation of poverty that the direct disbursement of money to the poor will not tolerably remedy.

Thus the essential priorities have the virtue of being as simple as they are compelling.

Let me speak of another set of priorities—one that many people would place even higher on the list than my initial three. They are, first, the elimination of racism in the United States, and second, the enlistment of the enthusiasm—or at least the tolerance—of the younger generation.

I have said that these priorities have to do with our salvation rather than with our survival. This is because their achievement would lift the spirit of America as if a great shadow had been removed from its soul. But like all salvations, this one is not near at hand. For unlike the first set of priorities, which is well within our power to accomplish, this second set lies beyond our present capabilities. Even if we manage to cut the military budget, to end poverty, to rebuild the cities, the bitter fact remains that we do not know how to change the deep conviction within the hearts of millions of Americans that blackness spells inferiority. Neither do we know how to win the enthusiasm of young people—and I mean the best and soberest of them, not the drop-outs and the do-nothings—for a society that is technocratic, bureaucratic, and depersonalized.

Thus the second set of priorities is considerably different from the first. It constitutes a distant goal, not an immediate target. Any projection of what America should try to become that does not include the goals of racial equality and youthful enlistment is seriously deficient, but any projection that does not expect that we will be a racist and alienated society for a long while is simply unrealistic.

This brings me to my third set of priorities—a set of tasks neither so simple as the first, nor so difficult as the second. I shall offer four such tasks—not in any particular order of urgency—as exemplifying the *kinds* of priorities we need in order to move from mere survival toward ultimate salvation.

I begin with a proposal that will seem small by comparison with the large-scale goals discussed so far. Yet, it is important for a society that seeks to lessen racial tensions and to win the approbation of the young. It consists of a full-scale effort to improve the treatment of criminality in the United States.

No one knows exactly how large is the criminal population of the United States, but certainly it is very large. Two million persons a year pass through the major prisons and "reformatories," some 300,000 residing in them at any given time. Another 800,000 are on probation or parole; a still larger number lurk on the fringes of serious misbehavior, but have so far escaped the law. Even the more humane institutions largely fail in their purposes. In New York State the rate of recidivism for crimes of comparable importance is 50 per cent. A recent FBI study of 18,000 federal offenders released in 1963 showed that 63 per cent had been arrested again five years later.

Indeed, as every criminologist will testify, prisons mainly serve not to deter, but to confirm and train the inmate for a career in criminality. These institutions exist not for the humanization but for the brutalization of their charges.

It must be obvious that an all-out effort to lessen criminality is not nearly so simple to achieve as slicing the military budget or tearing down the slums. But neither is it so difficult to achieve as racial tolerance. I suggest it is an objective well worth being placed high on the list of those "middle" priorities for which we are now seeking examples.

Recently, the Administration has declared the reform of prisons to be a major objective. Let us now see if this rhetoric will be translated into action.

My second suggestion is not unrelated to the first. Only it concerns not criminals, but those who represent the other end of the spectrum—the symbols of law and order, the police forces of America. I propose that an important item on the agenda must be an effort to contain and control a police arm that is already a principal reason for black anger and youthful disgust.

One way to minimize police abuse of Negroes is to minimize occasions for contact with them. The obvious conclusion is that black ghettos must be given the funds and the authorization to form their own police forces. Another necessary step is to lessen the contact of police forces with college youth; the legalization of marijuana would help in this regard. So would the training of special, highly paid, *unarmed,* elite police forces who would be used to direct all police actions having to do with civil demonstrations.

My third suggestion seemingly departs markedly from the first two. It concerns a wider problem than criminality or police misbehavior, but not a less pressing problem. It is how to rescue the environment from the devastating impact of an unregulated technology.

I need mention only a few well-known results of this ferocious process of destruction. Lake Erie is dead. The beaches at Santa Barbara are deserted. The air in New York is dangerous to breathe. We are drowning in a sea of swill; in a normal year the United States "produces" 142 million tons of smoke and fumes, seven million junked cars, twenty million tons of waste paper, forty-eight billion used cans, and fifty trillion gallons of industrial sewage. And presiding over this rampant process of environmental overloading is the most fearsome reality of all—a population that is still increasing like an uncontrollable cancer on the surface of the globe. I know of no more sobering statistic in this regard than that between now and 1980 the number of women in the most fertile age brackets, eighteen to thirty-two, will double.

Hence, I call for a different priority in dealing with this crucial question—not for less technology, but for more technology of a *different kind.* For clearly what we need are technological answers to technological problems. We need a reliable method of birth control suitable for application among illiterate and superstitious peoples. We need an exhaustless automobile, a noiseless and versatile airplane. We need new methods of reducing and coping with wastes—radioactive, sewage, gaseous, and liquid. We need new modes of transporting goods and people, within cities and between them.

The priority then is technological research—research aimed at devising the techniques needed to live in a place that we have just begun to recognize as (in Kenneth Boulding's phrase) our Spaceship Earth. There is a further consideration here, as well. Many people wonder where we can direct the energies of the engineers, draftsmen, scientists, and skilled workmen who are now employed in building weapons systems, once we cut our military budget. I suggest that the design of a technology for our planetary spaceship will provide challenge enough to occupy their attention for a long time. We have not hesitated to support private enterprise for years while it devoted its organizational talents to producing instruments of war. We must now begin to apply equally lavish support while private enterprise perfects the instruments of peace.

But to speak of priorities without mentioning education seems wrong, especially for someone in education. The question is, what is there to say? What is there left to declare about the process of schooling that has not been said again and again? Perhaps I can suggest just one thing, aimed specifically at the upper echelons of the educational apparatus. It is a proposal that the universities add a new orientation to their traditional goals and programs. I urge that they deliberately set out to become the laboratories of applied research into the future. I urge that they direct a major portion of their efforts toward research into, training for, and advocacy of programs for social change.

It may be said that there is no precedent for such an orientation of education toward action, and that the pursuit of such a course will endanger the traditional purity and aloofness of the academic community. The reply would be more convincing did not the precedent already exist and were not the purity already sullied. Scientists of all kinds, in the social as well as in the physical disciplines, have not hesitated to work on programs for social change—financed by the Department of Defense, the Office of Naval Research, NASA, etc.—programs designed to alter the world by high explosives in some cases, by cooptation or skillful propaganda in others.

Some members of the academic community, aware of the destruction they have helped to commit, have now begun to withdraw from contact with the war machine. That is to their credit. But what is needed now is for them to redirect their energies to the peace machine. We live in a time during which social experi-mentation—in the factory, in the office, in the city; in economic policy, in political institutions, in life-styles—is essential if a technologically dominated future is not simply to mold us willy-nilly to its requirements. The forces of change in our time render obsolete many of the institutions of managerial capitalism and centrally planned socialism alike; new institutions, new modes of social control and social cohesion now have to be invented and tried.

In part the university must continue its traditional role, studying this period of historic transformation with all the detachment and objectivity it can muster. But that is not enough. As Marx wrote: "The philosophers have only *interpreted* the world; the thing, however, is to change it." As the last item on my agenda, I would like to make the university the locus of action for the initiation of such change.

52. *How to Control the Military*

JOHN KENNETH GALBRAITH

The purpose of this pamphlet is to see the nature of the military power, assess its strengths and weaknesses and suggest the guidelines for regaining control. For no one can doubt the need for doing so.

The problem of the military power is not unique; it is merely a rather formidable example of the tendency of organization, in an age of organization, to develop a life and purpose and truth of its own. This tendency holds for all great bureaucracies, both public and private. And their action is not what serves a larger public interest, their belief does not reflect the reality of life. What is done and what is believed are, first and naturally, what serves the goals of the bureaucracy itself. Action in the organization interest, or in response to the bureaucratic truth, can thus be a formula for public disservice or even public disaster.

There is nothing academic about this possibility. There have been many explanations of how we got into the Vietnam War, an action on which even the greatest of the early enthusiasts have now lapsed into discretion. But all explanations come back to one. It was the result of a long series of steps taken in response to a bureaucratic view of the world—a view to which a President willingly or unwillingly yielded and which, until much too late, was unchecked by any legislative or public opposition. This view was of a planet threatened by an imminent takeover by the unified and masterful forces of the Communist world,

SOURCE. From the book *How to Control the Military* by John Kenneth Galbraith. Copyright © 1969 by John Kenneth Galbraith. Reprinted by permission of Doubleday & Company, Inc.

directed from Moscow (or later and with less assurance from Peking) and coming to a focus, however improbably, some thousands of miles away in the activities of a few thousand guerrillas against the markedly regressive government of South Vietnam.

There is first the military belief that whatever the dangers of a continued weapons race with the Soviet Union these are less than any agreement that offers any perceptible opening for violation. If there is such an opening the Soviets will exploit it. Since no agreement can be watertight this goes far to protect the weapons race from any effort at control.

Secondly, there is the belief that the conflict with communism is man's ultimate battle. Accordingly, one would not hesitate to destroy all life if communism seems seriously a threat. This belief allows acceptance of the arms race no matter how dangerous. The present ideological differences between industrial systems will almost certainly look very different and possibly rather trivial from a perspective of fifty or a hundred years hence if we survive. Such thoughts are eccentric.

Third, the national interest is total, that of man inconsequential. So even the prospect of total death and destruction does not deter us from developing new weapons systems if some thread of national interest can be identified in the outcome. We can accept 75 million casualities if it forces the opposition to accept 150 million. This is the unsentimental calculation. Even more unsentimentally, Senator Richard B. Russell, the leading Senate spokesman of the military power, argued on behalf of the Army's Sentinal Anti-Ballistic Missile System (the ABM) that, if only one man and one woman are to be left on earth, it was his deep desire that they be Americans. It was part of the case of the Manned Orbiting Laboratory (MOL) that it would maintain the American position in the event of extensive destruction down below.

Although Americans are probably the world's least competent conspirators— partly because no other country so handsomely rewards in cash and notoriety the man who blows the whistle on those with whom he is conspiring—we have a strong instinct for so explaining that of which we disapprove. In the conspiratorial view, the military power is a collation of generals and conniving industrialists. The goal is mutual enrichment; they arrange elaborately to feather each other's nest. The industrialists are the *deus ex machina;* their agents make their way around Washington arranging the pay-offs. If money is too dangerous, then alcohol, compatible women, more prosaic forms of entertainment or the promise of future jobs to generals and admirals will serve.

There is such enrichment and some graft. Insiders do well. H. L. Nieburg has told the fascinating story of how in 1954 two modestly paid aerospace scientists, Dr. Simon Ramo and Dr. Dean E. Wooldridge, attached themselves influentially to the Air Force as consultants and in four fine years (with no known dishonesty) ran a shoestring of $6,750 apiece into a multi-million dollar fortune and a position of major industrial prominence. (In 1967 their firm held defense contracts totalling $121,000,000.)

Also a part of the military power are the university scientists and those in such defense-oriented organizations as RAND, the Institute for Defense Analysis and Hudson Institute who think professionally about weapons and weapons systems and the strategy of their use. And last, but by no means least, there is the organized voice of the military in the Congress, most notably on the Armed Services Committees of the Senate and House of Representatives.

Once competitive bidding created an adversary relationship between buyer and seller and with numerous sellers, a special relationship with any one provoked cries of favoritism. But modern weapons are bought overwhelmingly by negotiation and in most cases from a single source of supply. (In the fiscal year ending in 1968, General Accounting Office figures show that 57.9 percent of the $43 billion in defense contracts awarded in that year was by negotiation with a single source of supply. Of the remainder 30.6 percent was awarded by negotiation where alternative sources of supply had an opportunity to participate and only 11.5 percent was open to advertised competitive bidding.) Under these circumstances, the tendency to any adversary relationship between the Services and their suppliers disappears. Indeed, where there are only one or two sources of supply for a weapons system, the Services will be as much interested in sustaining these firms as the firms are in being sustained.

Six things brought the military-industrial bureaucracy to its present position of power. To see these forces is also to be encouraged by the chance for escape.

First, there has been, as noted, the increasing bureaucratization of our life.

Second in importance in bringing the military-industrial complex to power were the circumstances and images of foreign policy in the late forties, fifties and early sixties.

Third, secrecy confined knowledge of Soviet weapons and responding American action to those within the public and private bureaucracy.

Fourth, there was the disciplining effect of personal fear.

Fifth, in the fifties and early sixties, the phrase "domestic priority" had not yet become a cliché.

Sixth and finally, in these years both liberal and conservative opposition to the military-industrial power were muted.

To see the sources of the strength of the military-industrial complex in the fifties and sixties is to see its considerably greater vulnerability now. The Communist imperium, which once seemed so fearsome in its unity, has broken up into bitterly antagonistic blocs. Moscow and Peking barely keep the peace. Fear in Czechoslovakia, Yugoslavia, and Roumania is not of the capitalist enemy but the great Communist friend. The more intimate calculations of the Soviet High Command on what might be expected of the Czech (or for that matter the Roumanian or Polish or Hungarian) army in the event of war in Western Europe must not be without charm. Perhaps they explain the odd military passion for the Egyptians. The Soviets have had no more success than has capitalism in penetrating and organizing the backward countries of the world. Communist and capitalist jungles are indistinguishable. Men of independent mind recognize that after twenty years of aggressive military competition with the Soviets our security is not greater and almost certainly less than when the competition began. And although in the fifties it was fashionable to assert otherwise ("a dictator does not hesitate to sacrifice his people by the millions") we now know that the Soviets are as aware of the totally catastrophic character of nuclear war as we are—and more so than our more articulate generals.

These changes plus the adverse reaction to Vietnam have cost the military power its monopoly of the scientific community. This, in turn, has damaged its claim to a monopoly of knowledge including that which depends on security classification.

Additionally, civilian priority has become one of the most evocative words in the language. Everywhere—for urban housing and services, sanitation, schools, police, urban transportation, clean air, potable water—the needs are huge and pressing. Because these needs are not being met the number of people who live in fear of an urban explosion may well be greater than those who are alarmed by the prospect of nuclear devastation. For many years I have lived in summers on an old farm in southern Vermont. In the years following Hiroshima we had the advance refugees from the atomic bomb. Now we have those who are escaping the ultimate urban riot. The second migration is much bigger than the first and has had a more inflationary effect on local real estate values.

Certainly the day when military spending was a slightly embarrassing alternative to unemployment is gone and, one imagines, forever.

With all of these changes has come a radical change in the political climate. Except in the darker reaches of Orange County and surburban Dallas (where defense expenditures also have their influence) fear of communism has receded. We have lived with the Communists on the same planet now for a half century. An increasing number are disposed to believe we *can* continue doing so. Communism seems somewhat less triumphant than twenty years ago. Perhaps the Soviet Union is yet another industrial state in which organization—bureaucracy—is in conflict with the people it must educate in such numbers for its tasks. Mr. Nixon in his many years as a political aspirant was not notably averse to making capital out of the Communist menace. But neither, if a little belatedly, was he a man to resist a trend. Many must have noticed that his warnings overt or implied of the Communist menace in his Inaugural Address were rather less fiery than those of John F. Kennedy eight years earlier.

During the summer of 1968, if I may recur once more to personal experience, I was concerned with raising money for Eugene McCarthy. We raised a great deal; the efforts with which I was at least marginally associated produced some $2.5 million. Overwhelmingly we got that money from businessmen. Opposition to the Vietnam War was, of course, the prime reason for this support. But concern over the military power was a close (and closely affiliated) second. When one is asking for money one very soon learns what evokes response.

Social concern, however inappropriate for a businessman, was most important but there were also very good business reasons for being aroused. In 1968, the hundred largest defense contractors had more than two-thirds (67.4 per cent) of all the defense business and the smallest fifty of these had no more in the aggregate than General Dynamics and Lockheed. A dozen firms specializing in military business (e.g., McDonnell Douglas, General Dynamics, Lockheed, United Aircraft) together with General Electric and A.T. & T. had a third of all the business. For the vast majority of businessmen the only association with the defense business is through the taxes they pay. Not even a subcontract comes their way. And they have another cost. They must operate in communities that are starved for revenue, where, in consequence, their business is exposed to disorder and violence and where materials and manpower are preempted by the defense contractors. They must also put up with inflation, high interest rates and regulation on overseas investment occasioned by defense spending. The willingness of American businessmen to suffer on behalf of the big defense contractors has been a remarkable manifestation of charity and self-denial.

Finally, all bureaucracy has a mortal weakness; it cannot respond effectively to attack. A bureaucracy under attack is a fortress with thick walls but fixed guns. It is a cliché, much beloved of those who supply the diplomatic gloss for the military power, that not much can be done to limit the latter or its budget—so long as "American responsibilities" in the world remain unchanged. And for others it is a persuasive point that to reduce the military budget will require a change in foreign policy.

Superpowers there are but superpowers cannot much affect the course of life within the countries they presume to see as on their side. Vietnam annual expenditures of $30 billion, a deployment of more than half a million men, could not much affect the course of development. In lands as diverse as India, Indonesia, Peru, and the Congo we have found that our ability to affect the development is even less. We have also found, as in the nearby case of Cuba, that a country can go Communist without any overpowering damage.

Our foreign policy has, in fact, changed. It is the Pentagon that hasn't. To argue that the military-industrial complex is now vulnerable is not to suggest that it is on its last legs. It spends a vast amount of public money, which insures the support of many (though by no means all) of those who receive it.

Nonetheless control is possible. I come to my final task. It is to offer a political decalogue of what is required. It is as follows.

1. The goal, all must remember, is to get the military power under firm political control. This means electing a President on this issue next time. This, above all, must be the issue in the next election.

2. Congress will not be impressed by learned declamation on the danger of the military power. There must be organization.

3. The Armed Services Committees of the two houses must obviously be the object of a special effort.

4. The goal is not to make the military power more efficient or more righteously honest. It is to get it under control.

5. This is not an anti-military crusade. Generals and admirals, and soldiers, sailors, and airmen are not the object of attack. The purpose is to return the military establishment to its traditional position in the American political system.

6. Whatever its moral case there is no political future in unilateral disarmament. And the case must not be compromised by wishful assumptions about the Soviets which the Soviets can then destroy. It can safely be assumed that nuclear annihilation is as unpopular with the average Russian as it is with the ordinary American, and that their leaders are not retarded in this respect. But it is wise to assume that within their industrial system, as within ours, there is a military-industrial bureaucracy committed to its own perpetuation and growth. This governs the more precise objectives of control.

7. Four broad types of major weapons systems can be recognized. There are first those that are related directly to the existing balance of power or the balance of terror vis-a-vis the Soviets. The ICBM's and the Polaris submarines are obviously of this sort; in the absence of a decision to disarm unilaterally, restriction or reduction in these weapons requires agreement with the Soviets. There are, secondly, those that may be added within this balance without tipping it drastically one way or the other. Beyond a certain number, more ICBM's are of this sort. Thirdly there are those that, in one way or another, tip the balance or seem to do so. They promise, or can be thought to promise, destruction of the second country while allowing the first to escape or largely escape. Inevitably, in the absence of a prospect for agreement, they must provoke response. An ABM, which seems to provide defense while allowing of continued offense, is of this sort. So are missiles of such number, weight and precision as to be able to destroy the second country's weapons without possibility of retaliation.

Finally there are weapons systems and other military construction and gadgetry which add primarily to the prestige of the Armed Services, or which advance the competitive position of an individual branch.

The last three classes of weapons do not add to such security as is provided under the balance of terror. Given the response they provoke, they leave it either unchanged or more dangerous. But all contribute to the growth, employment and profits of the contractors.

A prime objective of control is to eliminate from the military budget those things which contribute to the arms race or are irrelevant to the present balance of terror. This includes the second, third and fourth classes of weapons mentioned above. The ABM and the MIRV (the Multiple Independently-targeted Re-entry Vehicle) both of which will spark a new competitive round of a peculiarly uncontrollable sort, as well as manned bombers and nuclear carriers are all of this sort. Perhaps as a simple working goal some $5 billions of such items should be eliminated in each of the next three years for a total reduction of $15 billion.

8. The second and most important objective of control is to win agreement with the Soviets on arms control and reduction.

9. Independent scientific judgment must be mobilized—as guidance to the political effort, for advice to Congress and of course, within the Executive itself.

10. Control of the military power must be an ecumenical effort.

A few will find the foregoing an unduly optimistic effort. More, I suspect, will find it excessively moderate, even commonplace. It makes no overtures to the withdrawal of scientific and other scholarly talent from the military. It does not encourage a boycott on recruiting by the military contractors. It does not even urge the curtailment of university participation in military research. These, there should be no mistake about it, will be necessary if the military power is not brought under control. Nor can there be any very righteous lectures about such action. The military power has reversed constitutional process in the United States—removed power from the public and Congress to the Pentagon. It is in a poor position accordingly to urge use of regular political process. And the consequences of such a development could be very great—they could amount to an uncontrollable thrust to unilateral disarmament. But my instinct is for action within the political framework. This is not a formula for busy ineffectuality. None can deny the role of those who marched or picketed on Vietnam. But, in the end, it was political action that arrested the escalation and broke the commitment of the bureaucracy to this mistake. Control of the military power is a less easily defined and hence more difficult task. (To keep the military and its allies and spokesmen from queering international negotiations will be especially difficult.) But if sharply focused knowledge can be brought to bear on both weapons procurement and negotiation; if citizen attitudes can be kept politically effective by the conviction that this is the political issue of our time; if there is effective organization; if in consequence a couple of hundred or even a hundred members of Congress can be kept in a vigilant, critical and aroused mood; if the $5 billion annual goal can be kept sharply in mind; and if for the President this becomes visibly the difference between success and failure, survival and eventual defeat, then the military-industrial complex will be under control. It can be made to happen.

53. *Creating a National Food Plan*

DALE M. HOOVER AND

JAMES G. MADDOX

Recommendations

The United States needs a food policy which will include programs to supplement the incomes of poor people. We suggest the following guidelines for the development of an improved food-aid program for needy individuals.

1. The administration and budgets of the food programs to aid low-income families should be transferred out of the U.S. Department of Agriculture. Generally accepted principles of wise public policy dictate that these programs should be planned and administered as *food assistance programs* and not as adjuncts to, or derivatives from, farm commodity price support programs.

2. The direct distribution program should be replaced as rapidly as possible by a food stamp program.

3. The food stamp program should be made available to low-income families and individuals in all counties and independent cities in the United States throughout all months of the year.

4. The criteria for determining the eligibility of a family or an individual to participate in the stamp program should be the same in all areas of the country; the value of bonus stamps which an eligible recipient receives should be dependent on income and family size.

SOURCE. From *Looking Ahead* (Washington: The National Planning Association, October 1969).

5. Much greater supervision and control than now prevails will be necessary to achieve the recommendations suggested above. However, they are of sufficient importance to warrant full Federalization of the program if this is necessary to their achievement.

The particular form of the food stamp program which we consider most desirable would have the following features.

(a) Persons with no income and some families with very low incomes would receive free stamps equal to the cost of the minimum adequate diet.

(b) Persons with income above a specified level would be able to purchase stamps at less than face value, with the price varying in such a manner that a given percentage of income would be sufficient to purchase stamps equal to the cost of a minimum adequate diet for all income classes.

(c) Individual families would be free to purchase the amount of stamps they wish, up to the amount needed for an adequate diet.

(d) No income eligibility limits other than those implied by the cost of the minimum adequate diet and the rate at which maximum bonus stamps vary with income would be required or allowed.

(e) The administrator of the program should be empowered to establish the cost of the minimum adequate diet and to set the rate at which maximum bonus stamps—and the price of stamps—vary with income. This requirement would be necessary to allow limited Federal benefits to be extended equitably among the low-income population. No discrimination on the basis of residence arising from differences in state income eligibility levels would be allowed to continue.

Regardless of the exact form of the food stamp program chosen, three associated program activities should be undertaken or strengthened.

1. *Consumer education.* Income transfers alone cannot lead to adequate diets for all of the poor. An adequate educational program will require both professional home economists and lesser trained aides who specialize in communicating nutritional information to particular groups of the poor. A minimum educational program could probably be organized for about $30 million per year.

2. *Program evaluation.* Very little research has been conducted on the effects of the various food-aid programs despite the present emphasis on program planning and evaluation. Not only must participants be studied, but so must those families who have chosen not to participate in one or another of the programs. A research appropriation of $3 million might substantially improve the operation of future programs.

3. *Welfare program coordination.* In addition to proposals for a new food program based on benefits inversely related to earned income, the nation already has benefit-income variations incorporated in the programs of Old-Age Insurance,

Aid to Families with Dependent Children, public housing, rent subsidy, and mort-gage subsidy. It is possible that no one of these programs has serious disincentive effects on labor utilization taken alone. However, if a single family is eligible for both food aid and housing subsidization, it is possible that the net effect would be to seriously inhibit the response to work opportunities. The nation will not long be able to afford separate commodity programs which ignore the existence of other programs designed for the poor. Some system of program coordination and review within the Federal government is required.

54. *How to Bring the Impoverished into the Economy* V. THOMAS SULLIVAN

The United States is a big rich country—with numerous small poor countries inside it. This appears to be more and more the case, and more and more unnecessary. The industrial base and distribution system can provide for all the population, as it provides for most.

Today the question is how can the poor obtain economic benefits rapidly without initiating crushing tax-supported programs.

The attempt by management to understand rationally the socio-economic phenomenon of poverty is frequently met with frustration when oratory, emotionalism, politics and blind ideologies are substituted for hard, reliable data. Management's insistence on the application of systematic rationality in planning, developing goals and allocating resources has had little firm ground on which to build.

Putting first things first, the place to start is with the definition of the problem as it is currently stated, and then see if, by turning it around, leverage can be gained. Currently the problem is often stated thus: the amount of money that the poor have is too little to be useful, so the government should provide money to produce effective purchasing power. Let's turn that definition of the problem around and say for argument's sake that usefulness, not quantity of money, is the critical problem of the poor. In other words, increasing the efficiency of money will

SOURCE. Reprinted by permission from the *Columbia Journal of World Business,* November-December, 1969.

produce the same results as would increasing income artificially. This would not be a tax drain on the economy, but rather a stimulus. It could be faster, more humane, more respectful of the individual, administration-free and long-lasting.

In the industrialized developed United States, the basic problem of increasing the consumer's purchasing efficiency falls in the area of marketing. It is marketing which sets prices, lines, designs, distribution, style—the general selling strategy of the corporation. It is this marketing planning which must accept the blame for the current state of market affairs in the ghettos and among the poor. Or, to take the "blame" out of the equation, the poor are simply not being planned into the market stream of the country.

Marketing people are not writing plans which inclusively offer appropriate products and services to the bottom of the consumer market. This oversight effectively keeps the poor out of the main market stream.

Let's see how this works in a hypothetical case. A family defined as within the poverty level makes only $3,000 a year. This is hardly enough. Or is it? In Mexico City, if a family made that much they would not be rich, but they would enjoy a comfortable existence. Money is not the absolute criterion, but what the family can buy with their money becomes the determinant of their standard of living. Making available a spectrum of purchase opportunities to the poor consumer, so that participation in a suitable market stream is possible, is the real device for raising living standards.

Where does the spectrum of purchase opportunities, or the market stream, come from? And why is there one in Mexico City and a different one in New York? In essence, a spectrum of purchase opportunities, or the market stream, results from thousands of marketing decisions traditionally made to market to the most people the highest priced item possible. This process of optimizing profits is tempered by competition in a free economy, but it is natural that business will offer the most profitable product the mass market can afford.

In New York, this concentrates the spectrum of purchase opportunities among consumers earning a median family income of, say, $8,500 per year. In Mexico City, the spectrum of purchase opportunities is designed for a much lower mode, because the consumer income bulks lower. This is no attempt to equate national economies but to point out that the marketers of New York have moved their products and prices upward over the years as mass purchasing power moved upward. The poor who have not moved upward as fast as others, have been left behind with little selection in their spectrum of purchase opportunities. They have been forced to select among shoddy, second-hand, run-down choices—often even degrading choices.

So it turns out that what the consumer is not offered creates the problem. Must this problem exist? Must the poor be left permanently out of the market stream? It seems clear that the economic system is flexible. We only have to observe during a recession the phenomenon of marketing down by the appearance of economy models in every field. Taking this point of flexibility to its logical conclusion, consider how much in material benefits could be spread to the poor if marketers of the country tailored a product and service spectrum, or market stream, to the poor.

It is strange that a corporation will make a significant investment to establish operations overseas to market its products, where annual income is $500, and not make a specially-directed effort domestically to a group with an annual income five or six times as great.

One reason the poor have been receiving little attention from the marketers is that when markets are segmented on a population and income basis, the poor seem to represent, per capita, a small sales potential. The reason the poor represent such an apparently small per-capita sales potential is not because they have no desire to buy, nor because they have no money, but because marketers have designed and priced most products over their heads. Designing to sell to the middle- and upper-class consumer (the largest potential) is what the smart marketers do to cream the market. Selling to the poor, then, becomes by design inherently difficult, inefficient and almost impossible. The product doesn't "fit" the poor, sales do not follow, everyone soon agrees to cut losses and in a sense the businessman turns away.

Trading Down

It may be useful to look at some more specific reasons as to why business has turned its back on the poor as a market.

The fear of mass markets trading down is a fairly new concept, born of an affluent economy, and one not much discussed. The thought is that if the mass markets can trade up, they can also trade down, reducing per-unit return on a broad base while only slightly raising the number of new unit sales. The considerations of such theoretical profit-cutting and its corporate implications are usually enough to make most managers console themselves with the fact that the poor can always buy it second-hand.

This reason for not designing and marketing products and services to the poor is groundless. It is without basis not only because of the basic human aspiration for betterment, which prohibits the upper markets from trading down, but because it ignores new products which expand total consumption. It also ignores growing automation which permits profits on a continually lower selling price-per-unit basis.

Today with computerized controls permitting greater varieties of products and services to be manufactured efficiently, manufacturing has technically passed out of the single-minded era. The problem today is that, while efforts are made to innovate, the innovations are taking place to offer more selection to the largest market, the mass middle-class market. Little, if any, manufacturing innovation and tailoring is done for the poor market.

The gearing of a long manufacturing run to a strong sales curve has always been the ticket to success as a sales manager. Following the consumer crowd with the popular product or service represented success: the big product for the big market.

Even if special marketing approaches made available a new range of purchase opportunities to the poor (and the black poor especially) one item would stand in the way: credit. Credit is an emotional word with the poor. It should be. It is a fact of our society that a person's "credit-worthiness" is close to a judgment of character, honesty, integrity, personal value. If you have no credit and are poor, you cannot buy a car, travel freely or live as many others take for granted. Why are the poor considered by much of the credit industry to be bad risks? Are the poor more dishonest? Do they have a constitutional character flaw? Are they basically more careless?

There is no question that environmental deprivation and barren surroundings leave many poor citizens with a bewildered outlook. But what has happened to the poor since the old days when our God-fearing grandparents bought the player-piano for $5 down and $1 a week? They were honest people and responsible with credit. Are the poor today of less character? The answer is, of course, no. What appears to be the case is that the marketing of credit has followed the upward rise of purchasing power. As the purchasing power of the masses rose and the operational costs of credit administration increased, the change from weekly to monthly repayments was both economical and logical. For everyone but the poor. The poor still live a borderline existence from payday to payday. Asking a poor man to save from four paychecks to make a loan payment monthly is harder than asking another man to save and make his payment every four months. If someone asked middle-class people to make their mortgage payments and their car payments every four months, would not their "credit-worthiness" drop like a rock?

It appears, as with other marketing decisions, that the conscious decision to follow the mass market meant an unconscious decision to abandon the poor, especially the black poor. The black poor, so easily identifiable to the credit manager because of color, ghetto neighborhood, income and job classification, were almost perfectly designed out of the credit system or were victimized by it. Even if the black poor person got by the credit requirements designed for the middle classes, he would then have to repay on a monthly system designed for the middle classes. We can envision such a person having difficulties borrowing money, buying a product that's not designed for his needs, paying the money back to a tune he can't dance to. It is not hard to imagine the poor, and especially the black poor, confronted by such a system, vaguely wondering whether it had not been designed specifically to keep him out of the market economy.

The plight of the poor is not necessarily the inevitable result of the market economy. Quality of life for the poor could certainly be improved in a practical way if U.S. business marketed appropriate goods and services to them. This huge market lies within the greater, virtually undiscovered, market. Vast potential and vast pent-up demand certainly are its characteristics. Putting the profit motive in the picture for business participation in the national fight on poverty should turn this participation from a marginal contributory nature into one compellingly motivated by a dynamic force.

At this point the question becomes: is it moral to make a profit from the poor? Once business discovers the dimensions and characteristics of the poor as a market and designs products and programs to sell to it, it will not be long before efficient, first-rate business drives out of the ghettos the crooks, gypsters, fleecers and loan sharks who have held on to this market for years, only because of lack of competition. Is this immoral? It is more appropriate to ask the question another way: is it immoral to sell to the poor for a profit even if the results to the poor are better quality, greater variety and lower prices?

Where can managers who want to sell effectively to the huge lower market start? The greatest potential rests in imaginative social research rather than standard-variety marketing research, which may be too full of the terminology of the middle and upper classes, too full of clichés and standard groupings to break new ground. The very rich, as an example, have more in common with most other people today than does the poor person. Research may reveal that the poor are like other people, except that they have less money. Motivations and needs of the poor cannot be guessed at, and it is in this sense that marketing must accurately represent the poor to the corporation if both are to benefit.

Understanding the poor customer's unique needs, values and historical environment is the place to start. The opportunity and responsibility for marketing a suitable range of products and services to the poor rests with management, especially marketing management. The poor can benefit rapidly, and business can make a profit.

55. Outwitting the "Developed" Countries IVAN ILLICH

It is now common to demand that the rich nations convert their war machine into a program for the development of the Third World. The poorer four fifths of humanity multiply unchecked while their per capita consumption actually declines. This population expansion and decrease of consumption threaten the industrialized nations, who may still, as a result, convert their defense budgets to the economic pacification of poor nations. And this in turn could produce irreversible despair, because the plows of the rich can do as much harm as their swords. US trucks can do more lasting damage than US tanks. It is easier to create mass demand for the former than for the latter. Only a minority needs heavy weapons, while a majority can become dependent on unrealistic levels of supply for such productive machines as modern trucks. Once the Third World has become a mass market for the goods, products, and processes which are designed by the rich for themselves, the discrepancy between demand for these Western artifacts and the supply will increase indefinitely. The family car cannot drive the poor into the jet age, nor can a school system provide the poor with education, nor can the family icebox insure healthy food for them.

It is evident that only one man in a thousand in Latin America can afford a Cadillac, a heart operation, or a Ph.D. This restriction on the goals of development does not make us despair of the fate of the Third World, and the reason is simple.

SOURCE. Reprinted with permission from *The New York Review of Books*. Copyright © 1969 The New York Review.

We have not yet come to conceive of a Cadillac as necessary for good transportation, or of a heart operation as normal healthy care, or of a Ph.D. as the prerequisite of an acceptable education. In fact, we recognize at once that the importation of Cadillacs should be heavily taxed in Peru, that an organ transplant clinic is a scandalous plaything to justify the concentration of more doctors in Bogotá, and that a Betatron is beyond the teaching facilities of the University of São Paolo.

Unfortunately, it is not held to be universally evident that the majority of Latin Americans—not only of our generation, but also of the next and the next again—cannot afford any kind of automobile, or any kind of hospitalization, or for that matter an elementary school education. We suppress our consciousness of this obvious reality because we hate to recognize the corner into which our imagination has been pushed. So persuasive is the power of the institutions we have created that they shape not only our preferences, but actually our sense of possibilities. We have forgotten how to speak about modern transportation that does not rely on automobiles and airplanes. Our conceptions of modern health care emphasize our ability to prolong the lives of the desperately ill. We have become unable to think of better education except in terms of more complex schools and of teachers trained for ever longer periods. Huge institutions producing costly services dominate the horizons of our inventiveness.

We have embodied our world view into our institutions and are now their prisoners. Factories, news media, hospitals, governments, and schools produce goods and services packaged to contain our view of the world. We—the rich—conceive of progress as the expansion of these establishments. We conceive of heightened mobility as luxury and safety packaged by General Motors or Boeing. We conceive of improving the general well-being as increasing the supply of doctors and hospitals, which package health along with protracted suffering. We have come to identify our need for further learning with the demand for ever longer confinement to classrooms. In other words, we have packaged education with custodial care, certification for jobs, and the right to vote, and wrapped them all together with indoctrination in the Christian, liberal, or communist virtues.

In less than a hundred years industrial society has molded patent solutions to basic human needs and converted us to the belief that man's needs were shaped by the Creator as demands for the products we have invented. This is as true for Russia and Japan as for the North Atlantic community. The consumer is trained for obsolescence, which means continuing loyalty toward the same producers who will give him the same basic packages in different quality or new wrappings.

Industrialized societies can provide such packages for personal consumption for most of their citizens, but this is no proof that these societies are sane, or economical, or that they promote life. The contrary is true. The more the citizen is trained in the consumption of packaged goods and services, the less effective he seems to become in shaping his environment. His energies and finances are consumed in procuring ever new models of his staples, and the environment becomes a by-product of his own consumption habits.

The design of the "package deals" of which I speak is the main cause of the high cost of satisfying basic needs. So long as every man "needs" his car, our cities must endure longer traffic jams and absurdly expensive remedies to relieve them. So long as health means maximum length of survival, our sick will get ever more extra-ordinary surgical interventions and the drugs required to deaden their consequent pain. So long as we want to use school to get children out of their parents' hair or to keep them off the street and out of the labor force, our young will be retained in endless schooling and will need ever-increasing incentives to endure the ordeal.

Rich nations now benevolently impose a straightjacket of traffic jams, hospital confinements, and classrooms on the poor nations, and by international agreement call this "development." The rich and schooled and old of the world try to share their dubious blessings by foisting their pre-packaged solutions on to the Third World. Traffic jams develop in São Paolo, while almost a million northeastern Brazilians flee the drought by walking 500 miles. Latin American doctors get train-ing at the New York Hospital for Special Surgery, which they apply to only a few, while amoebic dysentery remains endemic in slums where 90 percent of the popula-tion live. A tiny minority gets advanced education in basic science in North America—not infrequently paid for by their own governments. If they return at all to Bolivia, they become second-rate teachers of pretentious subjects at La Paz or Cochibamba. The rich export outdated versions of their standard models.

The Alliance for Progress is a good example of benevolent production for under-development. Contrary to its slogans, it did succeed—as an alliance for the progress of the consuming classes, and for the domestication of the Latin American masses. The Alliance has been a major step in modernizing the consumption patterns of the middle classes in South America by integrating them with the dominant culture of the North American metropolis. At the same time, the Alliance has modernized the aspirations of the majority of citizens and fixed their demands on unavailable products.

Each car which Brazil puts on the road denies fifty people good transportation by bus. Each merchandised refrigerator reduces the chance of building a com-munity freezer. Every dollar spent in Latin America on doctors and hospitals costs a hundred lives, to adopt a phrase of Jorge de Ahumada, the brilliant Chilean economist. Had each dollar been spent on providing safe drinking water, a hundred lives could have been saved. Each dollar spent on schooling means more privileges for the few at the cost of the many; at best it increases the number of those who, before dropping out, have been taught that those who stay longer have earned the right to more power, wealth, and prestige. What such schooling does is to teach the schooled the superiority of the better schooled.

All Latin American countries are frantically intent on expanding their school systems. No country now spends less than the equivalent of 18 percent of tax-derived public income on education—which means schooling—and many countries spend almost double that. But even with these huge investments, no country yet succeeds in giving five full years of education to more than one third of its population; supply and demand for schooling grow geometrically apart. And what is true about schooling is equally true about the products of most institutions in the process of modernization in the Third World.

Continued technological refinements of products which are already established on the market frequently benefit the producer far more than the consumer. The more complex production processes tend to enable only the largest producer to continually replace outmoded models, and to focus the demand of the consumer on the marginal improvement of what he buys, no matter what the concomitant side effects: higher prices, diminished life span, less general usefulness, higher cost of repairs. Think of the multiple uses for a simple can opener, whereas an electric one, if it works at all, opens only some kinds of cans, and costs one hundred times as much.

This is equally true for a piece of agricultural machinery and for an academic degree. The midwestern farmer can become convinced of his need for a four-axle vehicle which can go 70 m.p.h. on the highways, has an electric windshield wiper and upholstered seats, and can be turned in for a new one within a year or two. Most of the world's farmers don't need such speed, nor have they ever met with such comfort, nor are they interested in obsolescence. They need low-priced transport, in a world where time is not money, where manual wipers suffice, and where a piece of heavy equipment should outlast a generation. Such a mechanical donkey requires entirely different engineering and design than one produced for the US market. This vehicle is not in production.

Most of South America needs paramedical workers who can function for indefinite periods without the supervision of an MD. Instead of establishing a process to train midwives and visiting healers who know how to use a very limited arsenal of medicines while working independently, Latin American universities establish every year a new school of specialized nursing or nursing administration to prepare professionals who can function only in a hospital, and pharmacists who know how to sell increasingly more dangerous drugs.

The world is reaching an impasse where two processes converge: ever more men have fewer basic choices. The increase in population is widely publicized and creates panic. The decrease in fundamental choice causes anguish and is consistently overlooked. The population explosion overwhelms the imagination, but the progressive atrophy of social imagination is rationalized as an increase of choice between brands. The two processes converge in a dead end: the population explosion provides more consumers for everything from food to contraceptives, while our shrinking imagination can conceive of no other ways of satisfying their demands except through the packages now on sale in the admired societies.

I will focus successively on these two factors, since, in my opinion, they form the two coordinates which together permit us to define underdevelopment.

In most Third World countries, the population grows, and so does the middle class. Income, consumption, and the well-being of the middle class are all growing while the gap between this class and the mass of people widens. Even where per capita consumption is rising, the majority of men have less food now than in 1945, less actual care in sickness, less meaningful work, less protection. This is partly a consequence of polarized consumption and partly caused by the breakdown of traditional family and culture. More people suffer from hunger, pain, and exposure in 1969 than they did at the end of World War II, not only numerically, but also as a percentage of the world population.

These concrete consequences of underdevelopment are rampant; but underdevelopment is also a state of mind, and understanding it as a state of mind, or as a form of consciousness, is the critical problem. Underdevelopment as a state of mind occurs when mass needs are converted to the demand for new brands of packaged solutions which are forever beyond the reach of the majority. Underdevelopment in this sense is rising rapidly even in countries where the supply of classrooms, calories, cars, and clinics is also rising. The ruling groups in these countries build up services which have been designed for an affluent culture; once they have monopolized demand in this way, they can never satisfy majority needs.

Underdevelopment as a form of consciousness is an extreme result of what we can call in the language of both Marx and Freud "*Verdinglichung*" or reification. By reification I mean the hardening of the perception of real needs into the demand for mass manufactured products. I mean the translation of thirst into the need for a Coke. This kind of reification occurs in the manipulation of primary human needs by vast bureaucratic organizations which have succeeded in dominating the imagination of potential consumers.

Let me return to my example taken from the field of education. The intense promotion of schooling leads to so close an identification of school attendance and education that in everyday language the two terms are interchangeable. Once the imagination of an entire population has been "schooled," or indoctrinated to believe that school has a monopoly on formal education, then the illiterate can be taxed to provide free high school and university education for the children of the rich.

Underdevelopment is the result of rising levels of aspiration achieved through the intensive marketing of "patent" products. In this sense, the dynamic underdevelopment that is now taking place is the exact opposite of what I believe education to be: namely, the awakening awareness of new levels of human potential and the use of one's creative powers to foster human life. Underdevelopment, however, implies the surrender of social consciousness to pre-packaged solutions.

The process by which the marketing of "foreign" products increases underdevelopment is frequently understood in the most superficial ways. The same man who feels indignation at the sight of a Coca-Cola plant in a Latin American slum often feels pride at the sight of a new normal school growing up alongside. He resents the evidence of a foreign "license" attached to a soft drink which he would like to see replaced by "Cola-Mex." But the same man is willing to impose schooling—at all costs—on his fellow citizens, and is unaware of the invisible license by which this institution is deeply enmeshed in the world market.

Some years ago I watched workmen putting up a sixty-foot Coca-Cola sign on a desert plain in the Mexquital. A serious drought and famine had just swept over the Mexican highland. My host, a poor Indian in Ixmiquilpan, had just offered his visitors a tiny tequila glass of the costly black sugarwater. When I recall this scene I still feel anger; but I feel much more incensed when I remember UNESCO meetings at which well-meaning and well-paid bureaucrats seriously discussed Latin American school curricula, and when I think of the speeches of enthusiastic liberals advocating the need for more schools.

The fraud perpetrated by the salesmen of schools is less obvious but much more fundamental than the self-satisfied salesmanship of the Coca-Cola or Ford representative, because the schoolman hooks his people on a much more demanding drug. Elementary school attendance is not a harmless luxury, but more like the coca chewing of the Andean Indian, which harnesses the worker to the boss.

The higher the dose of schooling an individual has received, the more depressing his experience of withdrawal. The seventh-grade dropout feels his inferiority much more acutely than the dropout from the third grade. The schools of the Third World administer their opium with much more effect than the churches of other epochs. As the mind of a society is progressively schooled, step by step its individuals lose their sense that it might be possible to live without being inferior to others. As the majority shifts from the land into the city, the hereditary inferiority of the peon is replaced by the inferiority of the school dropout who is held personally responsible for his failure. Schools rationalize the divine origin of social stratification with much more rigor than churches have ever done.

Until this day no Latin American country has declared youthful under-consumers of Coca-Cola or cars as lawbreakers, while all Latin American countries have passed laws which define the early dropout as a citizen who has not fulfilled his legal obligations. The Brazilian government recently almost doubled the number of years during which schooling is legally compulsory and free. From now on any Brazilian dropout under the age of sixteen will be faced during his lifetime with the reproach that he did not take advantage of a legally obligatory privilege. This law was passed in a country where not even the most optimistic could foresee the day when such levels of schooling would be provided for only 25 percent of the young. The adoption of international standards of schooling forever condemns most Latin Americans to marginality or exclusion from social life—in a word, underdevelopment.

The translation of social goals into levels of consumption is not limited to only a few countries. Across all frontiers of culture, ideology, and geography today, nations are moving toward the establishment of their own car factories, their own medical and normal schools—and most of these are, at best, poor imitations of foreign and largely North American models.

The Third World is in need of a profound revolution of its institutions. The revolutions of the last generation were overwhelmingly political. A new group of men with a new set of ideological justifications assumed power to administer fundamentally the same scholastic, medical, and market institutions in the interest of a new group of clients. Since the institutions have not radically changed, the new group of clients remains approximately the same size as that previously served. This appears clearly in the case of education. Per pupil costs of schooling are today comparable everywhere since the standards used to evaluate the quality of schooling tend to be internationally shared. Access to publicly financed education, considered as access to school, everywhere depends on per capita income. (Places like China and North Vietnam might be meaningful exceptions.)

Everywhere in the Third World modern institutions are grossly unproductive, with respect to the egalitarian purposes for which they are being reproduced. But so long as the social imagination of the majority has not been destroyed by its fixation on these institutions, there is more hope of planning an institutional revolution in the Third World than among the rich. Hence the urgency of the task of developing workable alternatives to "modern" solutions.

Underdevelopment is at the point of becoming chronic in many countries. The revolution of which I speak must begin to take place before this happens. Education again offers a good example: chronic educational underdevelopment occurs when the demand for schooling becomes as widespread that the total concentration of educational resources on the school system becomes a unanimous political demand. At this point the separation of education from schooling becomes impossible.

The only feasible answer to ever-increasing underdevelopment is a response to basic needs that is planned as a long-range goal for areas which will always have a different capital structure. It is easier to speak about alternatives to existing institutions, services, and products than to define them with precision. It is not my purpose either to paint a Utopia or to engage in scripting scenarios for an alternate future. We must be satisfied with examples indicating simple directions that research should take.

Some such examples have already been given. Buses are alternatives to a multitude of private cars. Vehicles designed for slow transportation on rough terrain are alternatives to standard trucks. Safe water is an alternative to high-priced surgery. Medical workers are an alternative to doctors and nurses. Community food storage is an alternative to expensive kitchen equipment. Other alternatives could be discussed by the dozen. Why not, for example, consider walking as a long-range alternative for locomotion by machine, and explore the demands which this would impose on the city planner? And why can't the building of shelters be standardized, elements be pre-cast, and each citizen be obliged to learn in a year of public service how to construct his own sanitary housing?

It is harder to speak about alternatives in education, partly because schools have recently so completely pre-empted the available educational resources of good will, imagination, and money. But even here we can indicate the direction in which research must be conducted.

At present, schooling is conceived as graded, curricular, class attendance by children, for about 1000 hours yearly during an uninterrupted succession of years. On the average, Latin American countries can provide each citizen with between eight and thirty months of this service. Why not, instead, make one or two months a year obligatory for all citizens below the age of thirty?

Money is now spent largely on children, but an adult can be taught to read in one tenth the time and for one tenth the cost it takes to teach a child. In the case of the adult there is an immediate return on the investment, whether the main importance of his learning is seen in his new insight, political awareness, and willingness to assume responsibility for his family's size and future, or whether the emphasis is placed on increased productivity. There is a double return in the case of the adult, because not only can he contribute to the education of his children, but to that of other adults as well. In spite of these advantages, basic literacy programs have little or no support in Latin America, where schools have a first call on all public resources. Worse, these programs are actually ruthlessly suppressed in Brazil and elsewhere, where military support of the feudal or industrial oligarchy has thrown off its former benevolent disguise.

Another possibility is harder to define, because there is as yet no example to point to. We must therefore imagine the use of public resources for education distributed in such a way as to give every citizen a minimum chance. Education will become a political concern of the majority of voters only when each individual has a precise sense of the educational resources that are owing to him—and some idea of how to sue for them. Something like a universal G.I. Bill of Rights could be imagined, dividing the public resources assigned to education by the number of children who are legally of school age, and making sure that a child who did not take advantage of his credit at the age of seven, eight, or nine would have the accumulated benefits at his disposal at age ten.

What could the pitiful education credit which a Latin American Republic could offer to its children provide? Almost all of the basic supply of books, pictures, blocks, games, and toys that are totally absent from the homes of the really poor, but enable a middle-class child to learn the alphabet, the colors, shapes, and other classes of objects and experiences which insure his educational progress. The choice between these things and schools is obvious. Unfortunately, the poor, for whom alone the choice is real, never get to exercise this choice.

Defining alternatives to the products and institutions which now pre-empt the field is difficult, not only, as I have been trying to show, because these products and institutions shape our conception of reality itself, but also because the construction of new possibilities requires a concentration of will and intelligence in a higher degree than ordinarily occurs by chance. This concentration of will and intelligence on the solution of particular problems regardless of their nature we have become accustomed over the last century to call research.

I must make clear, however, what kind of research I am talking about. I am not talking about basic research either in physics, engineering, genetics, medicine, or learning. The work of such men as Crick, Piaget, and Gell-Mann must continue to enlarge our horizons in other fields of science. The labs and libraries and specially trained collaborators these men need cause them to congregate in the few research capitals of the world. Their research can provide the basis for new work on practically any product.

I am not speaking here of the billions of dollars annually spent on applied research, for this money is largely spent by existing institutions on the perfection and marketing of their own products. Applied research is money spent on making planes faster and airports safer; on making medicines more specific and powerful and doctors capable of handling their deadly side-effects; on packaging more learning into classrooms; on methods to administer large bureaucracies. This is the kind of research for which some kind of counterfoil must somehow be developed if we are to have any chance to come up with basic alternatives to the automobile, the hospital, and the school, and any of the many other so-called "evidently necessary implements for modern life."

I have in mind a different, and peculiarly difficult, kind of research, which has been largely neglected up to now, for obvious reasons. I am calling for research on alternatives to the products which now dominate the market; to hospitals and the profession dedicated to keeping the sick alive; to schools and the packaging process which refuses education to those who are not of the right age, who have not gone through the right curriculum, who have not sat in a classroom a sufficient number of successive hours, who will not pay for their learning with submission to custodial care, screening, and certification or with indoctrination in the values of the dominant elite.

This counter-research on fundamental alternatives to current pre-packaged solutions is the element most critically needed if the poor nations are to have a livable future. Such counter-research is distinct from most of the work done in the name of the "year 2000," because most of that work seeks radical changes in social patterns through adjustments in the organization of an already advanced technology. The counter-research of which I speak must take as one of its assumptions the continued lack of capital in the Third World.

The difficulties of such research are obvious. The researcher must first of all doubt what is obvious to every eye. Second, he must persuade those who have the power of decision to act against their own short-run interests or bring pressure on them to do so. And, finally, he must survive as an individual in a world he is attempting to change fundamentally so that his fellows among the privileged minority see him as a destroyer of the very ground on which all of us stand. He knows that if he should succeed in the interest of the poor, technologically advanced societies still might envy the "poor" who adopt this vision.

There is a normal course for those who make development policies, whether they live in North or South America, in Russia or Israel. It is to define development and to set its goals in ways with which they are familiar, which they are accustomed to use in order to satisfy their own needs, and which permit them to work through the institutions over which they have power or control. This formula has failed, and must fail. There is not enough money in the world for development to succeed along these lines, not even in the combined arms and space budgets of the super-powers.

An analogous course is followed by those who are trying to make political revolutions, especially in the Third World. Usually they promise to make the familiar privileges of the present elites, such as schooling, hospital care, etc., accessible to all citizens; and they base this vain promise on the belief that a change in political regime will permit them to sufficiently enlarge the institutions which produce these privileges. The promise and appeal of the revolutionary are therefore just as threatened by the counter-research I propose as is the market of the now dominant producers.

In Vietnam a people on bicycles and armed with sharpened bamboo sticks have brought to a standstill the most advanced machinery for research and production ever devised. We must seek survival in a Third World in which human ingenuity can peacefully outwit machined might. The only way to reverse the disastrous trend to increasing underdevelopment, hard as it is, is to learn to laugh at accepted solutions in order to change the demands which make them necessary. Only free men can change their minds and be surprised; and while no men are completely free, some are freer than others.

5⑥. *The Ghetto as a Classroom: Beachhead College for Marketing — An Alternative to Classroom Learning* JOHN R. WISH

What is a Beachhead College?

A Beachhead College is an innovative, accredited learning center for students who want to explore learning through action within a community. The Beachhead is connected with the university, but located away from the campus. It is usually in the inner city. The students and their professor must be invited by an organization in the community interested in sponsoring a research project. The work done by the students enrolled in the Beachhead College is work needed in the community as defined by an organization in the community.

The Beachhead College concept was developed at Antioch College in Ohio in the mid-1960's. From Antioch, a group of students and a professor lived and worked in a community for one year. Beachheads are now operating in several cities. The Beachhead College that I initiated is connected with the University of Oregon and has been located in Portland.

Elements of organization in the Beachhead College for which I am responsible include the following parameters:

Size. Each unit should be limited to ten to thirty students who spend three to six months in the community. Such a size does not overwhelm the community.

Costs. Each student pays for his in-community experience as he pays for his on-campus experience—tuition, meals, and lodging included. If any project in the community results in revenue, that money is used by all students to reduce their out-of-pocket expenses.

Living arrangements. Each unit of students decide if they will live with families in the community or live together in communal style. There are problems and advantages to each style.

Academic credits. Credit must be given just as it is for other college work. At the University of Oregon, a maximum of 15 hours credit is given for the one term spent in the Beachhead College. Informal arrangements can be made with other professors so that the credit hours are counted in another department.

The University of Oregon Beachhead courses entitled "Consumer Problems of the Poor—I and II" are taken for 3 and 15 credits, respectively, in successive terms.

Grades. The students can choose either "Pass Differentiated" (A, B, C, No pass) or "Pass undifferentiated" (P, M). The grades are determined by an average of the student peers, the faculty member, and the community organization with whom the student works. Each of the above groups has 1/3 of the power in determining the final grade.

Instructor. A professor can work with 10 to 30 students maximum, and must be willing to devote a minimum of two days of 12 to 14 hours and one night each week. If he has 10 or more students working in the Beachhead College, he should have no other teaching responsibilities. (It's not the soft touch it first appears—30 students × 15 term hours—300 student credit hours.)

Preparation. A classroom course "Consumer Problems of the Poor—I," must be taken by the students to do the planning for successful field work. A number of students (about 50%) complete only the preparatory term. The decision is sometimes their own, sometimes their peers' and sometimes the professor's. The following books are very useful for their experience: David Caplovitz, *The Poor Pay More;* Eldridge Cleaver, *Soul On Ice; The Autobiography of Malcolm X;* Langdon Gilkey, *Shantung Compound,* and Richard Kim, *The Martyred.*

Passports and visas. No one legally may go to a foreign country unless (1) his government lets him go, and (2) the host country invites him. The permission from the professor and the student peers is a kind of a passport. That written invitation from a community organization (profit or non-profit) addressed to the professor, spells out the conditions under which each student is going into the community.

What Results from Beachhead College?

As a result of the Beachhead College we have better housing in Oregon, more information about the communities involved, and a new retail food store. More specifically:

Under the provisions of the Federal Housing Administration's Section 221H and 235J, students have worked with several churches to establish three nonprofit corporations for remodeling homes and reselling them at low-interest rates to low and moderate income families ($3000-$7000 per year). Over 80 families have moved into their own homes.

We engaged in a detailed study of church-owned vacant land in the state of Oregon. We found 87 acres in Portland alone with the idea that some of it could be available for housing for low and moderate income families. This past year we helped establish a nonprofit corporation to build housing under FHA Section 236 on some of that land.

In spring, 1969, we conducted a survey of 135 food stores each week for six weeks and demonstrated that in Portland, Oregon food prices DO NOT RISE ON WELFARE CHECK DAYS, AND ARE NOT HIGHER in low-income ghetto chain stores.

We acted as consultants to an OEO Community Action Agency in the black section of Portland for the demographic survey that became a part of the Model Cities Application.

Together with some members of the hip community, we formed a retail food store called "Friends-N-Food" which specializes in nonprocessed foods—especially bulk commodities and low-priced milk and cheese.

A less tangible result of the Beachhead College was that learning effectively took place outside of the classroom. Students became involved and received first-hand knowledge and experience that is often not known to them until they have "finished their education." The Beachhead experience allows the students to apply some of their book learning in a controlled and constructive atmosphere of the real world, while still working on a degree.

I think, then, that the intangible result is that professional educators, parents, and students must rethink what education is, where it is, and under what conditions it is. The successful field experience of the Beachhead College, and the T.V. series, "Sesame Street," convince me that the traditional classroom is limited in its application for learning.

57. *The U.S.'s Toughest Customer*

Midway through lunch at a fashionable Washington restaurant not long ago, a young man named Ralph Nader stopped suddenly and gazed down in disgust at his chef's salad. There, nestled among the lettuce leaves, lay a dead fly. Nader spun in his chair and jabbed both arms into the air to summon a waiter. Pointing accusingly at the intruder on his plate, he ordered: "Take it away!" The waiter apologized and rushed to produce a fresh salad, but Nader's anger only rose. While his luncheon companions watched the turmoil that had erupted around him, Nader launched into a detailed indictment of sanitation in restaurants. He pointed out that flies killed by insect spray often fall into food, thereby providing customers not only with an unappetizing bonus but also with a dose of DDT—or something even stronger.

Restaurant owners had better take heed. Nader is by now an almost legendary crusader who would—and could—use a fly to instigate a congressional investigation. As the self-appointed and unpaid guardian of the interests of 204 million U.S. consumers, he has championed dozens of causes, prompted much of U.S. industry to reappraise its responsibilities and, against considerable odds, created a new climate of concern for the consumer among both politicians and businessmen. Nader's influence is greater now than ever before. That is partly because the consumer, who has suffered the steady ravishes of inflation upon his income, is less willing to tolerate substandard, unsafe or misadvertised goods. It is also because

SOURCE. Reprinted by permission from *Time,* The Weekly Newsmagazine; Copyright Time Inc., 1969.

Nader's ideas have won acceptance in some surprising places. Last week, for example, Henry Ford II went farther than any other automobile executive ever has in acknowledging the industry's responsibility for polluting the air and asked—indeed, prodded—the Government to help correct the situation. The auto companies must develop, said Ford, "a virtually emission-free" car, and soon. Ford did not mention Ralph Nader, but it was not really necessary. Nader is widely known as a strong critic of the auto industry for, among other things, its pollution of the atmosphere.

Nader was able to force off the market General Motors' Corvair, which was withdrawn from production this year. Corvair's sales had plunged by 93% after Nader condemned the car as a safety hazard in his bestseller, *Unsafe at Any Speed.* That influential book, and Nader's later speeches, articles and congressional appearances, also forced the Department of Transportation to impose stricter safety standards on automobile and tire manufacturers.

Advocate, muckraker and crusader, Nader has also been almost solely responsible for the passage of five major federal laws. They are the National Traffic and Motor Vehicle Safety Act of 1966, the Wholesome Meat Act of 1967, the Natural Gas Pipeline Safety Act, the Radiation Control for Health and Safety Act and the Wholesale Poultry Products Act, all of 1968. This week Congress will almost certainly pass the Federal Coal Mine Health and Safety Act, which Nader and a group of insurgent mine workers supported against the wishes of complacent union leadership. The act contains stiff preventive measures against working conditions that can cause black lung.

Nader was the first to accuse babyfood manufacturers of imperiling the health of infants by using monosodium glutamate, a taste enhancer that medical research shows can cause brain damage in some animals. The three largest producers of baby food have since stopped using it. In addition, Nader's repeated warnings about the dangers of cyclamatcs and DDT helped to nudge the Department of Health, Education and Welfare to press research that led to recent federal restrictions on their use. From witness chairs and podiums, he has also taken aim at excessively fatty hot dogs, unclean fish, tractors that tip over and kill farmers, and the dangerous misuse of medical X-rays. He has revealed that some color-television sets were recalled for leaking excessive amounts of radiation. (The Federal Trade Commission has publicly warned viewers to sit at least six feet away from color tubes.)

The Erosion of Life

To many Americans, Nader, at 35, has become something of a folk hero, a symbol of constructive protest against the status quo. When this peaceful revolutionary does battle against modern bureaucracies, he uses only the weapons available to any citizen—the law and public opinion. He has never picketed, let alone occupied, a corporate office or public agency. Yet Nader has managed to cut through all the protective layers and achieve results. He has shown that in an increasingly computerized, complex and impersonal society, one persistent man can actually do something about the forces that often seem to badger him—that he can indeed even shake and change big business, big labor and even bigger Government.

"My job is to bring issues out in the open where they cannot be ignored," says Nader, chopping his hands, as he often does when he speaks. "There is a revolt against the aristocratic uses of technology and a demand for democratic uses. We have got to know what we are doing to ourselves. Life can be—and is being—eroded." To prevent that erosion, he unmercifully nags consumer-minded U.S. Senators, pushing them to pass new bills. When their committees stall, he phones them by day, by night, and often on Sundays. "This is Ralph," he announces, and nobody has to ask, "Ralph *who?*"

Nader today is widening his sights. A lawyer by training, he is investigating the affairs of Covington & Burling, the Washington law firm headed by former Secretary of State Dean Acheson. At one time or another, Covington & Burling has numbered among its clients 200 of the nation's 500 biggest corporations, and Nader wants to determine just how much influence the firm has inside the Government. Most of all, he is probing into the affairs of ossified federal bureaucracies. "We hear a lot about law and order on the streets," he says, with a mischievous twinkle in his eyes. "I thought we ought to find out how law and order operates in the regulatory agencies." How does it? "It doesn't."

Most Outstanding Man

He issued a report (now in hardcover) that scaldingly criticized the FTC and called for its reorganization; recently several FTC officials have agreed with him. He is examining laxity within agencies as diverse as the National Air Pollution Control Administration and the Federal Railroad Administration, which he says shares the blame for the fact that U.S. railways have 100 accidents a day, accounting for 2,400 deaths a year. "Regulatory agencies have failed by the most modest of standards," Nader contends, in great part because their top men are too cozy with the industries that they oversee and often use their Government jobs as stepping-stones to lucrative private careers in the same field. By his count, 75% of former commissioners of the Federal Communications Commission are employed or retained by the communications industry. This, he charges, amounts to a "deferred bribe." Agency officials who resign their jobs, Nader contends, should be barred from accepting immediate employment in the industry that they were supposedly policing.

To multiply the manpower for his campaigns, Nader has enlisted the help of vacationing students for the past two summers. Their Zola-like zeal for investigating bureaucracies has earned them the name "Nader's Raiders." Last year there were only seven Raiders, but this year the number grew to 102 law, engineering and medical students. The Raiders, who were paid a meager living allowance ($500 to $1,000 for ten weeks), delved energetically into the Department of Agriculture, the Food and Drug Administration, the National Water Pollution Control Administration, occupational health agencies, the Interstate Commerce Commission and several other fiefdoms.

In anticipation of their findings, which are due to be released beginning early next year, at least one ICC official has already resigned. Meanwhile, Nader and his Raiders have accused Government authorities in general of "systematically and routinely" violating the 2½-year-old Freedom of Information Act, which is supposed to entitle public access to much federal information. "If Government officials displayed as much imagination and initiative in administering their programs as they do in denying information about them," he says, "many national problems now in the grip of bureaucratic blight might become vulnerable to resolution." In line with that philosophy, one group of Raiders last month filed a suit in federal court to force the Civil Aeronautics Board to release findings on passenger complaints. Nader expects similar suits to be filed soon against the Departments of Labor and Agriculture.

Over the long run, the inspiration that Ralph Nader is providing for young Americans may prove as important to the country as his own lone battle. The Harvard Law School newspaper has somewhat generously called him "the most outstanding man ever to receive a degree from this institution," which has counted among its graduates Oliver Wendell Holmes and Felix Frankfurter. Nader is a major hero in most law schools. Two of last summer's Raiders canvassed Texas colleges and returned with 700 applications for next summer.

Critics and Champions

Nader is not universally loved for his efforts. New Left revolutionaries condemn him because he wants to improve the economic system rather than tear it down. Businessmen complain that he is a publicity-seeking gadfly and that he can be self-righteous to the point of arrogance. His most obvious weakness is that he sometimes exaggerates for effect, as when he said that frankfurters are "among the most dangerous missiles this country produces." But many businessmen, whatever their feelings about Nader's methods, applaud his accomplishments and concede that he is an important and often valuable critic. Last month a study committee of the U.S. Chamber of Commerce deplored "the tardiness of business in responding constructively" to consumers' criticism. The committee called on sellers to "expand information regarding safety, performance and durability of products." Nader insists that he is not "anti-business" but simply "pro-people." He often jokes that he is as much a foe of the funeral industry as Jessica Mitford but that while she only wrote a book, "I'm trying to reduce the number of their customers."

Occasionally the people whom Nader is trying to help seem more resentful of his efforts than do his corporate targets. On his taxi rides through Washington, cabbies regularly berate him because they must now pay for seat belts and 28 other pieces of mandatory safety equipment. Nader sympathizes with them but argues that the automakers could reduce prices by at least $700 per car if they would do away with costly annual style changes. Even Lyndon Johnson, who signed the 1966 auto-safety bill into law, has found some Nader innovations irritating. On a drive across his Texas ranch, L.B.J. noticed a spot on the windshield of his new Chrysler and groped for the washer and wiper knobs. Still unfamiliar with the Nader-inspired safety feature of non-protruding knobs, Johnson pawed at the dashboard in vain while he continued to drive. Utterly frustrated, he turned to a passenger and muttered: "That goddamned Nader."

What makes Nader so effective today? Much of the answer lies in his lawyer's dedication to hard facts. He makes accusations almost daily that would be libelous if untrue; yet no one has ever sued him on his charges against companies or products. He collects facts everywhere—from his audiences on campus speaking tours, from obscure trade journals and Government publications, from interviews with high officials, from secret informers in public office and private industry, from thousands of letters addressed simply to "Ralph Nader Washington, D.C." Nader receives more mail than the majority of U.S. Senators and Congressmen, reads all the letters—but can answer few.

His first inkling that all was not well with the Corvair's suspension system came from a disgruntled General Motors auto worker who wrote him a letter. In *Unsafe at Any Speed,* Nader went on to single out the sporty car's rear-suspension system as an example of hazardous compromise between engineering and styling. At certain speeds and tire pressures, or in certain types of turns, he charged, the rear wheels could "tuck under," causing a driver to lose control. G.M., which eventually redesigned the system, at first did not even recall the model for checking. But executives were disturbed enough by Nader's charges to hire a Washington law firm to look into the matter. The lawyer, in turn, engaged the Vincent Gillen private detective agency to trail Nader. Purely on a fishing expedition that was to find nothing, the agency's head urged his men to uncover what they could about Nader's "women, boys, etc." Tipped by friends that investigators were looking into his private life, Nader charged publicly that he was being harassed. G.M.'s use of grade-B spy-movie tactics was fully exposed when its president, James Roche (now chairman), was summoned before a Senate subcommittee and twice apologized to Nader for the company's investigation.

In his battle for pipeline-safety legislation, Nader secured important technical data from an engineer who was fighting the installation of a gas main near his home.

He first learned of the damage that pipeline explosions could cause from a professor whom he met at an M.I.T. conference. "Sometimes the things these professors casually drop at conferences send me up the wall," says Nader.

Though Nader has rarely done his fighting in the courtroom, he has exerted a profound influence on the law. Before his auto-safety crusade, accident injuries were blamed on faulty drivers—not faulty cars. In order to collect damages, an accident victim was usually required to prove negligence on the part of a manufacturer. But Nader contended that automakers should build "crashworthy" cars that would not cause bodily injury in a "second collision" after the accident itself. The second-collision concept is now recognized by many courts. A 22-year-old Pennsylvania college student, who suffered permanent injury when the roof of a car buckled in an accident, recently won the right to use the "second-collision" principle in a damage suit against General Motors. U.S. District Judge John A. Fullam ruled that the roof should have been built to withstand the car's roll-over and that automakers are required "to provide more than merely a movable platform capable of transporting passengers from one point to another." Since the second-collision principle could be applicable to other products as well, manufacturers may become more safety-conscious and design their products to avoid injury in case of mishap.

The New Citizenship

The entire legal profession must be reformed, Nader maintains, if society is to alleviate its ailments. "The best lawyers should be spending their time on the great problems—on water and air pollution, on racial justice, on poverty and juvenile delinquency, on the joke that ordinary rights have become," he says. "But they are not. They are spending their time defending Geritol, Rice Krispies and the oil-import quota."

That is changing, in no small part because of Nader. Of the 39 *Harvard Law Review* editors who will be graduated next June, not one intends to join a high-paying Wall Street law firm. Instead, most plan to enter neighborhood agencies or government service—and represent the individual against the institutions. Nader believes that the rise of the youthful protester, which began in the '60s, will accelerate into the '70s. "You watch," he predicts. "General Motors will be picketed by young activists against air pollution."

Student demonstrators, he believes, will increasingly choose to become student investigators. Many of them will move to Washington and, like Nader, spend their early careers prowling among the Government filing cabinets, searching for examples of abuse and seeking means of reform in the existing system. "This is a new form of citizenship," Nader says. At heart, he is teaching the oldest form of citizenship: that one man, simply by determined complaining, can still accomplish a great deal in a free society.

58. *On How to Be a Constructive Nuisance*   HARRISON WELLFORD

(with assistance from James Turner and John Esposito)

We shall summarize the chief characteristics of Nader's approach and then suggest some ways in which they can be applied to environmental problems.

Winning Credibility Through Accuracy

First if you speak out for reform, you must remain free of special interests with axes to grind. Offers of support must be scrutinized to be sure there are no hidden ties. There must be no holds barred on the search for information or the use of it, even if personal financial sacrifice is required.

Second, you must do the tedious and unglamorous research which ensures that your reports are marked with the highest accuracy in the smallest details. Especially in technical areas, where established experts are quick to impute emotionalism to unestablished critics, all charges must be supported by a mountain of sifted evidence.

Third, you must amass the technical skills appropriate to the issue. Whether the problem is pesticides, auto safety, rural poverty, or air pollution, the vital issues are complex and technical. They demand the interdisciplinary expertise of doctors, lawyers, economists, scientists, engineers, and other people with special skills. Working together on task forces, such groups escape the narrow channels of graduate training and make sure that all sides of a problem are covered. The reign of

SOURCE. From *The Environmental Handbook,* ed. by Garrett de Bell. Copyright © 1970 by Garrett de Bell. A Ballantine/Friends of the Earth Book.

the expert on environmental issues is one of the major defenses of polluters. The interdisciplinary task force concept gives credibility to research and allows the group to talk back to the expert in his own language.

Identifying the Equities

There are basic human rights at stake in environmental issues as well as social wrongs. The silent violence of pollution is an offense to moral values. Specifying the equities, the right and wrong of an issue, provides a yardstick for assessing blame and enforcing accountability of public and private officials.

Fuzzy judgments about the shared responsibility of government officials, the polluters and private citizens are simply inaccurate and encourage compromises which stultify reform. There is no natural law which gives companies the right to pollute. They assumed it and they should now bear the major burden of cleaning up after themselves. Moreover, insistence on the human rights at stake in the war on pollution helps bureaucrats get off the fence. The typical administrator sees himself as a man in the middle, an arbitrator between two competing interests. There is little incentive for him to seek out an abstract public interest on his own.

Empirical Research to Isolate the Pressure Points

The vital point of leverage in a policy arena is rarely apparent at first glance. It might be a government official or an entire agency; it might be a "recognized expert"; it might be a corporation president. Finding the point or points against which to apply pressure requires hard empirical research. Without this kind of effort, internal agency or corporate decisions which determine policy for millions will remain unrecorded history. Never has there been a greater gap between library research using printed documents and empirical research inside a decision-making body. The facts of vital decisions rest in the memories of participants, in interoffice memos which are never made public, in meetings at which no transcript is taken, and in telephone calls which go unrecorded. If one is investigating a public agency, it is essential to insist that one interview personnel all the way down the hierarchical chain. Exposure to the fresh air of citizenship has been known to make some bureaucrats hysterical, but it is the only way to break through the public relations curtain so carefully drawn by the top administrators.

We are convinced that the vital points of leverage in a policy area cannot be discovered at distance sitting in a library. For example, which public official has the greatest day-to-day impact on pesticide policy? Do we look for him in the Science Advisory Council in the White House? In the pesticide branch of the Food and Drug Administration? In the Pesticide Regulation Division of the Department of Agriculture? In the Fish and Wildlife Service of the Department of Interior? Or in some obscure congressional subcommittee? Even examining agency regulations setting jurisdictions is little help. There is an interdepartmental agreement which on its face gives the Food and Drug Administration, the Public Health Service, the Pesticide Regulation Division, and the Fish and Wildlife Service a shared role in seeing that pesticides are safe for people and their environment as well as effective in use. Only empirical observations of the agencies at work would reveal that Dr. Harry Hays, director of the Pesticide Regulations Division of USDA, routinely registers proposed pesticides over the objections of the Public Health Service and Fish and Wildlife Service. He has regarded the interdepartmental agreement as a dead letter. Still further research would reveal that none of the manifold agencies involved with pesticides feels directly responsible for testing proposed pesticides for long range effects, in order to prevent the introduction of new ecological time-bombs such as DDT and 245-T. For pesticides, PRD is the point of leverage on which environmental activists should focus. As a general principle, it is futile to rail against unpleasant outcomes if one will not take the effort to master the details of the policy process which yielded the outcome. You will always end up hitting the wrong target.

The Proper Name Approach

A study of pollution which does not name the polluters and the public officials in their sway is destined for the archives before it has been read. While weakness in institutional structure may ultimately be the culprit, the temperament and values of individual personalities in the institutional slots have immediate impact on policy. Failure to hold individuals accountable allows them to substitute corporate irresponsibility for individual conscience. For example, Dr. Hays of the Pesticide Regulation Division of USDA must be made to realize that he will lose his comfortable obscurity if he continues to neglect evidence of environmental hazards in registering new pesticides. For the purpose of getting information from recalcitrant officials, the prospect of seeing their name in print and their actions exposed is more threatening than any law. How many environmental activists know the names of the chief polluters in their community: who is the head of the local plastics factory or public utility? On the national level, how many know the names of the men who run General Motors, U.S. Steel, or Union Oil? If pollution control is to come in time, the names of these men will have to become words not to be heard on the lips of children.

Getting the Facts

On environmental problems, where there are so many *ex cathedra* claims to inside knowledge by putative experts, good information is absolutely essential.

Environmental activists need reliable facts not only to inform themselves about where the problems are, but also to free public officials from specious information which convinces them that the problems do not exist. In challenging American intervention in the Vietnamese War, student critics were rebuked by their elders with the assertion that the American government must have secret information which justified its action. In the new war against environmental pollution, students now criticizing the nonintervention of government are hushed by new claims of inside information, this time coming from scientists on industry payrolls, government officials with Ph.D.'s, and cost accountants adept at demonstrating (with appropriate graphs and charts) that pollution is an acceptable cost. The insiders were wrong on Vietnam and they should not go unchallenged on environmental issues. Charles Frankel, in a recent memoir on his service in the State Department, tells it like it is. "I used to imagine," he states, "when the government took actions I found inexplicable, that it had information I didn't have. But after I had served in the government for some months, I found that the issue was more complex: often the government does know something that people on the outside don't, but it's something that isn't so."

Pollution is a crime compounded of ignorance and avarice. Ignorance exists at the very top where men in high places daily make decisions about weapons, pesticides, and pollution tolerances with only a vague idea, if any, of their ecological implications. In his memoirs, the English Prime Minister Clement Attlee admitted that he concurred in President Truman's decision to drop the bomb without knowing anything about fallout or the genetic effects of an atomic explosion, even though the genetic effects of radiation were well known in the scientific community (and H. J. Muller had won a Nobel Prize for demonstrating war as far back as 1927). To paraphrase Clemenceau, war on pollution is too serious a matter to be left to the experts, whether they are prime ministers, presidents, or the head of PRD.

Environmental activists must get information, not only to arm themselves, but to disarm the experts. Like every act in the environmental field, however, this is easier said than done. After a summer spent investigating federal agencies we concluded that the "relationship between free access to information and responsible government is very direct. All of the agencies we have studied enjoy large discretionary power over the programs they administer. Under the agency's legal structure, they can go one way or another; they can delay action, decide what portion of the law to enforce or not to enforce, and even adamantly refuse to carry out programs mandated by Congress. These agencies are more agencies of discretion than of law. . . ." (Quoted from *The People's Right to Know: A Status Report on the Responsiveness of Some Federal Agencies to the People's Right to Know about Their Government,* by Ralph Nader, Gary Sellers, Reuben Robertson, John Esposito, Harrison Wellford, James Turner, and Robert Fellmeth, published in the

Congressional Record, September 3, 1969.) When the public doesn't have free and rapid access to information, the individual official exercising discretion often becomes progressively more attached to special interests. The reason is not far to seek. As Dean Landis pointed out in his *Report on the Regulatory Agencies to the President-elect in 1960,* "it is the daily machine-gun like impact on both agency and its staff of industry representation that makes for industry orientation on the part of many honest and capable members as well as staffs." If local and federal agencies are not to become simply service stations for pollution lobbyists, there must be countervailing pressure from environmental activists. The latent reformers in the agency must be given bargaining power with which to resist.

Author Index

Subject Index

pollution and, 187, 188

Path to market, *see* Distribution
Pollution, 14, 26, 28, 48, 146, 149, 170
  antipollution costs, 235, 238-239
  attack on, 367-371
  in future world, 311, 317-319
    consumption and, 314-315
    posterity and, 316-317
  governmental action and, 234-235,
    238-239
    municipalities, 238
  industry and, 233-239
    antipollution companies, 234
    antipollution measures, 233-239
    expenditures, 235
    oil industry, 237-238
    production and, 189-191, 196,
    228-232
    steel industry, 236-237
  life expectancy and, 170
  marketing and, 146, 149
  Nixon administration and, 226
  overpopulation and, 187, 188
  pesticides, 192-194, 368-369
  types of, 228-229
  of water, 187-191, 234, 235, 236,
  238
    industry and, 189-191, 196
    municipal waste and, 188-189
    remedy, 191
  see also Environment

Poverty, 13, 33, 47, 147-148, 153, 170,
  213, 214, 329
  housing and, 217-218, 219
    ghetto case study, 243-251
  marketing and, 343-347
  national food program and, 340-342
  race and, 279-280, 329, 346
  sales abuses and, 209-212, 360
Power companies, pollution and, 235-236
Price systems, urban problems and, 79-88
  income redistribution, 81, 83, 84
  "merit goods," 81, 86-87
  property tax, 79-80
  rationing by price, 82
  scale and choice, 84-85, 86
  tolls, 80, 81
  transportation price, 85-86, 87
  wages, 82-83
Product innovation, *see* New products
Proxmire, William, 226
Puerto Ricans, New York housing and,
  243-251

Quintana, Harry, 247

Racism, *see* Minority discrimination
Ramo, Simon, 334
Raytheon Company, market channel
  and, 51
Reference groups, 121-125
  marketing and, 122-125
    advertising, 125
    brand choice, 123-124
    product choice, 123-124
  Negroes and, 294
  theory of, 121-122
    behavior and, 122
Research and development, future pros-
  pects, 146
  of markets, 51, 53-54
  see also New products
Reuss (Congressman), 226
Robinson, Vernon, 248
Roche, James, 365
Rockefeller, John D., 110, 237
Rodriguez, Connie, 250
Rosen, Philip, 249
Rouse, James, 259
Russell, Richard B., 334

Saudi Arabia, defense spending (1967),
  169
Sears Roebuck Company, in Latin
  America, 54
Selective Service System, youth
  attitude to, 289
Self-fulfilling prophecy, 290-296
  definition, 291
  marketing and, 293-296
  social problems and, 293-296
  in social sciences, 291-292
Shirer, William, 307-308
Smith, Nathan, 248
Social change, business and, 29-35
  corporation challenged, 150-164
    youthful attitudes vs., 151-161
  management and, 24, 26-28
  marketing and, 12-18
    corporate involvement, 17
  symptoms of, 15-16
  youth and, 151-160, 287-289
Social class, income and, 128
  marketing and, 129-131, 135-136
    car market, 129-130
  U.S. class structure, 126-128, 131
    mobility, 131
Social development, management and, 27